Internationalization of TESOL Teacher Education

NEW PERSPECTIVES ON LANGUAGE AND EDUCATION

Founding Editor: Viv Edwards, *University of Reading, UK*

Series Editors: Phan Le Ha, *University of Hawaii at Manoa, USA*, Joel Windle, *Monash University, Australia* and Kyle R. McIntosh, *University of Tampa, USA.*

Two decades of research and development in language and literacy education have yielded a broad, multidisciplinary focus. Yet education systems face constant economic and technological change, with attendant issues of identity and power, community and culture. What are the implications for language education of new 'semiotic economies' and communications technologies? Of complex blendings of cultural and linguistic diversity in communities and institutions? Of new cultural, regional and national identities and practices? The New Perspectives on Language and Education series will feature critical and interpretive, disciplinary and multidisciplinary perspectives on teaching and learning, language and literacy in new times. New proposals, particularly for edited volumes, are expected to acknowledge and include perspectives from the Global South. Contributions from scholars from the Global South will be particularly sought out and welcomed, as well as those from marginalized communities within the Global North.

All books in this series are externally peer-reviewed.

Full details of all the books in this series and of all our other publications can be found on http://www.multilingual-matters.com, or by writing to Multilingual Matters, St Nicholas House, 31–34 High Street, Bristol, BS1 2AW, UK.

NEW PERSPECTIVES ON LANGUAGE AND EDUCATION: 127

Internationalization of TESOL Teacher Education

Global and Critical Perspectives

Edited by
Vander Tavares

MULTILINGUAL MATTERS
Bristol • Jackson

DOI https://doi.org/10.21832/TAVARE8936
Library of Congress Cataloging in Publication Data
A catalog record for this book is available from the Library of Congress.
Names: Tavares, Vander, editor.
Title: Internationalization of TESOL Teacher Education: Global and Critical Perspectives/Edited by Vander Tavares.
Description: Bristol; Jackson: Multilingual Matters, [2025] | Series: New Perspectives on Language and Education: 127 | Includes bibliographical references and index. | Summary: "This book examines internationalization practices, policies and experiences within TESOL teacher education. The chapters offer empirical, conceptual and theoretical engagements with the internationalization of TESOL teacher program curricula from both global and critical perspectives"— Provided by publisher. Identifiers: LCCN 2024034780 (print) | LCCN 2024034781 (ebook) | ISBN 9781800418936 (hardback) | ISBN 9781800418929 (paperback) | ISBN 9781800418950 (epub) | ISBN 9781800418943 (pdf)
Subjects: LCSH: English language—Study and teaching—Foreign speakers—Case studies. | English teachers—Training of—Case studies. |
LCGFT: Essays. Classification: LCC PE1128.A2 I596 2025 (print) | LCC PE1128. A2 (ebook) | DDC 428.0071/1—dc23/eng/20241021
LC record available at https://lccn.loc.gov/2024034780
LC ebook record available at https://lccn.loc.gov/2024034781

British Library Cataloguing in Publication Data
A catalogue entry for this book is available from the British Library.

ISBN-13: 978-1-80041-893-6 (hbk)
ISBN-13: 978-1-80041-892-9 (pbk)

Multilingual Matters
UK: St Nicholas House, 31–34 High Street, Bristol, BS1 2AW, UK.
USA: Ingram, Jackson, TN, USA.
Authorised Representative: Easy Access System Europe - Mustamäe tee 50, 10621 Tallinn, Estonia, gpsr.requests@easproject.com.

Website: https://www.multilingual-matters.com
X: Multi_Ling_Mat
Facebook: https://www.facebook.com/multilingualmatters
Blog: https://www.channelviewpublications.wordpress.com

Copyright © 2025 Vander Tavares and the authors of individual chapters.

All rights reserved. No part of this work may be reproduced in any form or by any means without permission in writing from the publisher.

The policy of Multilingual Matters/Channel View Publications is to use papers that are natural, renewable and recyclable products, made from wood grown in sustainable forests. In the manufacturing process of our books, and to further support our policy, preference is given to printers that have FSC and PEFC Chain of Custody certification. The FSC and/or PEFC logos will appear on those books where full certification has been granted to the printer concerned.

Typeset by Techset Composition India(P) Ltd, Bangalore and Chennai, India.

Contents

Contributors vii

Introduction 1

Part 1: Challenges to the Internationalization of TESOL Education Around the World

1 Engagements with Internationalization in Norwegian TESOL Education: Reproducing or Confronting Ideologies? 17
   Ingrid Rodrick Beiler and Vander Tavares

2 Internationalization in Vietnam's English Language Teacher Education Curriculum: Toward a Localized English Teacher Education Framework 33
   Anh Ngoc Trinh, Nhung Hong Thi Nguyen and Anh Lan Thi Tran

3 Inclusion/Exclusion of TESOL in the 'True' Internationalization of Japan's Higher Education 48
   Yoko Kobayashi

4 Higher Education English Teachers' Ideologies on Translanguaging: Monolingual Mindset Meets Internationalization 63
   Md. Sadequle Islam and Sílvia Melo-Pfeifer

Part 2: Identifying Trends, Knowledges and Skills to Support Internationalization

5 Harnessing Teacher Identity for Globalization and Internationalization of TESOL Curricula 81
   Manfred Man-fat Wu

6 Internationalizing TESOL Teacher Education by Connecting Global and Local Practices from a 'Teacher Agency' Perspective 96
   Zhenjie Weng

7   Approaches and Practices for Intercultural Knowledge
    Development in Internationalizing TESOL Teacher Programs:
    An Overview of the Field   112
    Chiew Hong Ng, Yin Ling Cheung and Weiyu Zhang

Part 3: Exploring the Potential of Study Abroad and Virtual Exchange Experiences in TESOL

8   The Value of Virtual Exchange in Internationalizing the
    TESOL Curriculum: Centering Global Competencies   131
    Zuzana Tomaš and Anna Slatinská

9   Two Tales of Study Abroad: The Role of Class   146
    Hyun-Sook Kang

10 Master's TESOL Returnees' Career Dilemmas in China:
    The Need to Prepare Teachers for Careers Beyond the
    United States   161
    Jialing Wang

11 Japanese Pre-Service English Teachers' Reflections on Study
    Abroad Experiences: Developing Intercultural Competence
    through ELF Awareness   178
    Ayako Suzuki

Part 4: Fostering Decolonization through Internationalization

12 Contesting Native Speakerism in Language Teacher Identity
    Construction: A Case Study of a Short-Term Study Abroad
    Program   195
    Hyesun Cho

13 Toward Antiracist TESOL Teacher Education: Centering
    Transnational BIPOC Students and Communities   211
    Eunjeong Lee and Chatwara Suwannamai Duran

14 Future Preparers of TESOL Teachers: Construction of
    Decolonizing Community Space by Weaving International
    Identities   226
    G. Sue Kasun, Saniha Kabani and J. Nozipho Moyo

    Index   240

Contributors

Hyesun Cho is Professor of TESOL at the University of Kansas, USA. Her research interests include language teacher identity, critical literacy and study abroad teacher education for social justice. Her recent books are *Transnational Teacher Identities* and *Korean as a Heritage Language from Transnational and Translanguaging Perspectives,* both by Routledge.

Chiew Hong Ng is Senior Lecturer at the National Institute of Education, Nanyang Technological University, Singapore. She specializes in reading pedagogies and teacher cognition. She has published in *Changing English, Education and Information Technologies, International Journal of TESOL Studies* and *The European Journal of Applied Linguistics and TEFL.*

Nhung Hong Thi Nguyen is Dean at the Faculty of English Language Teacher Education, University of Languages and International Studies, Vietnam National University Hanoi (VNU). Her areas of interest include English language teaching, English language teacher education and training and internationalization of higher education.

Saniha Kabani is a doctoral student at Georgia State University pursuing the program Teaching and Learning with a focus on Teaching and Teacher Education. With over eight years of experience in teaching and mentoring, she is dedicated to fostering inclusive learning environments where every student can thrive. Her research interests include critical mentorship and equity-oriented coaching for multiethnic and multilingual students in critical mathematics.

Hyun-Sook Kang is Associate Professor of Global Studies in Education in the Department of Education Policy, Organization & Education at the University of Illinois, Urbana-Champaign. She studies global mobility and language learning and practice, with implications for teacher education online and on campus.

Sue Kasun is Professor of Language Education at Georgia State University. A bilingual Spanish-English speaker, she researchers Mexican-origin youth and their intersection with transnationalism, teacher education and, more recently, connecting Indigenous knowledge with formal education.

Yoko Kobayashi is Professor in the Faculty of Humanities and Social Sciences, Iwate University and the author/editor of *The Evolution of English Language Learners in Japan: Crossing Japan, the West and South East Asia* and *Attitudes to English Study among Japanese, Chinese and Korean Women: Motivations, Expectations and Identity*.

Anh Lan Thi Tran is a Lecturer at the Faculty of English Language Teacher Education, University of Languages and International Studies, VNU. Her research interests include teacher education and professional development, mentoring, language assessment and teacher research. She has worked in several projects on teacher education, teacher professional development and school–university partnership in Vietnam.

Eunjeong Lee is Assistant Professor of Applied Linguistics and Rhetoric and Composition at University of Houston. Her research centers around language-minoritized writers, language ideologies and decolonial language and literacy education. Her work has appeared in *Written Communication*, *Journal of Language, Identity and Education*, *World Englishes* and other refereed journals.

Yin Ling Cheung is Associate Professor and Associate Dean at National Institute of Education, Nanyang Technological University, Singapore. She specializes in second language writing. She co-edited *Advances and Current Trends in Language Teacher Identity Research* (Routledge, 2015). She has published in *System* and *Journal of English for Academic Purposes*.

Manfred Man-fat Wu is affiliated with the Institute for Research in Open and Innovative Education, School of Open Learning, Hong Kong Metropolitan University. His publications are mainly on applied linguistics, and also cover a range of topics, including philosophy of language and philosophy of education. Manfred has been an editor of *Theory and Practice in Language Studies* for more than 10 years.

Sílvia Melo-Pfeifer is Full Professor at the Faculty of Education at the University of Hamburg (Germany) in the field of language teacher education (French and Spanish didactics). Her research interests include pluralistic approaches in language learning, teaching and in teacher education and the use of arts-based approaches in research in applied linguistics.

Julien Nozipho Moyo is a PhD student at Georgia State University in the Teaching and Language program with a focus on language and literacy. She is from Zimbabwe and is of Kalanga heritage. She is also fluent in isiNdebele. Her areas of interest are instruction in and preservation of indigenous languages and international education. Nozipho has experience teaching ESOL and Spanish at the high school level.

Anh Ngoc Trinh is a Lecturer in the Faculty of English Language Teacher Education, University of Languages and International Studies, VNU. She has presented and published papers internationally. Her research areas of interest include internationalization of the curriculum, curriculum development, teacher education, homeschooling, social emotional learning (SEL).

Ingrid Rodrick Beiler is Associate Professor of English at Oslo Metropolitan University. She has a PhD from the University of Oslo, which is a linguistic ethnography of English writing and language ideologies in multilingual classrooms in Norway. Her research interests include the sociolinguistic status of English, translingual practices and epistemic justice in secondary and adult education. Her work has been published in journals including *the Modern Language Journal*, *TESOL Quarterly* and *Language Policy*.

Md. Sadequle Islam is Assistant Professor of English at the University of Chittagong (Bangladesh). Currently, he is pursuing his PhD at the University of Hamburg, Germany. His research interests are translanguaging, L1 in L2 learning, technology in ELT and second language acquisition. He is also a lifetime member of the Bangladesh English Language Teachers' Association (BELTA).

Anna Slatinská serves as Senior Lecturer at Matej Bel University in Banská Bystrica, Slovakia, teaching at the Faculty of Arts (Department of English and American Studies). Her scholarly interests and expertise include English language teaching methodology; intercultural communication; developing global skills: language, culture, identity and cultural heritage; and service-learning.

Chatwara Suwannamai Duran is Associate Professor of Applied Linguistics at University of Houston. Her work has appeared in *Linguistics and Education*, *Race Ethnicity and Education*, *TESOL Quarterly*, *Theory into Practice* and several refereed volumes. Her book *Language and Literacy in Refugee Families* (2017) showcases multi-year ethnographic study with Karenni refugee families in the US.

Ayako Suzuki is a professor at the College of Humanities at Tamagawa University, Japan, where she teaches undergraduate and graduate courses in EAP, sociolinguistics and multicultural education. At the university, she has also been involved in running the Center for English as a Lingua Franca. She has researched and published in the area of ELT, ELF and intercultural citizenship.

Vander Tavares is Associate Professor of Education at Inland Norway University of Applied Sciences, Norway and holds a PhD from York University, Canada. His research interests include language teacher identity development, critical second language education, internationalization of higher education and identity in multilingual/multicultural contexts. In 2021, he was the recipient of the *Equity, Diversity and Inclusion (EDI) Award* by the Canadian Bureau for International Education (CBIE).

Zuzana Tomaš is Professor of ESL/TESOL at Eastern Michigan University where she teaches and researches TESOL teacher education courses. She is a co-author of *Fostering International Student Success in Higher Education*, a Fulbright scholar and director of several Study Abroad and Virtual Exchange programs.

Jialing Wang is Assistant Research Professor in the Department of Applied Linguistics at the Pennsylvania State University (PSU). Her research focuses on internationalization of higher education and second language education. She received a DEd in Higher Education from PSU and an MEd in TESOL from the University of Georgia.

Zhenjie Weng, PhD, is Assistant Professor of English Language at the Language and Culture Center at Duke Kunshan University in China. Her specialization is in second, foreign and multilingual language education, and her research mainly focuses on language teacher education. She has published articles in leading journals in the field, such as *TESOL Journal*, *International Journal of Qualitative Studies in Education* and *Teaching in Higher Education* on language teacher identity, emotions, agency and expertise.

Weiyu Zhang is Language Specialist at Southeast Asian Ministers of Education Organization, Regional Language Centre, Singapore. Her research interests include discourse analysis, academic writing and English for Research Publication Purposes. She has published in *Journal of English for Academic Purposes*, *Ibérica* and *Journalism Studies*.

Introduction

These days, the word *internationalization* typically appears next to *higher education*. After all, on a conceptual level, the internationalization of higher education has been a topic of extensive research since the early 2000s, when scholars in the field of international education engaged in attempts to define internationalization of higher education as a framework or approach in light of increased mobility across educational spaces (e.g. Knight, 2004; Qiang, 2003). While for some the internationalization of language education might seem like something new if we are referring to a systematic process with established philosophical foundations and educational aims, for others, the term might seem unoriginal, if we are to consider that language education has always been enveloped in an international essence. On a wide spectrum of possibilities, language education can be about promoting, on one hand, unity and cooperation, while on the other hand, displacement and dominance, since all relations between people are embedded in some degree of power.

In most, if not all parts of the world, language education has historically held an international orientation through the foreignization of languages, language use and language users. In the case of English language education, an entire academic field of study has been built on the foreignization of English with varying preferences in terminology. Two simple examples are EFL ('English as a Foreign Language' – the language is ascribed a foreign status for the other speaker) and TESOL[1] ('Teaching English to Speakers of Other Languages' – those who do not speak English are ascribed a foreign/othered identity) (Shin, 2006). Other labels for English may include English as an international, world, or global language, English as a lingua franca, and more recently, global Englishes. Despite the ideological differences behind these terms, all of them construe teaching and learning English as something dynamic that spans across or beyond regional and national borders. These transcultural flows continue to challenge fixed ideologies behind English language education, such as those of language ownership and epistemic validity (Kumaravadivelu, 2012).

Issues related to epistemic and methodological plurality are not unique to English language teaching and learning, however. Processes and rationales aimed at internationalizing education, as in bringing international perspectives or practices into education, are also not neutral or apolitical (Guzmán-Valenzuela, 2023). This understanding leads us to ask questions such as whose perspectives and interests these processes and rationales reflect, who is included/excluded in the 'international' and how any decisions can and will reinforce existing hierarchies in education. An ethical commitment to internationalization of education must critically and urgently consider questions related to equity and inclusion so that all can benefit equally from an internationalized education. Both in English language education and internationalization, Western perspectives have dominated from theory to practice, resulting in further invisibility of minoritized groups or the replacement of local knowledges and practices (Guo *et al.*, 2022; Tavares, 2022). Yet, these issues do unfold discretely, as English has been the language through which internationalization has been operationalized, thus creating a mutually reinforcing and intricate interplay between the two.

Taking such issues into consideration, this volume approaches internationalization of language education within the context of TESOL teacher education. It gathers critical and international perspectives on different facets of internationalization, such as pedagogical practices, concepts and experiences within the policy, curricular and institutional dimensions of teacher education through the voices of researchers, teacher educators, pre- and in-service teachers of English in China, Germany, Japan, Korea, Norway, Vietnam and the United States. In doing so, this volume seeks to diversify TESOL teacher education from an internationalization perspective that not only brings together the local and the global (Pennycook, 2006), but also aims to sensitize current and future teachers (and teacher educators) to these *glocal* perspectives in ways that can positively inform their teaching (Olmedo & Harbon, 2010). In the subsequent section of this introduction, the context for this volume will be presented, followed by a summary of the chapters included.

Internationalization of Teacher Education: Insights and Affordances

Teacher education is directly influenced by the evolving global challenges and changes facing society. To remain responsive and responsible educators, teachers 'need to keep pace with rapidly developing knowledge areas and approaches to learning and assessment, use new technologies, [and] promote equality and social justice' (Lourenço, 2018: 158) with the overall aim of supporting the academic learning and individual growth of all learners. Despite the presence of a global character in education, teacher education, in particular, tends to focus on training teachers for the national context by positioning one language and culture (typically the majority ones) as the compass for decision-making in relation to teaching methods, assessment and professional development, even when international activities or experiences are embedded in teacher education (Sieber & Mantel, 2012). As Lourenço (2018) argued, this is an important part of teacher education, but an overwhelmingly national orientation 'is not sufficient to educate individuals to act and live in this complex world' (2018: 158–159), characterized by growing political, socioeconomic and climatic instability that affects all.

To internationalize teacher education does not simply entail the addition of international visits or content to the curriculum. Yet, for many, internationalization may reflect Knight's (2004) seminal definition of the concept, from which the process of *integrating* something global has been prioritized. Moving beyond integration, a core component of internationalization of teacher education is a critical reconceptualization of language, culture and, more importantly, knowledge: what knowledge is, how and where it may be co-constructed, and by whom. Therefore, internationalization requires new epistemological engagements in all dimensions of teacher education to avoid an internationalized curriculum that includes the international, but in a manner that perpetuates social inequality and injustice (Stein, 2017). Internationalization of (teacher) education must aim for 'reciprocal or transformative outcomes, such as challenging and/or broadening students' worldviews, reframing the power dynamics of intercultural relationships, or enhancing epistemic equity between different communities and nations' (Buckner & Stein, 2020: 160).

Another important component of the internationalization of teacher education is the dissemination of knowledge between local and global contexts. This practice can contribute to creating a dialogue between different arenas of teacher education (e.g. local, national, international) so as to promote cross-cultural learning of social justice issues whose lessons and insights may be incorporated in our own immediate teacher education contexts (Olmedo & Harbon, 2010), thereby raising a critical awareness of broader topics and challenges in the field for future teachers. Internationalization activities that can support the dissemination of knowledge as well as other pedagogical goals may include mobility of student teachers and teacher educators; diversifying teaching, learning and research, especially through international collaboration; the implementation of international activities 'at home' and through innovative approaches or modalities, such as virtual technology and exchange; mutual changes to teacher education programs as a result of international partnership; and institutional, regional and national policies designed to promote cooperation (Kehm & Teichler, 2007), while maintaining a critical reflexivity in all groups involved throughout any of such processes.

The internationalization of teacher education is tied to the development of several skills and dispositions in pre- and in-service teachers. From internationalizing a language teacher education program in the United States through a carefully designed study abroad program in Spain, Colón-Muñiz *et al.* (2014) found that linguistic and cultural immersion contributed meaningfully to developing student teachers' awareness of themselves as communicative and cultural beings, meaning that the students paid more attention to their own language use and reflected more on their own cultural behavior. Another important outcome was greater empathy for future immigrant students learning English in the United States, which included a better understanding of culture shock and linguistic barriers. The student teachers demonstrated change to their pedagogy in terms of not making assumptions about learners based on language or culture, valuing learners' cultural capital and better understanding the complexity of intercultural relations, which the authors considered to be tied to the development of intercultural skills.

Most research on internationalization of language teacher education has focused on study-abroad opportunities for pre-service teachers. This research has called attention to the need to avoid positioning participating student teachers as educational tourists in international settings. Baecher and Chung (2020) provided an example of such a possibility through the experiences of English language teachers from New York teaching English and learning Spanish while also being a local household member in Costa Rica. The authors reported that the in-service teachers developed a range of intercultural skills and critical perspectives on language education as they questioned curriculum designs, identified language ideologies and valued new and existing relationships in the local setting. The authors recommend that language teacher education programs create a formal credit-bearing component that builds on the internationalization activity, 'rather than moving the teaching experience abroad as if it were just another practicum site' (2020: 47–48). This formal component should prepare student teachers and teacher educators from pre-departure to the conclusion of the experience, and include the voices of community members as well.

As technological advances continue to permeate teacher education, internationalization also becomes possible through virtual exchange and study abroad. Virtual opportunities have the potential to include a wider range of student teachers, considering the cost and time associated with participating in traditional exchange or study abroad programs. Hilliker (2020) found that virtual exchange can enable TESOL student teachers to recognize linguistic and cultural stereotypes, apply theoretical knowledge and develop empathy for language learners. In a similar vein, Pu and Weng (2023) demonstrated the potential of virtual collaboration among English language teachers in developing interculturality, reflexivity and *glocality* in teaching. Speaking to its potential, the authors argued that 'virtual exchange was not just a course activity, but a pedagogical tool to drive meaningful projects across physical borders that supported participation and reification' in the student teachers' online communities of practice (2023: 474).

Another dimension of language teacher education internationalization research has considered comprises the experiences of teacher educators, though to a lesser degree. When reflecting on her experiences as a teacher educator to international student teachers in a diverse setting in the United States, Kim (2023) explained that paying attention to her cultural identity and membership, which in some ways converged, but in others diverged from the students', contributed to enhancing her critical self-reflection and pedagogy. In turn, she experienced 'a greater appreciation and understanding of diversity' (2023: 17), which had the potential to approximate her socially and emotionally to the students in the program. Differently from Kim (2023), teacher educators who go abroad may also experience emotional, intellectual and (inter)cultural development that leads to the same skills and dispositions which student teachers cultivate (Williams & Grierson, 2016), including empathy for the other and knowledge of power relations between groups.

Organization and Main Themes

This volume is organized into four parts, which reflect diverse engagements with internationalization. The first part of this volume explores the challenges and gaps in internationalization frameworks and discourses in TESOL teacher education, bringing to light the influence of language and political ideologies. The second part considers trends, knowledges and skills needed to support internationalization efforts in TESOL teacher education. This part identifies the need to build on teacher identity, agency and intercultural knowledge. The third part examines the potential of study abroad and virtual exchange initiatives from perspectives of global and intercultural competence, ideologies of race and ethnocentrism for professional development and language awareness. The final part engages with decolonial perspectives on the internationalization of TESOL teacher education to challenge native-speakerism, racism and monoculturalism.

In Chapter 1, Ingrid Rodrick Beiler and Vander Tavares consider manifestations of internationalization in English teacher education programs in Norway. Through a critical discourse analysis that rests on an internationalization perspective considerate of the influence of neoliberalism on English language education, including the intersection of neoliberalism and language ideologies, the authors examine publicly available documents of several English teacher education programs in Norway. The analysis demonstrates that prominent English language models oscillate between the Anglo-American native speaker and the competent (elite) European user of English as a Lingua Franca, positioning perspectives on language (use) originating from Global South contexts as supplemental. Additionally, the material benefit of internationalization largely flows to government-sponsored Norwegian centers abroad. Thus, the authors conclude that engagements with internationalization in Norwegian teacher education reinforce Western and European superiority, in which native speakers and (elite) European non-native speakers comprise the primary poles of speakerhood in ways that do not disrupt a neoliberal internationalization agenda or dominant ideologies about language and culture. The authors identify that greater attention to social justice in English teacher education in Norway is needed.

In Chapter 2, Anh Ngoc Trinh, Nhung Hong Thi Nguyen and Anh Lan Thi Tran discuss internationalization dimensions in Vietnam's English language teacher education (ELTE) curriculum development and implementation as well as the possibilities of internationalization in ELTE curriculum renovation through a proposed framework of English Language Teacher Competency. The qualitative data were drawn from content and thematic analysis of 46 ELTE curriculum frameworks of 39 universities and colleges specialized in ELTE across the country. Internationalization of the curriculum (IoC) refers to the incorporation of international, intercultural and/or global dimensions into the content of the curriculum as well as the learning outcomes, assessment tasks, teaching methods and support services of a program of study. Drawn from this conceptualization, the authors postulate that social-constructivism and a competency-based approach are perceived as global and international dimensions, and therefore recognized and embedded in the development of learning outcomes and teaching methodologies in Vietnam's ELTE curriculum, even though they were not explicitly and substantially demonstrated across the curriculum and in the documents of all investigated institutions. The authors argue that incorporating foreign-born theories in a purposeful way could support efforts to renovate an ELTE curriculum and enhance possibilities for the internationalization of ELTE.

In Chapter 3, Yoko Kobayashi examines the overlooked question of why symbolic internationalization invites no criticism from inside and outside (e.g. governing boards of universities, ministries of education). TESOL studies conducted by and with predominantly western male native English-speaking teachers working in Japan's higher education have revealed that these visible foreigners are assigned to the symbolically international but practically peripheral role of fabricating institutions as the site of culturally diverse communities. Drawing on analyses of Japan's higher education policies, Kobayashi attributes stakeholders' silence to an academic and disciplinary hierarchy, resulting in their low expectation toward low-ranked programs and teaching/administrative staff, including TESOL and liberal arts. Meanwhile, Kobayashi also argues that Japan's liberal arts departments are spared from closures because they cater to the needs of: (1) internationalization-minded, predominantly female high school students who adhere to global English ideologies and (2) a Japaneseness-oriented business world that favors the employment of monolingual university graduates with a liberal arts degree. Addressing the exclusion that affects TESOL and its members, Kobayashi discusses both plausible concerns and future directions so that the globally celebrated, academically marginalized and ideologically charged TESOL can endorse true internationalization as a professional community.

In Chapter 4, Md. Sadequle Islam and Sílvia Melo-Pfeifer contextualize their inquiry around the prevailing discussions about whether it is beneficial or detrimental to navigate across various linguistic resources in the language classroom in different linguistic contexts (mono, bi or multilingual) from primary to higher education. In this chapter, the authors discuss English language teachers' ideologies toward translanguaging and its use in higher education TESOL classrooms in Germany. Based on classroom observations, the authors show that though the TESOL classrooms are governed by a monolingual English-only policy, frequently recalled by the teacher, translanguaging is still used as a resource in several ways, both by students and teachers. The interviews with teachers portray a more strict and implicit exclusion and disaffirmation of the use of other languages or language varieties. The authors approach the mismatch between the ideology and practice of translanguaging in TESOL in German higher education through the lens of internationalization as a goal in higher education and examine the language policies promoted at the university to achieve internationalization.

In Chapter 5, Manfred Man-fat Wu argues that the internationalization of TESOL teacher education curricula informed by globalization requires teacher educators to develop and possess a unique make-up of their teacher identity to nurture future-ready teachers. A review and analysis of literature to date related to globalization, language teaching identity and internationalization of TESOL teacher education indicate that to enact an internationalized curriculum, teacher educators need to possess dispositions that embrace diverse perspectives on culture and language when it comes to English. Another mission for internationalized TESOL teacher education is to produce teachers who are equipped with relevant pedagogical knowledge and skills on global citizenship. Among the elements in global citizenship, morality – more specifically duty to others and its actualization – is an essential trait for both TESOL educators and students. The identity of teacher educators should also be infused with respect for personhood possessing rights on a global scale. To achieve the above aims, Wu proposes that teacher training curricula should include personal reflections on the roles of self as teachers and the English language in the internationalized curricula to support a transformation of TESOL teacher education curricula in the context of internationalization.

In Chapter 6, Zhenjie Weng considers how the increased mobility of English language teachers around the world has helped to reveal some of the weaknesses of TESOL teacher education curricula when preparing international teacher candidates (ITCs). For example, in a MATESOL program in a Canadian university, the ITCs criticized native speakerism, promoted multilingualism in practice and reconstructed their identity as future agents of change; however, after returning to their home country, most of them were unable to actualize their reconstructed identity owing to restricted contextual factors. This global–local disconnection has been a long-lasting problem in TESOL. One proposed solution to the disconnection is to provide more context-specific elective courses to the increasingly diverse teacher populations. However, with the complexity and uncertainty embedded in the increased mobility of teachers, those context-specific courses might not always be helpful. Weng therefore introduces a conceptual tool, namely teacher agency (TA), which also serves as a critical lens, that TESOL teacher candidates can draw upon for their future practice regardless of the location of their workplace. Through reviewing literature that unpacks the current issues in internationalizing TESOL teacher education and demonstrating how TA as a conceptual tool can be used to address the issues, Weng emphasizes the need to integrate TA in TESOL teacher education to prepare teacher candidates to be agents of change in their local contexts.

In Chapter 7, Chiew Hong Ng, Yin Ling Cheung and Weiyu Zhang maintain that TESOL teachers have to develop students' global and intercultural competences to appropriately cultivate cross-cultural understanding. While there is no lack of research on intercultural knowledge development, there is scant systematic research on intercultural knowledge development in internationalizing TESOL teacher program in terms of these research questions: (1) What are the approaches and practices for intercultural knowledge development in internationalizing TESOL teacher programs? (2) What are the factors that facilitate or hinder teachers' intercultural knowledge development in the TESOL classrooms? The authors reviewed 30 relevant articles following a literature search performed to help answer those questions. Speaking to researchers, teacher educators, pre-service and in-service teachers in TESOL, the authors propose that developing intercultural knowledge within the internationalization of TESOL teacher programs can be approached through English medium education, program development, curriculum and syllabus design, courses, and pedagogical practices such as the use of projects that cultivate intercultural knowledge.

In Chapter 8, Zuzana Tomaš and Anna Slatinská examine the value of virtual exchanges (VEs) for TESOL teacher candidates in the ESL and EFL contexts. VEs engage two groups of students from different cultural contexts in collaborating online, often on a shared product. Recent scholarship on VEs has shown a variety of benefits for teachers, including increased confidence to teach, improved ability working in multicultural settings, enhanced global competence, digital literacy and problem-solving skills. To add to this important body of research, the authors explore teacher candidates' perceived value of VEs, the nature of pedagogical products developed during the VE and self-reported changes in the teacher candidates' global competence. Specifically, teacher candidates worked together to co-create free online English books aimed at newcomer learners (e.g. an Afghan English learner in Michigan, a Ukrainian refugee in Slovakia) as requested by teachers in both contexts. Teacher candidates from the two universities then used the ebooks in Zoom-based lessons with actual English learners in Slovakia. After describing the program, the authors discuss implications of using globally centered VEs in the TESOL curriculum.

In Chapter 9, Hyun-Sook Kang explores how social class plays a role in Korean college students' ideology about English learning in relation to a short-term study-abroad program in the US. Class has garnered growing scholarly attention as a factor that shapes access to and the nature of a sojourning experience. This study examined how class, defined as global mobility and access to cultural and social capital, influenced the motivation for and beliefs about English learning, as illustrated in two participants, Larry and Fiona, who showed a contrast in international mobility. As part of a cohort of 10 teacher candidates from the same sending university, they participated in a four-week program that focused primarily on promoting students' English skills for classroom instruction purposes and cultivating their awareness of multiculturalism. Thematic analysis of student reflections and interviews during the program suggests disjunctures between the two participants in their prior international experience, their motivation for English learning and their beliefs about the ideal English speaker they aspired to become. Considering these findings, Kang discusses implications for future research, study-abroad program development and the internationalization of TESOL programs.

In Chapter 10, Jialing Wang argues that ethnocentrism plagues TESOL programs in the US and impairs effective and adequate training for teaching English in international contexts. Concurrently, career outcomes of international TESOL graduates who leave the host country after graduation are opaque. Wang critically explores the career paths of Master's TESOL holders who returned to China after completing their degrees and examines the barriers to transfer western pedagogical practices to language classrooms in China. This study considers 11 semi-structured interviews with Chinese returnees who graduated from a TESOL master's program at a public US university between 2014–2021. Participants were employed in one of four types of institutions: private educational companies, public schools, international schools or higher education institutions. Regardless of their institution, they face challenges in applying the knowledge and skills gained from TESOL education in the US. Based on the findings, Wang demonstrates how imperative it is for TESOL programs to better understand the contexts in which their graduates will teach, and provide professional development opportunities that prepare them for practical realities they may face teaching English outside the US.

In Chapter 11, Ayako Suzuki focuses on 10 Japanese pre-service English teachers who had the opportunity to develop ELF awareness before and after their long-term study abroad and explores their perceptions of the significance of multilingual and multicultural experiences during SA through semi-structured reflective interviews conducted eight months after the completion of their study abroad (SA). SA has become a recommended practice for English language teachers in many countries, including Japan, and has begun to be incorporated into university teacher training curricula. Although SA is widely perceived to enhance English language proficiency and intercultural competence, research has shown that without educational support to cultivate awareness of English as a lingua franca (ELF), SA participants may not be able to achieve these developments. This is because the lack of ELF awareness may challenge them when engaging in intercultural interactions, which are essentially multilingual and multicultural. The findings revealed that those with developed ELF awareness were able to see their intercultural competence positively and locate their local ELT within the wider context of global English language use. Building on these findings, Suzuki highlights the importance of integrating pre- and post-SA educational interventions to develop ELF awareness into teacher training curricula.

In Chapter 12, Hyesun Cho presents a qualitative case study of a short-term study-abroad program co-founded and directed by herself at a Midwestern university in the United States. Cho examines language teacher identity construction from a critical perspective and aims to elucidate how native English-speaking student teachers negotiate their language teacher identities through critical reflections while teaching English as a foreign language (EFL) in Korean secondary classrooms during study abroad. Cho makes recommendations for teacher educators who strive to infuse a critical perspective into a short-term study-abroad program by contesting the dominant language ideology perpetuated in the field of TESOL, such as native speakerism.

In Chapter 13, Eunjeong Lee and Chatwara Suwannamai Duran discuss the praxis of cultivating antiracist TESOL teacher education. While laudable, the internationalizing movement of TESOL programs has received criticisms for performing a 'lip service' to antiracism and social justice without challenging what and who counts as a legitimate language, speaker and teacher, keeping intact the working of colonial, monolingual ideologies and nationalist frameworks. What does pedagogical praxis to reimagine and reorient to these terms from racialized and language-minoritized communities-centered perspectives look like and entail? How can this work extend efforts to internationalize TESOL teacher education and simultaneously to eradicate inequalities in English language teaching and learning? The authors grapple with these questions, situating their discussion within a public-serving university in Houston. The authors focus on their praxis to build antiracist TESOL teacher education and the significance of a transnational, community-centered perspective that center BIPOC, transnational and multilingual students' rich lived experiences and knowledge of different languages and literacies. They conclude by arguing that beyond highlighting onto-epistemological diversity, TESOL teacher education must center inequities and injustices entangled with people's lived experiences of such diversity to cultivate antiracism and social justice.

In Chapter 14, G. Sue Kasun, Saniha Kabani and J. Nozipho Moyo present their experiences of decolonizing the internationalization of language education. The decolonizing community space was co-constructed by a transnationally minded professor and two doctoral students. Each student was from varying language, ethnic and geographic identities, united in their experiences of teaching in the United States' southeastern region. Collaboratively, the authors purposefully developed a reading list which primarily focused on identity and its multifaceted intersections with race, culture and raciolinguistics along with the positioning of identity in the international realm. During the learning process, the professor received a cancer diagnosis. As a result, the students were led to take ownership of their learning in dialog with their professor. Their community wealth extended beyond the learning environment in support of one of the community members: the professor. Authentic *cariño* was reflected as the students offered emotional support, coordinated a post-op recovery schedule, provided meals for the professor's family, care-taking and formed new relationships with extended members of the professor's community. By upholding a decolonizing community space, the authors lived out the values of Ubuntu and ummah. This auto-ethnographic reflective piece provides readers an opportunity to reframe roles of teacher/educator/care-giver in their international efforts toward creating spaces of learning.

This volume makes a timely contribution to scholarship on the internationalization of TESOL teacher education. It will be of interest to graduate students, faculty, researchers, policymakers, curriculum designers and especially teacher educators. Developing and participating in internationalized experiences in TESOL teacher education from a critical and responsive place affords teachers and teacher educators growth in numerous domains, including in relation to understanding the importance of a global perspective in TESOL in the first place. Olmedo and Harbon (2010: 86–87) argued that international experiences not only help with language proficiency development, but 'also sensitize teachers to the frustrations that their own students face when in classrooms taught in a national language that they do not understand'. As intense transnationalism continues to characterize the 21st century in response to war, displacement and other motives, it is essential that (English) language teachers can understand, support and empower students learning English in an unfamiliar place and in times of challenge.

Note

(1) In this volume, TESOL is not employed with the aim of perpetuating processes of foreignization. Rather, it is used, first, to serve as a site of critique *per se*, and second, to help contextualize its ideological foundations, values and roles in different geopolitical areas, some of which are critically explored through the chapters in this volume.

References

Baecher, L. and Chung, S. (2020) Transformative professional development for in-service teachers through international service learning. *Teacher Development* 24 (1), 33–51.

Buckner, E. and Stein, S. (2020) What counts as internationalization? Deconstructing the internationalization imperative. *Journal of Studies in International Education* 24 (2), 151–166.

Colón-Muñiz, A., SooHoo, S. and Brignoni, E. (2014) Language, culture and dissonance: A study course for globally minded teachers with possibilities for catalytic transformation. *Teaching Education* 21 (1), 61–74.

Guo, Y., Guo, S., Yochim, L. and Liu, X. (2022) Internationalization of Chinese higher education: Is it westernization? *Journal of Studies in International Education* 26 (4), 436–453.

Guzmán-Valenzuela, C. (2023) Unveiling the mainstream narrative and embracing critical voices in the era of internationalisation in higher education: Considerations from Latin America. *Compare: A Journal of Comparative and International Education*, 1–19.

Hilliker, S. (2020) Virtual exchange as a study abroad alternative to foster language and culture exchange in TESOL teacher education. *TESL-EJ* 23 (4), 1–13.

Kehm, B.M. and Teichler, U. (2007) Research on internationalisation in higher education. *Journal of Studies in International Education* 11 (3–4), 260–273.

Kim, H.J. (2023) Culturally responsive pedagogy amid the internationalization of teacher education: Self-study of teaching international teacher candidates in US teacher education program. *Studying Teacher Education*, 1–22.

Knight, J. (2004) Internationalization remodeled: Definition, approaches, and rationales. *Journal of Studies in International Education* 8, 5–31.

Kumaravadivelu, B. (2012) Individual identity, cultural globalization, and teaching English as an international language: The case for an epistemic break. In L. Alsagoff, S.L. McKay, G. Hu and W.A. Renandya (eds) *Principles and Practices for Teaching English as an International Language* (pp. 9–27). Routledge.

Lourenço, M. (2018) Internationalizing teacher education curricula: Opportunities for academic staff development. *On the Horizon* 26 (2), 157–169.

Olmedo, I. and Harbon, L. (2010) Broadening our sights: Internationalizing teacher education for a global arena. *Teaching Education* 21 (1), 75–88.

Pennycook, A. (2006) *Global Englishes and Transcultural Flows*. Routledge.

Pu, C. and Weng, S. (2023) Developing teacher candidates' global teaching competence through virtual exchange. *Asia-Pacific Journal of Teacher Education* 51 (5), 458–479.

Qiang, Z. (2003) Internationalization of higher education: Towards a conceptual framework. *Policy Futures in Education* 1 (2), 248–270.

Shin, H. (2006) Rethinking TESOL from a SOL's perspective: Indigenous epistemology and decolonizing praxis in TESOL. *Critical Inquiry in Language Studies* 3 (2–3), 147–167.

Sieber, P. and Mantel, C. (2012) The internationalization of teacher education: An introduction. *Prospects* 42 (1), 5–17.

Stein, S. (2017) The persistent challenges of addressing epistemic dominance in higher education: Considering the case of curriculum internationalization. *Comparative Education Review* 61 (S1), S25–S50.

Tavares, V. (2022) Neoliberalism, native-speakerism and the displacement of international students' languages and cultures. *Journal of Multilingual and Multicultural Development,* 1–14.

Williams, J. and Grierson, A. (2016) Facilitating professional development during international practicum: Understanding our work as teacher educators through critical incidents. *Studying Teacher Education* 12 (1), 55–69.

Part 1

Challenges to the Internationalization of TESOL Education Around the World

1 Engagements with Internationalization in Norwegian TESOL Education: Reproducing or Confronting Ideologies?

Ingrid Rodrick Beiler and Vander Tavares

This chapter considers manifestations of internationalization in English teacher education programs in Norway. Through a critical discourse analysis that rests on an internationalization perspective sensitive to the influence of neoliberalism on English language education, including the intersection of neoliberalism and language ideologies, the authors examine publicly available documents of several English teacher education programs in Norway. The analysis demonstrates that prominent English language models oscillate between the Anglo-American native speaker and the competent (elite) European user of English as a Lingua Franca, positioning perspectives on language (use) originating from Global South contexts as supplemental. Additionally, the material benefit of internationalization largely flows to government-sponsored Norwegian centers abroad. Thus, the authors conclude that engagements with internationalization in Norwegian teacher education reinforce Western and European superiority, in which native speakers and (elite) European non-native speakers comprise the primary poles of speakerhood, in ways that do not disrupt a neoliberal internationalization agenda or dominant ideologies about language and culture. The authors identify that greater attention to social justice in English teacher education in Norway is needed.

Introduction

The internationalization of higher education involves the integration of international and intercultural perspectives and experiences into the fabric of academic institutions. At a curricular level, internationalization can enrich the educational experiences of faculty and students by including diverse teaching and learning methods, global content and international collaboration through short- and long-term exchanges (Leask, 2015). However, internationalization has also become increasingly entangled in neoliberal practices and discourses of higher education. When it comes to language, internationalization has further intensified the commercialization of English and therefore widened the global gap between different groups of students based on (in)equality of access to language education and, by extension, academic mobility (Bailey, 2023). Despite these challenges, internationalization can also embody a critical ethos through which students, in particular, can be empowered to identify and potentially confront the injustices sustained by coloniality and neoliberalism.

In this chapter, we consider how Norwegian teacher programs that qualify students to teach English to speakers of other languages (TESOL) engage with internationalization. English language education is thoroughly integrated into the education system in Norway, being a compulsory subject for the first 11 years of school (Norwegian Directorate for Education and Training [NDET], 2020). Additionally, some Norwegian institutions offer both undergraduate and graduate degrees that are taught fully or mostly in English, including TESOL programs. As the broader TESOL field continues to critically wrestle with ideological issues of English language education, such as native speakerism and monolingual norms, we seek to explore how TESOL programs in Norway approach these issues through possible engagements with internationalization. We employ a critical content analysis to identify the extent to which orientations toward native speakerism and global English are present in TESOL programs in Norway. Subsequently, we focus on two TESOL programs and examine how they differ in terms of values of neoliberal education and elements of native speakerism. We conclude by discussing the implications of such engagements for future teachers of English in Norway.

Internationalization of English Language Education through a Neoliberal Lens

Neoliberalism surfaced as an economic and political framework of governance in the mid-19th century. Individual freedom, free markets, deregulation and limited government intervention have been some of the priorities of a neoliberal paradigm since its emergence (Wrenn, 2014). Such priorities have gradually redesigned the relationship between the state and the individual: neoliberal states, corporations and organizations work to protect first the interests of 'the market' rather than those of individuals. The influence of neoliberalism today is such that it has captured many domains of life, including schooling and education. Institutions of higher education, which have been historically responsible for professional training, including that of future teachers, have also experienced a shift in their role and purpose in society. Operating largely through a corporative-capitalist model (Olssen & Peters, 2005), institutions of higher education make decisions on their programming considering economic gain that benefits primarily the (funding) state. On a secondary level is benefit to students, yet in relation to their employment success instead of intellectual development (Zepke, 2018), as the former has more consequential implications for the economy.

Language education has not been immune to neoliberal pressures and interests. Language is now highly commercialized and commodified, and consequently treated as a product (Heller, 2010). English, for instance, is shaped by language (teaching and learning) organizations functioning in Global North Anglophone 'industries', which determine the value and use of the language, both of which are then sold internationally to Southern language markets. Private language learning centers have emerged as profitable enterprises, especially with the continuous development of technology that tailors language instruction according to the clientele (see Shin, 2016). Targeted on the neoliberal agenda of English language education are often individuals who acquired English as a first language and can thus be marketed as 'native speakers' (Alshammari, 2021). Here, what sells is being a 'native speaker' of English, rather than first having adequate teaching and language qualifications for the profession. Furthermore, elevating 'native speaker' teachers of English in a profit-seeking business also implicitly divulges the message to students that they should strive to sound like their teachers to succeed educationally and linguistically (Tavares, 2022a).

Under the influence of neoliberalism, markets, trade and communication have gone from local to global. In this new business context, English remains the privileged language, or the lingua franca, which is promoted as giving English language teachers and students access to the global economy. Two ideological consequences are worth mentioning. First, 'English as a lingua franca' (ELF) is not free of repercussions. ELF may be understood as 'a contact language between persons who share neither a common native tongue nor a common (national) culture, and for whom English is the chosen foreign language of communication' (Firth, 1996: 240). For countries where English is not an official language, proficiency in English is encouraged and rewarded, therefore expanding and naturalizing the use of English as a lingua franca where multiple varieties come together. However, questions continue to be posed about the interplay between ELF and local languages and dialects, cultural identities and power (Canagarajah, 2006; Chvala, 2020). Furthermore, despite the prominence and well-received shift toward ELF (and other perspectives on English as an international language), it remains unclear how much of English language pedagogy is conceptualized, especially in English language teacher education programs, from an ELF stance.

This point raises a second ideological implication of the neoliberalization of the English language. With its focus on commercialization, neoliberalism preserves and multiplies the prominence of native speakerism in English language education. As an ideology, native speakerism refers to the belief that 'native speakers' of English are linguistically and culturally superior, and thus better suited as models for teaching compared to non-native speakers. Because the native speaker of English has been turned into a 'brand' and 'branding strategy', many institutions of business and education may prioritize hiring native speakers for teaching positions (Daoud & Kasztalska, 2022) or use them to promote educational services, such as cultural excursions, academic exchanges, trainings and workshops (e.g. Kubota, 2016a), including for future teachers of English. Yet native speakerism is not an ideology of language alone. In the international English language business, race and ethnicity intersect with language (Tavares, 2022b). White, native speakers of English from particular Anglophone settings remain privileged in educational contexts that reflect a neoliberal take on English (Ramjattan, 2019).

The British and American English 'native speakers' have historically been the two dominant points of reference in English language native speakerism. These two models have existed based on the 'standard' variety of British and American English which, while important for some pedagogical applications, neglect other, often minoritized, varieties and dialects within their nation states. Recently, however, efforts grounded in multicultural pedagogy have drawn more attention to linguistic variety: both intra-linguistic (within one English) and interlinguistic (different types of English and English relative to other languages). Neoliberal multiculturalism thus works to recognize and celebrate linguistic diversity; yet it does not *confront* the processes of hierarchization and othering that remain in place (Kubota, 2015). This issue has direct implications for the internationalization of English language studies and teacher education. That is, although ESOL education is now more diversified with references to world Englishes (Kachru, 1992), ELF, and other more flexible English constructs, many ESL programs and teacher education programs still elevate, subtly or explicitly, British or American standards.

Study Context

English has no official status in Norway, but it is considered a core school subject, compulsory for the first 11 years of school. The subject is governed by a national curriculum, most recently revised in 2020 (NDET, 2020). One significant change in this curriculum was to remove references found in the previous curriculum to Great Britain and the United States and 'other English-speaking countries' as target sources of literature and societal knowledge (NDET, 2013). Instead, the new curriculum refers generically to 'English-language' literature and 'the English-speaking world' (NDET, 2020). This revision may reflect changing perceptions of English in Norway, increasingly viewed as a lingua franca for communication across national and linguistic backgrounds, as well as a language for personal use in spare-time activities, service encounters, education and work. Nevertheless, British and American native-speaker ideologies persist among some teachers and students (Chvala, 2020; Rindal, 2019). English teaching largely occurs in the context of public schools, with little privatization of primary and secondary education generally or language education specifically.

Similarly, TESOL education is offered as a component of broader teacher education programs at 13 public universities or colleges. In integrated five-year teacher education programs leading to primary (grades 1–7) or upper primary to lower secondary certification (grades 5–10), students generally take a series of English courses that combine content (e.g. English grammar, children's literature) with teaching methods. In programs leading to secondary certification (grades 8–13), it is more common to take one or more foundations courses in English language, literature, or culture and a separate course in general pedagogy and English didactics. In the latter case, teacher education students may take their English courses with others who are not seeking teacher certification. All newly certified teachers in Norway must have a master's degree, but the credit requirements for English differ according to grade level, either 30 ECTS for the primary grades (1–7) or 60 ECTS for upper primary to lower secondary (5–10) or secondary (8–13) certification. In addition, students may elect to take further credits in English, for instance to specialize in English at the master's level.

Case and Methods

Our study is a critical discourse analysis of publicly available, online program information for English courses offered toward teacher education in Norway. Critical discourse analysis considers how asymmetrical relations of power are expressed in the details of text and talk and how these reflect and relate to broader societal discourses (Blackledge, 2008). We compiled program documents for analysis through redundant web searches, which we cross-referenced with two online databases[1] of higher education programs in Norway. Through this process, we developed a list of all relevant institutions (see Table 1.1) and program types, including primary teacher education (*grunnskolelærer 1–7* [GLU1-7]), upper primary to lower secondary teacher education (*grunnskolelærer 5–10* [GLU5-10]), integrated secondary teacher education (*lektorprogram*) and one-year foundations courses in English (*årsstudium*). The last program type may also be taken by students in teacher education, for instance those working toward a BA in English. For each program, we analyzed any of the following that were publicly available online: overall program

Table 1.1 Ideological orientations in Norwegian TESOL programs

Institution	Native speaker orientations	UK/US dichotomy	Global English orientations
Inland Norway U. of Applied Sciences	Moderate	No	Moderate
Nord University	Moderate	Yes*	Prominent
Norwegian U. of Science and Technology	Moderate	No	Prominent
Oslo Metropolitan University	Weak	No	Prominent
UiT The Arctic University of Norway	Prominent	Yes	Weak
University of Agder	Prominent	Yes	Weak
University of Bergen	Prominent	Yes	Weak
University of Oslo	Prominent	Yes	Weak
University of South-Eastern Norway	Moderate	Yes	Moderate
University of Stavanger	Prominent	Yes	Weak
Volda University College	Prominent	Yes*	Moderate
Western Norway U. of Applied Sciences	Moderate	Yes*	Moderate
Østfold University College	Prominent	Yes	Weak

*Only in 1 of 3–4 programs of study.

information, overall course plans and course descriptions. These documents are institutionally sanctioned and remain relatively constant for several years, thus providing better insight into official institutional discourses.

Given the delimited scope of institutions certifying English teachers in Norway, our first level of analysis seeks to broadly characterize engagements with internationalization across all relevant institutions. For the sake of comparability, we considered the first 30–60 ECTS in English offered, comprising required bachelor's level courses. Thus, we have excluded masters-level courses in English, as well as separate courses in English didactics and pedagogy (in Norwegian, *praktisk-pedagogisk utdanning*). At this broad level of analysis, we identified and categorized geopolitical (e.g. the United States) and societal domains (e.g. the labor market) and language-oriented concepts (e.g. English as a lingua franca) that frame or structure the programs. Each researcher undertook an independent reading of the course plans, information and documents. At this stage, we highlighted textual content, especially from course titles, learning outcomes and course descriptions, that related to the domains and concepts mentioned previously. Notes were then added to the marked-up text to establish connections between text and the categorizations. Subsequently, the researchers met to discuss, compare and refine preliminary findings in collaboration.

Our second level of analysis consists of a closer examination of program documents from two institutions that offer all three possible levels of English teacher certification (i.e. grades 1–7, 5–10 and 8–13), namely Nord University and the University of Agder. These two institutions were selected for the breadth of their English course offerings and their contrasting ideological orientations, which we arrived at as a result of the procedures of our first level of analysis. Furthermore, neither of the authors has worked at either institution, thus ensuring a greater degree of analytical distance. At this level of analysis, we consider textual descriptions within the documents at a lexical, phrasal, or full sentence level that may signal any of the concepts discussed previously, such as globalization, neoliberalism, diversity and native speakerism. We also examine the contextualizing description of these broad concepts. For instance, we considered 'American' or 'British' English or literature to be explicit, specific references that contextualize native speakerism.

We approach our analysis from a combination of first-hand experience teaching in comparable programs in Norway and from cultures of English teacher education and practice in multiple international contexts. Ingrid has nearly 10 years of experience as an English teacher educator in Norway, in addition to previous education and teaching experience in the United States, Palestine and Iraq. She is usually positioned as a White bilingual native speaker of Norwegian and dominant American English, though she is plurilingual. Vander has over a decade of experience teaching and designing courses in ESOL at colleges and universities in Canada, where he also completed his TESOL training. He is a White and plurilingual transnational to Norway, where he works as a teacher educator within both English language and non-English language teacher education programs.

Findings

Ideological orientations across institutions

In this section, we provide an overview of ideological orientations in TESOL program documents across all institutions that offer English teacher education in Norway. We consider the extent to which program information manifests native speaker and global English orientations, recognizing that both may be present at the same institution or even in the same document (see Hult, 2017). First, within native speaker orientations, we include elements such as content and standards related to Inner Circle countries (Kachru, 1992), for instance British history or General American pronunciation. In some cases, the apparently neutral term 'English-speaking countries' can also be understood to refer to Inner Circle countries based on context. From a qualitative perspective, we characterize the native speaker orientation across program documents at each institution as either prominent, moderate, or weak. These categorizations reflect, respectively: extensive/consistent, partial/inconsistent, or rare/incidental reference to native speaker standards or context. Second, we identify whether specific English-dominant countries, usually the United Kingdom and the United States, comprise a structuring element of course offerings or course content at institutions. Third, we identify 'global English' orientations through the use of theoretical terms such as world Englishes, English as an international language, or ELF, as well as through reference to 'the English-speaking world' or 'English-speaking countries', without implicit or explicit specification of the term as applying to Inner Circle countries. We also characterize global English orientations as either prominent, moderate or weak, employing the same criteria of relative frequency and prominence as for native speaker orientations. The categories are illustrated through case descriptions below. A categorization of ideological orientations across Norwegian TESOL programs is presented in Table 1.1.

The categorization in Table 1.1 demonstrates the ideological tensions present at all TESOL institutions in Norway, as both native speaker and global English orientations can be found across programs. Nonetheless, most institutions display prominent native speaker orientations, a fact that breaks with the relatively weak native speaker orientations in the Norwegian national curriculum in English (NDET, 2020). One strong instantiation of such native speaker orientations is captured by the third column, which indicates that all institutions with prominent native speaker orientations employ demonyms or standards related to the United States or United Kingdom – or the dichotomy between the two – as structuring elements in one or more of their programs of study, for instance by requiring courses in British and American literature or area studies (e.g. University of Bergen, University of South-Eastern Norway, Østfold University College) or by defining relevant varieties of English as Received Pronunciation and General American English (e.g. UiT The Arctic University of Norway, University of Oslo, University of Stavanger). Only one of 13 institutions (Oslo Metropolitan University) displays a weak native speaker orientation across program types and, conversely, a prominent global English orientation.

A few institutions emerge with a significantly mixed ideological profile, simultaneously displaying prominent or moderate native speaker *and* global English orientations. The University of South-Eastern Norway is a telling case in this respect, where discourses differ significantly between, on the one hand, programs for primary and lower secondary school teachers and, on the other hand, the year-long foundations course in English and the program for secondary school teachers. The former programs display much stronger global English orientations, focusing for instance on 'intercultural learning'[2] (English 1, GLU1-7) and 'English as a world language' (English 2, GLU5-10). In contrast, the course plan for the foundations course in English states that it 'places emphasis on Great Britain and the USA'. Similarly, the integrated secondary teacher program requires courses titled American Studies and British and Commonwealth Studies, thus reproducing the UK/US dichotomy as a dominant discursive and ideological structure, while also extending attention to the formerly colonized Other.

Similarly, at several other institutions that offer multiple different English programs (e.g. the Norwegian University of Science and Technology, Volda University College, Østfold University College), native speaker orientations seem most strongly expressed in year-long foundations courses and mostly weakly expressed in primary and lower secondary teacher education, where the course descriptions are often quite closely tied to the national curriculum in English. Indeed, the varying strength of institutional orientations may to some extent relate to which types of programs are offered and analyzed. For example, Oslo Metropolitan University, whose program documents display weak native speaker orientations and prominent global English orientations, only offers primary and lower secondary teacher education. Conversely, the program documents analyzed for the University of Oslo, more firmly oriented toward native speaker standards, concern a year-long foundations course, also taken by secondary teacher education students. These contrasts may illustrate the impact of institutional histories and subject traditions on the knowledge object of English teacher education.

Nonetheless, institutions with similar program offerings do also display significantly different orientations. We will analyze two such contrasting cases next, the University of Agder and Nord University, both medium-sized universities on a Norwegian scale (11,000–13,000 students), with multiple campuses and types of TESOL program offerings.

Case 1: University of Agder

The University of Agder represents a strong case of native speaker orientations, especially as expressed in program documents for the year-long foundations course in English, also taken as part of the secondary teacher education program. Both programs' introduction webpages emphasize the global status of English, yet closely align this apparent global English orientation with native speaker traditions. In the introduction to the foundations course, potential students can read: 'English is the dominant language in the world today. Therefore, it is important to be able to write and speak English and to have knowledge of British and American culture'. In this framing, the global status of English does not entail diversification or democratization of standards, but rather reinforcement of Anglo-American hegemony, as students purportedly need British and American cultural knowledge to succeed in a world where English dominates. Furthermore, prospective students are told that 'English *opens up* the possibilities' (our emphasis) in private and public sectors, as well as academia 'across the entire world', embodying a neoliberal discourse of internationalization, in which English becomes a globally profitable resource. Moreover, the importance of studying English for personal and intellectual growth is absent – a feature of neoliberal language education (Tavares, 2022a).

The connection between native speaker ideologies and global English is somewhat more subtle in the presentation of English for secondary level teachers, where British literature and American culture and history are the only examples given alongside apparently geographically open terms such as 'the most relevant cultures where English is used' or 'great English-language cultures'. Further specification of these terms requires consulting the program plan, for which students are referred to the English foundations course. Here, it becomes apparent that three of six required courses concern American and British Literature or 'Anglo-American' (original) society, alongside courses in English phonetics (covering standard British and American pronunciation), grammar and academic language use. These final three courses all frame English in terms of structure and systems, emphasizing stabilized, prestigious varieties. Across all course descriptions, there are only two mentions of contexts beyond the United States, United Kingdom or Norway. First, American and British Literature (Part II) includes 'selected Anglophone literature' which must be understood as something other than the previous three bullet points on 'American and British' content. Second, the course 'Anglo-American contemporary challenges in a historical perspective' (all original) includes one mention of the Commonwealth. Thus, when English is described as 'the global language of our time', the program appears to imagine a centripetal globalization, which reinforces powerful native speaker models, traditions and knowledge.

These orientations and emphases are important to understanding internationalization in the program because the foundations course plan states, under the header 'internationalization', that 'English is an international subject, and international and intercultural topics are addressed in the programme'. That is, readers are referred to the nature of the subject itself as the basis for internationalization, which must be understood, based on the framing, structure and content of the program, to comprise an internationalization oriented toward the United States and United Kingdom. Indeed, a 'longstanding agreement' with the Norwegian Study Centre in York (England) is the next point mentioned under the description of internationalization, along with mention of longer-term options in 'English-speaking countries' (all original). With respect to the integration of short-term study abroad in York, English teacher education at the University of Agder is more typical than unusual among Norwegian TESOL programs, as also evident in Case 2.

The primary and lower secondary English teacher courses at Agder feature less explicit native speaker orientations than the previously described programs. Instead, these programs are characterized by implicit orientations toward global English and to the Norwegian context. The courses follow a structural division that is common to English teacher education for these school grades in Norway, between English language and English literature and culture. The language courses largely emphasize 'English as a system' and comparison with the structure of Norwegian, though also using multilingualism as a resource, in line with the national curriculum in English (NDET, 2020). The second of two language courses in each program further aims to develop knowledge of 'English as a world language', although this is presented alongside a unitary and homogenous conception of 'the grammatical and phonological structure of the English language'. In courses covering literature and culture, target knowledge domains include 'the English-speaking world', 'English-speaking countries', 'English-language literature' and literature and texts 'from the English-speaking world'. None of these areas is defined more precisely, such that they are open to interpretation. In some cases, they are linked to the development of intercultural competence and culture-general skills and attitudes such as facilitation and tolerance, which might suggest a more open orientation toward global English. Still, the denomination 'English-speaking countries' might be considered narrower, since one presumably needs a critical mass of English speakers for the country, anthropomorphized, to be considered 'English-speaking'. In this sense, the 'international' is enveloped and constrained by the Anglophone. Indeed, the Norwegian Study Center in York comprises the only destination for student mobility that is integrated into the courses.

Case 2: Nord University

Nord University provides a contrast to the University of Agder because of relatively weak native speaker orientations – though moderate in one of four programs – and explicit global English orientations across program types. Furthermore, Nord University is one of the only institutions to feature weak native speaker orientations and strong global English orientations in its English foundations course and secondary teacher education, a pattern more common to primary and lower secondary education programs.

Across the four program documents available for the foundations course in English (a program introduction, program description and two component course descriptions), the geopolitical referent is consistently defined as 'the English-speaking world' (original). Key words in the program and course descriptions emphasize interculturality, cultural hybridity and diversity within 'the English-speaking world'. This orientation is clearly communicated in the first sentence of the program description: 'As citizens of the world, we need good English skills and intercultural awareness' (original). Whereas the comparable program introduction at Agder links English dominance to a need for British and American cultural knowledge, the initial program framing at Nord focuses on the individual in relationship with the other in the world, who therefore needs intercultural awareness to use English. This orientation toward interculturality and diversity becomes especially clear in the description of the second of two component courses, where course aims include developing 'knowledge about language contact, society and culture in the English-speaking world and about multiculturalism and multilingualism', 'intercultural awareness and critical thinking' and the ability to 'compare and contrast cultures, and develop the appreciation of cultural differences and intercultural competence' (all original). There are no comparable references to specific countries or varieties of English. Thus, despite an illustration photo with the British flag on the introduction page and a short obligatory trip to the Norwegian Study Centre in York integrated into the first course, the overall framing and course content portray English as a resource for interacting respectfully with a range of (plurilingual) interlocutors in diverse contexts, where English may not be the dominant language.

The orientation toward diversity and hybridity is perhaps even more clear in the course description of English for secondary teachers, where English itself is decentered initially. The document opens with a philosophical question:

> What do you know when you know a language? We look for answers to this by considering the English language: how it is pronounced, how words, phrases and sentences are constructed, how it is acquired by children, how it is used in social context, how English varies in different parts of the English-speaking world and how the language has changed, and continues to change, over time.

This description frames the study of language as primary and English and 'the English-speaking world' as simply an instantiation and means of developing an understanding of language. Here, in contrast to Agder, English is subsumed under the international and not vice-versa. This broader scope is also reflected in the conceptualization of the object of study: English not only as a structured system, but also as it is used in social context and as it varies and changes across time, place and social affiliation. Several course aims repeat the dual emphasis on language learning generally and English specifically, for instance to 'critically evaluate discussions in media about linguistics and English language'. This may be understood as an aim grounded in students' immediate context, as emphasized also in the subsequent aim, to 'communicate the relevance of linguistics and English for education, life skills, democratic participation and sustainable social development in our age', which reproduces cross-curricular themes from the national curriculum in English (NDET, 2020). Overall, the orientation to English education might be described as glocal (Guilherme & Souza, 2019), requiring local contextualization while opening up to international interaction.

These orientations generally characterize the primary and lower secondary education courses at the institution as well, especially the two primary teacher courses (English 1A and 1B) and two parallel courses for upper primary and lower secondary teachers. The first course (English 1A) specifies three domains of English that comprise relevant knowledge: English in the world, in Norway and in the national curriculum. The second course (English 1B) specifies the aim to develop knowledge about 'various cultures in Norway and across the world and their relevance to primary ELT'. Thus, English is conceived as glocal and pedagogical, with an emphasis on cultural diversity.

It is also noteworthy that both English 1A and 1B emphasize, to varying levels, traditional skills and experiences that are devalued by neoliberal education. In English 1B, there is a focus on the self in coexistence with the other, wherein relationships are encouraged. Students are expected to 'be a good language model' for children and to 'work alone and in collaboration with others to develop learning practices related to the children's language learning'. As such, personal development occurs both individually and collectively and, equally important, for the benefit also of the other (in this case, children). In short, such skills and experiences reject an individualist model of self-development espoused by neoliberal education, in which students must compete, rather than collaborate, with one another and always prioritize the self (Tavares, 2022a).

However, the second two courses for upper primary and lower secondary teachers (English 2A and 2B) shift to a pronounced native speaker orientation, reproducing the structuring dichotomy of British vs. American literature and culture as the stated content of the respective courses. Ideological tensions are nonetheless apparent in these course descriptions, as neither the United Kingdom nor United States are named in any course aims. In English 2A, the aims refer generically to 'society, history, and forms of cultural expression in English-speaking countries'. In English 2B, the aims focus on 'English-speaking countries', 'English as a world language' and 'intercultural competence'. This apparent contradiction raises the possibility that the course description maintains vestiges of traditional content, oriented toward the native speaker, while having been partly revised with a stronger orientation toward global English. Another possibility is that British and American cultures in fact define apparently open references to 'English-speaking countries' and 'English as a world language', as in the program documents at the University of Agder. These programs also integrate a trip to York, which further sediments the traditional role of England as a locus of internationalization, at Nord as at Agder.

Discussion

The two cases that we analyzed represent relative but not complete contrasts, as elements of both native speaker and global English orientations are present across the cases. Two phrases that lend ambiguity to these orientations, sometimes causing them to converge, include 'English-speaking countries' and 'the English-speaking world'. Based on context, these denominations may either signal openness to English use across the world or, quite narrowly, a reinforced focus on those countries and parts of the world traditionally defined as 'English-speaking'. In the latter instance, Norwegian TESOL programs often focus only on standardized, stabilized varieties of English in Great Britain and the United States, ignoring even former British settler-colonies such as Australia, Canada and New Zealand, not to mention former colonies across the Caribbean, Africa and Asia, as targets for international engagement and language use. These delimitations constrict conceptions of successful communication and normative ways of being in English. Yet even if 'English-speaking countries' and 'the English-speaking world' are defined broadly, the act of boundary-making is necessarily exclusionary. If there is literature from the English-speaking world, there must also be literature that is *not* from the English-speaking world, or else it would simply be called literature. Thus, attempts to open up the geographical reference of the English language still maintain distinctions between places that *do* or *do not* serve as legitimate language models and, by extension, as desirable sites of internationalization. We suggest that a glocal approach to English, with simultaneous attention to global functions and local appropriation across various contexts, might provide a more complex and equitable foundation for internationalization in Norwegian TESOL education (see Canagajarah, 2006; Guilherme & Souza, 2019). This dual awareness of the local and global is already present in Norwegian English teachers' reflections on English in their own context (Chvala, 2020) and might be extended to discuss and understand the multiple dynamics of English elsewhere in the world (e.g. Hult, 2017).

From a neoliberal language education perspective, including English-language models other than the United States and the United Kingdom can be seen as a deviation from 'standard' international practice. Although this is, we argue, an important, ethical 'deviation' that must be made, internationalization through engagement with the *othered* is not easily marketable, as institutions of higher education are embedded in an international educational market where competition, mobility patterns and market trends that 'sell' co-exist, sometimes even in conflict. Thus, we highlight the possibility that engagements toward the international in TESOL education in Norway reinforce Western, neoliberal, native-speaker ideologies in an intersecting fashion, and to some extent, also racial ideologies, as native speakerism in English oriented toward the United States and United Kingdom cannot be detached from the White speaker (Kubota, 2015; Tavares, 2022b). By maintaining the order as such, international engagements in TESOL education in Norway keep future teachers 'away from real-world problems' (Kubota, 2016b: 490) and miss out on the important need to involve students in critical English language (teacher) education in relation to language-based injustices from a global perspective. This raises the issue of the *purpose* of English language education, in a more holistic sense: to replicate the sociopolitical order or to transform it.

Conclusion and Implications

In this study, we have considered engagements with internationalization in sanctioned institutional discourses of TESOL education in Norway, through publicly available program documents. This scope of analysis necessarily excludes details of program implementation such as reading lists, course topics and assignments. Furthermore, we have not considered English-specific content in general didactic and pedagogical courses or master's level courses. Ideological orientations contrary to those in the analyzed program documents may operate at these other program levels, both toward native speaker and global English orientations. Thus, future research might usefully consider in-depth, multilevel analyses of ideological orientations in Norwegian TESOL education, for instance through ethnographic methods.

Overall, our analysis points to a strong orientation toward the British and American native speaker in most TESOL programs in Norway, notably including three of Norway's four most renowned institutions: the University of Oslo, University of Bergen and UiT The Arctic University of Norway. Most often, strong orientations to native speakerism are, not surprisingly, accompanied by weak orientations to global English. The mandatory exchange to the University of York in many programs may also be seen as a site, both physical and ideological, where traditions are preserved. In light of the critical changes and discussions taking place within TESOL scholarship, including lingua franca, raciolinguistic (e.g. Kubota, 2015; Ramjattan, 2019), multilingual, plurilingual and translingual approaches to English language education, we conclude that, at a surface level, most TESOL programs in Norway remain generally ideologically conservative.

Notes

(1) studievalg.no; utdanning.no
(2) Unless otherwise noted, all program document quotes are our translations from Norwegian.

References

Alshammari, A. (2021) Job advertisements for English teachers in the Saudi Arabian context: Discourses of discrimination and inequity. *TESOL Journal* 12 (2), 1–13.
Bailey, L. (2023) *Challenging the Internationalisation of Education: A Critique of the Global Gaze*. Taylor and Francis.
Blackledge, A. (2008) Critical discourse analysis. In Li Wei and M.G. Moyer (eds) *Blackwell Guide to Research Methods in Bilingualism and Multilingualism* (pp. 296–310). Blackwell.
Canagarajah, S.A. (2006) Negotiating the local in English as a lingua franca. *Annual Review of Applied Linguistics* 26, 197–218.
Chvala, L. (2020) Teacher ideologies of English in 21st century Norway and new directions for locally tailored ELT. *System* 102327. https://doi.org/10.1016/j.system.2020.102327

Daoud, S. and Kasztalska, A. (2022) Exploring native-speakerism in teacher job recruitment discourse through Legitimation Code Theory: The case of the United Arab Emirates. *Language Teaching Research*. https://doi.org/10.1177/13621688211066883

Firth, A. (1996) The discursive accomplishment of normality: On 'lingua franca' English and conversation analysis. *Journal of Pragmatics* 26, 237–259.

Guilherme, M. and Souza, L.M.M. (2019) *Glocal Languages and Critical Intercultural Awareness: The South Answers Back*. Routledge.

Heller, M. (2010) The commodification of language. *Annual Review of Anthropology* 39, 101–114.

Hult, F.M. (2017) More than a lingua franca: Functions of English in a globalised educational language policy. *Language, Culture and Curriculum* 30 (3), 265–282. https://doi.org/10.1080/07908318.2017.1321008

Kachru, B.B. (1992) *The Other Tongue: English Across Cultures*. University of Illinois Press.

Kubota, R. (2015) Race and language learning in multicultural Canada: Towards critical antiracism. *Journal of Multilingual and Multicultural Development* 36 (1), 3–12.

Kubota, R. (2016a) The social imaginary of study abroad: Complexities and contradictions. *The Language Learning Journal* 44 (3), 347–357.

Kubota, R. (2016b) The multi/plural turn, postcolonial theory, and neoliberal multiculturalism: Complicities and implications for applied linguistics. *Applied Linguistics* 37 (4), 474–494.

Leask, B. (2015) *Internationalizing the Curriculum*. Routledge.

Norwegian Directorate for Education and Training (2013) English subject curriculum. https://www.udir.no/kl06/ENG1-03/

Norwegian Directorate for Education and Training (2020) Curriculum in English. https://www.udir.no/lk20/eng01-04?lang=eng

Olssen, M. and Peters, M.A. (2005) Neoliberalism, higher education and the knowledge economy: From the free market to knowledge capitalism. *Journal of Education Policy* 20 (3), 313–345.

Ramjattan, V.A. (2019) The white native speaker and inequality regimes in the private English language school. *Intercultural Education* 30 (2), 126–140.

Rindal, U. (2019) PhD revisited: Meaning in English: L2 attitudes, choices and pronunciation in Norway. In U. Rindal and L.M. Brevik (eds) *English Didactics in Norway – 30 Years of Doctoral Research* (pp. 335–355). Scandinavian University Press.

Shin, H. (2016) Language 'skills' and the neoliberal English education industry. *Journal of Multilingual and Multicultural Development* 37 (5), 509–522.

Tavares, V. (2022a) Exploring the impact of notions of success based on native-speakerism, individualism and neoliberalism on ESL students' identities. In A.J. Daghigh, J.M. Jan and S. Kaur (eds) *Neoliberalization of English Language Policy in the Global South* (pp. 153–172). Springer.

Tavares, V. (2022b) Neoliberalism, native-speakerism and the displacement of international students' languages and cultures. *Journal of Multilingual and Multicultural Development*, 1–14.

Wrenn, M. (2014) Identity, identity politics, and neoliberalism. *Panoeconomicus* 61 (4), 503–515.

Zepke, N. (2018) Student engagement in neo-liberal times: What is missing? *Higher Education Research and Development* 37 (2), 433–446.

2 Internationalization in Vietnam's English Language Teacher Education Curriculum: Toward a Localized English Teacher Education Framework

Anh Ngoc Trinh, Nhung Hong Thi Nguyen and Anh Lan Thi Tran

Internationalization of English language teacher education (ELTE) has become an imperative rather than a necessity since teachers are perceived as pivotal in the internationalization agenda (Childress, 2010; Green & Whitsed, 2013). Nonetheless, the area has received insufficient attention and witnessed a dearth of scholarly investigations in Vietnam. To address the paucity, this chapter discusses internationalization dimensions in Vietnam's ELTE curriculum development and implementation and the possibilities of internationalization in ELTE curriculum renovation through a localized framework of ELTE. The qualitative data were drawn from content and thematic analysis of 46 ELTE curriculum frameworks of 39 universities and colleges specializing in ELTE nationwide. Internationalization of the curriculum (IoC) refers to 'the incorporation of international, intercultural, and/or global dimensions into the content of the curriculum as well as the learning outcomes, assessment tasks, teaching methods, and support services of a program of study' (Leask, 2015: 9). Drawn from this conceptualization, the chapter postulates that social constructivism and competency-based approaches in the examined curricula are perceived as global and international dimensions. These approaches were embedded in the development of program outcomes and could be observed in the choice of teaching methodologies and assessment methods even though they were not explicitly and substantially stated across the curricula. The chapter argues that the intentional incorporation of foreign-born theories could support renovating an ELTE curriculum, however, they should be carefully considered to align with local contexts.

Introduction

During the last few decades, there have been increasing calls for teacher education programs worldwide to address the needs of an interdependent and globalized world. Many teacher education institutions have accordingly internationalized their programs in numerous ways to meet societal needs. Some institutions send pre-service teachers abroad or increase the number of international pre-service students, whereas others adopt global perspectives in their curricula, or apply international pedagogies in classroom practices. Within such a changing educational landscape, ELTE is not an exception. Strengthening the quality of ELTE programs toward a more globalized and internationalized direction has become an imperative rather than a necessity in the internationalization agenda (Childress, 2010; Green & Whitsed, 2013).

The IoC is concerned with the curriculum itself, with the efforts to incorporate 'international, intercultural and/or global dimensions into the content of the curriculum as well as the learning outcomes, assessment tasks, teaching methods and support services of a program of study' (Leask, 2015: 9). Indeed, different factors, including global, regional, national and local ones, interact with each other to shape the internationalization of the curriculum. Among these, the integration of foreign-born theories and approaches to curriculum development and implementation is a common practice.

One of the visible dimensions of an internationalized curriculum is how the program goals and outcomes are defined, created, implemented and assessed in light of Western-based theories. Current ELTE models worldwide are oriented toward a competency-based approach to the development of program outcomes. Program-level competencies, integrating knowledge, skills and attitudes required in higher education or the workplace, play a crucial role in preparing students for their future educational and employment contexts (Johnstone & Soares, 2014). Recent research into the development of program goals and outcomes emphasizes the adoption of 21st-century knowledge, skills and entrepreneurial competencies (Boyles, 2012). Typical and impactful models include the partnership for 21st-century skills with the 4Cs model or the 6Cs by Fullan and Langworthy (2014). Trilling and Fadel (2009) added cross-cultural understanding, communication and media fluency, computing and ICT fluency, and career and learning self-reliance besides critical thinking and problem-solving, creativity and innovation, collaboration, teamwork and leadership. These competencies play a crucial role in educating 21st-century teachers, helping them prepare for increasingly complex environments and meet different learning needs of students in the modern world.

Another dimension in the IoC agenda is the application of Vygotsky's social constructivist theory which emphasizes the social context of learning in which knowledge construction is achieved through social interaction. An ELTE program developed considering the social constructivist theory supports pre-service teachers' active cognitive engagement, helping them connect new knowledge to their existing experiences. It values holistic pre-service teachers' development and recognizes the powerful impact of socially oriented learning models.

More than ever, it is critical for an ELTE program to create experiences that lead to deep learning through purposefully integrating diverse academic content with experiences that facilitate a deliberate development of skills, thinking and knowledge necessary for learners to become lifelong learners. Fullan and Langworthy (2014) introduced the concept of new pedagogies, emphasizing new collaborative learning models between learners and teachers, with a focus on deep learning goals. In this approach, teachers design, construct and assess authentic learning experiences and assessments, leveraging existing tools and resources to maximize content learning within the context of knowledge, skills and attitudes development. In the new approach, the quality of a teacher is evaluated based on their pedagogical competence which is a system of teaching strategies and the ability to foster collaborative relationships with learners in empowering the learning process (Fullan & Langworthy, 2014). This perspective on empowering the learning process is also mentioned by Kumaravadivelu (2013) when describing the teacher training model for language teachers, stressing that teachers need to become self-determining individuals and undergo self-transformation. Farrell (2008) introduced a teacher education model that underscores self-reflection/experiential learning and views learners as active participants in their learning process, encouraging systematic reflective practice, exploring beliefs and engaging in classroom practice to take responsibility for their development throughout their careers (Farrell, 2015). Through this approach, language teachers can better bridge or narrow the gap between theory/practice present in many language teacher education programs.

While arguing that institutions' adoption of foreign-born theories or approaches in their curricula might encompass an internationalization dimension, we aim to identify the extent to which such theories are embedded through the localization process in ELTE curricula in Vietnam. This chapter first sets the background to the study by outlining the contextual impacts of Vietnam's foreign language development and internationalization policies. Secondly, it briefly reports how qualitative data were analyzed before presenting the approaches to ELTE curriculum development and implementation. Lastly, it provides a critical discussion about the adoption of a localized ELTE framework where Western-based theories are incorporated in ELTE curricula should align with the current policies in the local context.

Contextual Background

Internationalization of curriculum, with a focus on learners' competencies, has been positioned as an impetus for Vietnam's political, economic and sociocultural enhancement. Vietnam has issued policies and implemented practices to strengthen the national education quality as well as to meet the increasing needs of a globalized world. After the issuance of Circular 07/2015/TT-BGDDT on the required competencies of graduates in 2015 and the National Qualifications Framework in 2016, Circular 20/2018/TT-BGDDT on professional standards and competencies of school teachers was an additional attempt aiming to promote competency-based approach in teacher education programs. In response to the uncertainties and the swiftly changing nature of the 21st century, the new National General Education Curriculum 2018 issued under Circular 32/2018/TT-BGDDT set a range of competencies as desirable outcomes for Vietnamese students to achieve at different levels. This new curriculum serves as a strong call for attention to learners' competency development and necessitates a careful review of current teacher education programs at higher education levels.

In ELTE, more efforts have been made by the government through the National Foreign Languages Project (commonly known as the NFLP), and the introduction of English as a compulsory subject from Grade 3. Since 2008, the NFLP has been funded with a budget of nearly US$500 million, targeting leveraging English proficiency for Vietnamese students and teachers across levels as well as providing professional opportunities for teachers by 2020. As a part of the project, a localized language competency framework and a standardized English proficiency test, VSTEP, were tailored to the context of English use in Vietnam in 2014. Since its introduction, the test has been commonly used in high-stakes exams for entry or graduation of both undergraduate and postgraduate programs. With the extension of the NFLP from 2017 to 2025, the goal was set as '100% of the graduates from ELTE programs to meet the requirements of the professional standards and the ETCF by 2025' (MOET, 2018: 3). In 2020, the Framework for Language Teacher Competencies (FLTC) was officially introduced by the Ministry of Education and Training (MOET) as a revised version of the English Language Teacher Competence Framework (ETCF) developed in 2013 by international and local experts. This document was considered 'a guide for language teacher education institutions in developing, improving and renovating the education programs' (MOET, 2020: 1).

Data Collection and Data Analysis

The qualitative data for this chapter were drawn from the first phase of a national project conducted between 2019 and 2021 by an expert team working in key ELTE universities across Vietnam, among whom two co-authors were the main investigators. This project collected 46 ELTE curriculum frameworks and selected course syllabi of 39 universities and colleges for qualitative analysis. The curriculum frameworks were coded based on the regional locations of the surveyed universities and colleges, followed by a number indicating the order of collected data in the data collection process. Accordingly, data were coded into the following regions: Northern Central Coast (BTB), Northeast (DB), Red River Delta (DBSH), Southwest (TNB), Southeast (DNB), Central Coastal (DHTB), South Central Coast (NTB), Northwest (TB), Central Highlands and South-Central Coast (TN). The curriculum framework coded as 'DBSH-CD8' represents the 8th college in the Red River Delta region, while 'DBSH1' represents the 1st university in the Red River Delta region.

Qualitative data analysis refers to 'finding a way through multiple layers of meaning' (Bryman, 2016: 565), where identifying themes is the most crucial aspect. We used content and thematic analysis to interpret data in particular contexts and make sense of the broader system based on connecting sets of relevant data. By focusing on the content, we identified the existence, significance and relationships of the words and sentences in the text, thus making inferences about messages in program goal statements and program outcomes of ELTE curricula in universities and colleges (Marshall & Rossman, 2014). We also analyzed programs' stated teaching methodologies and assessment practices through thematic analysis which involved identifying and categorizing codes from texts and then searching for themes to make sense of the data based on theory (Bryman, 2016).

The Adoption of Foreign-born Approaches in Vietnam's ELTE Curriculum Development

In this section, we examine the extent to which ELTE institutions apply foreign-born theories through an analysis of their curriculum frameworks and course syllabi.

Competencies described in program goal statements

Data analysis indicates that ELTE institutions adopted a competency-based toward developing program goals and outcomes. These goals were categorized into two groups: one denoting the competencies required for the 21st century, and the other describing the portraits of expected ELTE graduates who possess required competencies for the teaching career.

In the first group, competencies required for the 21st century were stated explicitly in the goal statements. Some institutions aim to develop graduates' 'abilities to work', 'to be a good person' and 'to succeed in life' (DHTB3); 'collaboration and creativity' (DBSH4), 'quality, efficiency, professionalism, integrity' (BTB1), 'quality, efficiency, creativity and contribution to the community' (NTB3) or 'self-study and research, creative thinking and the application of acquired knowledge' (BTB-CD4). More particularly, competencies described in the goal statements emphasize the social demands of the local communities, such as 'to meet the requirements of human resources' and 'to contribute to the socio-economic development of the province and other localities' (TN-CD1); the needs of the country, such as 'learning for the nation, learning for innovation, creativity, and integration' (TN1); the needs of the employers, such as 'increasing practicality to enhance students' competencies and meet the requirements of employers' (DB4).

In the second group, to portray an expected image of an ELTE graduate, 23 out of 39 institutions (58.97%) emphasize the knowledge, skills, teaching capacity and professional ethics of pre-service teachers. One typical goal statement is: 'The program provides students with the knowledge and pedagogical skills in English to shape and develop their personality, professional ethics, knowledge, and basic and necessary skills to achieve professional success in the field of teaching, education, and English use' (TB1). Similar to this, other programs' goal statements appear to reflect a traditional view of teaching in which an English language teacher is seen as a professional who possesses the so-called 'traditional' knowledge base (Shulman, 1987), including pedagogical knowledge, skills and professional ethics.

In contrast, the program goal statements of 12 out of 39 institutions, accounting for 30.76%, portray an image of an English language teacher in the era of change and innovation. Besides the professional knowledge, skills and professional ethics, an English teacher in this new view needs to possess other competencies such as creativity, the ability to continue learning and the ability to adapt to societal changes. An instance of program goals is described as follows:

> Providing teachers with good quality, being able to teach English at schools and higher education institutions; being highly adaptable, possessing good knowledge of English, being equipped with knowledge of teaching, knowledge of learners in specific contexts, being flexible, having good communication and problem- solving skills and self-learning ability, being well prepared for further education… (DB4)

This view of teaching reflects Freeman and Johnson's (1998) conceptualization of interrelated components that constitute teaching activities: 'the teacher and the learner, the context of teaching activities, and pedagogical methods' (1998: 405).

Competencies described in program outcomes

Among those institutions portraying the image of a pre-service EFL teacher in the new era of change and innovation, six universities (DHTB1, DBSH4, DNB2, DNB3, DB3, NTB3) presented program outcomes that correspond to their program goal statements. When examining the lists of program outcomes of these institutions, we could identify global, international and intercultural competencies that represent internationalization dimensions. Table 2.1 provides further detail.

As can be seen, these program outcomes comprise competencies required for the 21st century (e.g. creativity, critical thinking, problem-solving) and competencies that align with the Foreign Language Teacher Competency Framework (FLTCF) such as technological literacy, cultural competency, language proficiency, teaching competencies and professional development.

However, the program outcomes described in many institutions' curriculum frameworks were about specific subject knowledge and skills, specifically linked to teaching English as a subject rather than integrating into developing comprehensive competencies for school students as

Table 2.1 Examples of global, international and intercultural competencies as program outcomes in ELTE curricula

Creativity	Having a creative and critical thinking mindset to continuously improve one's expertise and apply it to teaching to help students develop appropriate creative and critical thinking skills corresponding to their educational level. (DBSH4)
Critical Thinking and Problem Solving	Having a mindset of creativity and critical thinking to continuously enhance one's language proficiency and apply it to teaching, to assist students in developing appropriate creative and critical thinking skills that align with their educational level. (DBSH4) Being able to analyze situations in learning, identifying and articulating problematic situations in learning. (DBSH4)
Technology Literacy	Being able to analyze student profiles: psychological characteristics, abilities, needs and goals. (DB2)
Teaching Competencies	Being able to plan lessons, and choose the appropriate approaches, methods and techniques of teaching (DBSH5)
Professional Development	Being able to self-direct and adapt to different work environments; developing self-learning and accumulating knowledge and experience to enhance professional expertise. (DBSH3)
Language Proficiency	Being able to use the English language for communication skills (listening, speaking, reading, writing). (DBSH3) Achieving level 5 within the 6-level Foreign Language Competency Framework in Vietnam or an equivalent to C1 of the Common European Framework of Reference for Languages for English. (DBSH3)
Cultural Competency	Having a solid understanding of cultural and social knowledge and arts, developing critical thinking skills, forming effective language learning methods and understanding the history of world civilizations and the cultures of ASEAN countries. (DBSH3)

required by the 2018 National General Education Curriculum. In addition, the idea that pre-service EFL teachers need to achieve a 'good' English language proficiency level (Level 5 in the six levels of the Foreign Language Competency Framework) still appears to reflect the requirement of a 'native-like' or 'near-native' proficiency level with a 'generic command of English' (Freeman, 2020). There is no emphasis on how teachers use English in their classroom instruction or English-for-Teaching. According to Freeman (2020), ELTE program outcomes should shift their focus toward teachers' confidence in applying language skills in practical settings rather than solely measuring their mastery of general English.

Social Constructivism in Program Goals, Content, Teaching and Assessment

The shift toward social constructivism is expected to bring about fundamental changes in program outcomes, structural components, teaching methods and assessment in ELTE programs (Freeman & Johnson, 1998). The underpinnings of social constructivism in an ELTE curriculum can be observed in the five characteristics that promote learner-centeredness in program philosophies, outcomes, teaching and assessment (Fullan & Langworthy, 2014; Roberts, 1998). Below are the characteristics used to analyze features of social constructivism in the curriculum frameworks of the studied institutions.

(1) There is a transition from English language knowledge transfer to a human-centered approach (providing future teachers with English language knowledge, with specific competencies and values).
(2) There is a transition from providing the knowledge of the 'English language' subject including the knowledge of pedagogies to a practical approach to help pre-service teachers become active learners and learn how to become English language teachers in real-world contexts.
(3) The program should emphasize the idea that learning is a process of experiencing and reflecting, and the learning or education process should also create an environment where learners can have real teaching experiences and receive direct guidance in specific teaching contexts. Through this, learners can reflect and draw necessary experiences.
(4) The overall program goals are to educate individuals who can be self-directed and responsive to educational innovations, enhance learner capacity, promote learner autonomy, foster practical skills and prepare learners with adaptability to the employment market, professional skills and understanding of the working environment.
(5) Teaching and assessment focus on creating learning situations and tasks that allow pre-service teachers to experience and construct knowledge with interactions with instructors, peers and students.

Features of social constructivism identified in the program goals of the studied institutions include 'putting the learner at the center' (DBSH-CD2) or 'creating conditions for self-study and research, encouraging creative thinking and the application of acquired knowledge' (BTB-CD4). Besides, there was evidence of how the studied institutions show an alignment between their claimed teaching and assessment approaches and their curriculum contents.

Table 2.2 summarizes how the curriculum frameworks address the issue of learner-centeredness in their teaching assessment approach and curriculum contents in six institutions in which x indicates that no relevant information was found and v indicates that relevant information was found. As can be seen from the table, among the six training institutions, only DHTB1 demonstrates a relative consistency and alignment between the approach and the content. When examining its framework curriculum and course syllabi, we are concerned about the factors in these documents that promote and enhance learner capabilities, increase learner autonomy, foster practical skills, prepare learners for adaptability in the job market, develop work skills and provide an understanding of the work environment. With regards to the first feature, this institution had stated evidence of how they incorporated reflective practices into teaching and practical components of the curriculum. In the fifth feature, for example, the program content of DHTB1 allows learners to engage in experiential learning and actively construct knowledge on their own. These features align well with the roles of learners as owners of the active learning process (Beck & Kosnik, 2006; Freeman & Johnson, 1998), or the development of the teaching profession via social interaction, research and practical experience in an education environment in teacher education (Johnson & Golombek, 2018).

However, the alignment to social constructivism was inconsistently demonstrated in the teaching and assessment methods employed by other institutions. In the curriculum frameworks and syllabi accessible to us, some institutions described their teaching and assessment activities including presentation, simulation, role-play, group project and reflection. These

Table 2.2 The characteristics of an ELTE curriculum with a focus on learner-centeredness (Fullan & Langworthy, 2014; Roberts, 1998)

Curriculum characteristics	DBSH-CD2	DB-CD2	TB-CD4	DB4	BTB-CD3	DHTB1
Feature 1	x	X	x	x	x	v
Feature 2	x	X	x	x	x	v
Feature 3	x	X	x	x	x	v
Feature 4	x	X	x	x	x	v
Feature 5	x	X	x	x	x	v

(x: No relevant information found; v: Relevant information found) were described as features of social constructivism in teaching and learning methods suggested by Chu *et al.* (2017) and competency-based assessment by Do (2019). However, the examination of other institutions' curriculum frameworks and course syllabi shows that the described teaching and assessment methods in the course syllabi still followed a traditional content-oriented approach. The course descriptions often repeat phrases such as 'The course equips students with knowledge of…', and the teaching methods account for 70–80% as teacher-centered methods based on a fixed content schedule, which might not allow students to exercise their activeness and creativity.

Toward a Localized Teacher Education Framework for Internationalization

The analysis of ELTE curriculum frameworks from different institutions indicates the adoption of foreign-born theories including social constructivism and competency-based approaches to some extent. At the same time, there is also evidence of the integration of national policies and regulations in education and language teacher education into the curricula.

Brewer and Leask (2012) claim that IoC is normally critiqued for its tendency to formulate hegemony of Western perspectives, the risk of the re-colonization of knowledge production, and knowledge dissemination resulting from uncritical and unselective curriculum borrowing practices. The export and import of Western higher education practices across the globe are in line with the unprecedented growth of global transactions and the dominance of English as the lingua franca. This viewpoint is shared by many scholars whose work particularly focuses on internationalization practices in Asian higher education contexts (Steiner-Khamsi & Waldow, 2012; Tran *et al.*, 2018).

It might be argued that integrating principles of social constructivism and a competency-based approach or any other Western ideologies in an ELTE curriculum may run the risk of re-colonization of knowledge production in Vietnam. However, such adoption can be justified owing to the changing nature of the teaching profession and its feasibility in the Vietnamese educational context. Embedding these international dimensions in the ELTE curriculum supports the possibilities of internationalization in Vietnamese education as a whole and in ELTE particularly. More importantly, features of these two foreign-born theories and possibly other conceptual dimensions were already localized into a framework for English language teacher education in Vietnam via national policies. For example, competencies regarding creativity, adaptability, problem-solving or the ability to enact the profession in changing contexts are defined and described in both Circular 07/2015/TT-BGDDT and the 2016 National Qualifications Framework. The fact that Circular 07/2015/

TT-BGDDT described the expected learning outcomes as comprising knowledge, skills, attitudes and professional accountability might explain why most institutions include the phrase 'the course equips students with the knowledge of ...' in their program goal statements. In addition, such phrases as 'learning for the nation' and '...contribution to the socio-economic development' in program goals of many institutions have indeed been used in government policy documents in recent decades as different ways to emphasize national strategies for strengthening local human resources and global integration.

Within teacher education, Circular 20/2018/TT-BGDDT dictates professional standards that require teachers to constantly self-study and plan for professional development and to develop competencies for learners. While these are global competencies, some standards are particularly traditional expectations of a teacher in Vietnamese culture. While a teacher's ethics and values are described as the number-one standard for a Vietnamese teacher, the ability to provide consultation and support to learners and build a safe and democratic educational environment for students are also key standards. Confucianism, with its tradition of fondness for learning and special respect for teachers, scholars, students and mentors, has become a fundamental element in shaping Vietnam's culture (Pham & Fry, 2004). Therefore, a teacher is expected to be a role model and to support the student's growth.

For English language teacher education, the issuance of the FLTC developed by international and local experts in the middle of 2020 was significant evidence of how international dimensions are embedded and localized in shaping the portrait of an English language teacher in the Vietnamese current context. This framework is the typical representation of '*glonacal heuristic theory*' proposed by Marginson and Rhoades (2002) who suggested that the *global*, the *national* and the *local* dimensions interlock with each other and national history, languages, cultures and political systems generate varying considerations of global factors.

The study of program goals and program outcomes in curriculum frameworks of Vietnamese teacher education institutions indicates the so-called alignment to educational policies and the aforementioned frameworks (i.e. FLTC Framework and the National Qualifications Framework). In reality, despite certain limitations in the implementation process, these national policies and frameworks have raised teachers' awareness of desirable competencies and somehow assisted institutions considering issues of teachers' low language proficiency or lack of pedagogical skills, while seeking ways to promote purposeful professional development (Vu & Phan, 2020). Such alignment also indicates that institutions have considered national interests, policies and strategies in shaping the framework for English language education in their process of internationalizing education (Marginson *et al.*, 2011; Maringe & Foskett, 2010).

Since most students in the Vietnamese educational system are domestic and learn English as a foreign language, the nature of social and academic contexts in Vietnam is unlikely to offer rich conditions for pre-service teachers to develop teaching pedagogies that allow them to work in international teaching contexts like in other Western countries. In such circumstances, pre-service teachers are encouraged to review and reflect on their teaching practices before imaging, revising, planning, acting and evaluating any possibilities of internationalizing their teaching courses in their future jobs (Leask, 2015). The adoption of social constructivism as the underlying theory to construct pedagogies and curriculum decisions might allow them to go beyond the boundaries of their training and develop their pedagogies to internationalize their teaching for their future students' global awareness and possibly get ready to teach in international teaching contexts in the future. In addition, thanks to the escalation of technology-enhanced learning, pre-service teachers of English in Vietnam are offered numerous opportunities to gain access to a range of professional development workshops and seminars offered by experts around the world. It can be argued that once equipped with the philosophies of learning and professionalism nurtured and boosted in their ELTE programs, pre-service teachers would be more likely to be empowered to navigate their learning and teaching as autonomous professionals.

Kitano (1997) differentiated three levels of curriculum change in multicultural contexts including exclusive, inclusive and transformed. The first only focuses on Westernized content and didactic pedagogies. The second level includes alternative, international and comparative perspectives. The last level highlights a transformative paradigm that encourages interrogation and critical reflections on disciplinary knowledge. Sharing with Kitano (1997), Banks' (2007) four-level model also involves integration and transformation but adds a level of social action in which students are empowered to take actions because of their transformed learning experiences. The adoption of social constructivism as the theoretical ground for the development, implementation and renovation of curriculum in ELTE programs in Vietnam shows high possibilities for transformation in the curriculum itself and among teachers. Also, it correlates with the transformative approach to IoC which has been received as the most difficult to be applied in the literature (Joseph, 2013). The reason is that social constructivism allows teachers more chances to be exposed to diverse cultural and social contexts in which they learn and reflect. Hence, it not only incorporates global, international and especially intercultural dimensions into formal curriculum areas but also emphasizes student experiences that encourage critical, reflective practices to obtain transformative learning outcomes. The paradigmatic shift across the curriculum allows students to exercise reflections upon their disciplinary knowledge and interrogate conventional assumptions (Tangney, 2018). This process reflects the transformation level suggested by Banks (2007), Bond *et al.* (2003), Joseph (2013) and Kitano (1997).

It is also argued that the transformative approach to IoC aligns with the view of curriculum as praxis and the ontological, epistemological dimensions of knowing, acting and being (Barnett & Coate, 2005).

Conclusion and Implications

Drawing from the conceptualization of IoC (Leask, 2015), social-constructivism theory, competency-based approach and other multiple conceptual dimensions, the chapter provides an epistemological understanding of the case of Vietnam's ELTE curriculum development in light of curriculum internationalization. While the underpinning concepts and theories are perceived as global and international dimensions, they should be localized in the development of program goals and outcomes as well as carefully considered in the implementation of teaching and assessment practices of ELTE curricula in Vietnam.

In our imaginaries, fundamental changes could be undertaken to develop a localized English language teacher education curriculum framework. Firstly, the program outcomes should be designed to develop specific competencies of pre-service teachers, emphasizing the formation and development of professional skills and competencies in a multicultural and rapidly changing educational landscape. Secondly, rather than building a specialized and content-heavy program for a specific educational level, the program structure should be balanced between general and specific knowledge domains to facilitate the development of competencies, so that ELTE can foster dynamism, autonomy, creativity, flexibility and enable pre-service teachers to adapt to various environments. Thirdly, teaching and learning activities in a localized curriculum should clearly define the role of the instructor as an interactive facilitator who supports and co-constructs knowledge with the learners. The curriculum focuses on human development and emphasizes the learner and the learning-to-teach process by highlighting various personal and professional engagement activities pre-service teachers can participate in throughout their program. Fourthly, the assessment activities in the program can focus on developing pre-service teachers' competencies including their ability for self-learning, self-research and lifelong learning. Lastly, the localized curriculum should encourage a shift in the teacher education model by closely partnering universities and schools, gradually bridging the gap between the academic environment at universities and the practical reality of schools in the current context of Vietnam's socioeconomic development. The portraits of graduate teachers in the ELTE curriculum are those who can transform their knowledge, skills and attitudes into addressing challenges or adapting to new situations. Instead of constructing competency standards as a list of separate knowledge, skills and attitudes, their specific competencies involve graduates' ability to perform authentic tasks at a chosen educational level.

References

Banks, J. (2007) Approaches to multicultural curriculum reform. In J.A. Banks and C.A.M. Banks (eds) *Multicultural Education; Issues and Perspectives* (6th edn, pp. 247–270). Wiley.
Barnett, R. and Coate, K. (2005) *Engaging the Curriculum in Higher Education*. Open University Press.
Beck, C. and Kosnik, C.M. (2006) *Innovations in Teacher Education: A Social Constructivist Approach*. State University of New York Press.
Bond, S., Qian, J. and Huang, J. (2003) *The Role of Faculty in Internationalizing The Undergraduate Curriculum and Classroom Experience*. Canadian Bureau for International Education.
Boyles, T. (2012) 21st century knowledge, skills, and abilities and entrepreneurial competencies: A model for undergraduate entrepreneurship education. *Journal of Entrepreneurship Education* 15, 41.
Brewer, E. and Leask, B. (2012) Internationalization of the curriculum. In D.K. Deardorff, H. de Wit and J.D. Heyl (eds) *The SAGE Handbook of International Higher Education* (pp. 245–266). Sage.
Bryman, A. (2016) *Social Research Methods*. Oxford University Press.
Childress, L. (2010) *The Twenty-First Century University: Developing Faculty Engagement in Internationalization*. Peter Lang.
Chu, S.K.W., Reynolds, R.B., Tavares, N.J., Notari, M. and và Lee, C.W.Y. (2017) *21st Century Skills Development Through Inquiry-Based Learning*. Springer.
Do, A.D. (2019) Towards competency-based student assessment. Retrieved from https://moet.gov.vn/giaoducquocdan/giao-duc-trung hoc/Pages/default.aspx?ItemID=6273
Farrell, T.S. (2008) Promoting reflective practice in initial English language teacher education: Reflective microteaching. *Asian Journal of English Language Teaching* 18, 1–15.
Farrell, T.S. (2015) *Reflective Language Teaching: From Research to Practice*. Bloomsbury Publishing.
Freeman, D. (2020) Arguing for a knowledge-base in language teacher education, then (1998) and now (2018). *Language Teaching Research* 24 (1), 5–16.
Freeman, D. and Johnson, K.E. (1998) Reconceptualizing the knowledge-base of language teacher education. *TESOL Quarterly* 32 (3), 397–417.
Fullan, M. and Langworthy, M. (2014) *A Rich Seam: How New Pedagogies Find Deep Learning*. Pearson.
Green, W. and Whitsed, C. (2013) Reflections on an alternative approach to continuing professional learning for internationalization of the curriculum across disciplines. *Journal of Studies in International Education* 17 (2), 148–164.
Johnson, K.E. and Golombek, P.R. (2018) Informing and transforming language teacher education pedagogy. *Language Teaching Research*, 136216881877753. https://doi.org/10.1177/1362168818777539
Johnstone, S.M. and Soares, L. (2014) Principles for developing competency-based education programs. *Change: The Magazine of Higher Learning* 46 (2), 12–19.
Joseph, C. (2013) Internationalizing the curriculum: Economic rationalist or transformative approach. *ASA Footnotes* 41.
Kitano, M.K. (1997) What a course will look like after multicultural change. In A.I. Morey and M. Kitano (eds) *Multicultural Course Transformation in Higher Education: A Broader Truth* (pp. 18–30). Allyn and Bacon.
Kumaravadivelu, B. (2012) *Language Teacher Education for a Global Society: A Modular Model for Knowing, Analyzing, Recognizing, Doing, and Seeing*. Routledge.
Leask, B. (2015) *Internationalizing the Curriculum*. Routledge.
Le, V.C. (2020) English language teaching in Vietnam: Aspirations, realities, and challenges. In V.C. Le, H.T.M. Nguyen, T.T.M. Nguyen and R. Barnard (eds) *Building*

Teacher Capacity in English Language Teaching in Vietnam: Research, Policy, and Practice (pp. 7–22). Routledge.

Marginson, S. and Rhoades, G. (2002) Beyond national states, markets, and systems of higher education: A glonacal agency heuristic. *Higher Education* 43 (3), 281–309.

Marginson, S., Kaur, S. and Sawir, E. (2011) Global, local, national in the Asia-Pacific. In S. Marginson, S. Kaur and E. Sawir (eds) *Higher Education in the Asia-Pacific: Strategic Responses to Globalization* (pp. 3–34). Springer Netherlands.

Maringe, F. and Foskett, N. (2010) *Globalization and Internationalization in Higher Education: Theoretical, Strategic and Management Perspectives.* Continuum International Pub. Group.

Marshall, C. and Rossman, G.B. (2014) *Designing Qualitative Research.* Sage Publications.

Ministry of Education and Training (2008) Decision to approve plan on 'Teaching and learning foreign languages in the national educational system for the period 2008–2020.' Hanoi, Vietnam.

Ministry of Education and Training (2020) Document No 2069/BGDĐT-NGCBQLGD re Guidelines on using the Competence Framework for School English Language Teachers. Hanoi. Vietnam.

MOET (2018) Issue regulations on professional standards for preschool teachers (Circula No. 26/2018/TT-BGDĐT). https://thuvienphapluat.vn/van-ban/Giao-duc/Thong-tu-26-2018-TT-BGDDT-chuan-nghe-nghiep-giao-vien-mam-non-402061.aspx

Pham, L.H. and Fry, G.W. (2004) Education and economic, political, and social change in Vietnam. *Educational Research for Policy and Practice* 3 (3), 199–222.

Roberts, J. (1998) *Language Teacher Education.* Routledge

Shulman, L. (1987) Knowledge and teaching: Foundations of the new reform. *Harvard Educational Review* 57 (1), 1–23.

Steiner-Khamsi, G. and Waldow, F. (eds) (2012) *Policy Borrowing and Lending: World Yearbook of Education 2012.* Routledge.

Tangney, S. (2018) The development of a reflective tool for internationalisation of the curriculum. *Innovations in Education and Teaching International* 55 (6), 640–649.

Tran, L.T., Phan, H.L.T. and Marginson, S. (2018) The 'advanced programmes' in Vietnam: Internationalising the curriculum or importing the 'Best Curriculum' of the West? In L.T. Tran and S. Marginson (eds) *Internationalisation in Vietnamese Higher Education* (pp. 55–75). Springer.

Trilling, B. and Fadel, C. (2009) *21st Century Skills: Learning for Life in Our Times.* John Wiley and Sons.

Vu, H.H. and Phan, L.H. (2020) Interrogating troubling issues in Vietnam's English language teacher education. In A.B.M. Tsui (ed.) *English Language Teaching and Teacher Education in East Asia: Global Challenges and Local Responses* (pp. 217–234). Cambridge University Press.

3 Inclusion/Exclusion of TESOL in the 'True' Internationalization of Japan's Higher Education

Yoko Kobayashi

Teaching English to Speakers of Other Languages (TESOL) studies conducted by and with predominantly western male native English-speaking teachers working in Japan's higher education have revealed that these visible foreigners are assigned to the symbolically international but practically peripheral role of fabricating institutions as the site of culturally diverse communities. This chapter examines the overlooked question of why such symbolic internationalization invites no criticism from inside and outside (e.g. governing boards of universities, the Ministry of Education). Drawing on analyses of Japan's higher education policies, this chapter attributes stakeholders' silence to an academic and disciplinary hierarchy, resulting in their low expectation toward low-ranked programs and teaching/administrative staff, including TESOL and liberal arts. Meanwhile, this chapter argues that Japan's liberal arts departments are spared from closures because they cater to the needs of: (1) internationalization-minded, predominantly female high school students who adhere to global English ideologies and (2) a Japaneseness-oriented business world that favors the employment of monolingual university graduates with a liberal arts degree. Addressing the exclusion that affects TESOL and its members, this chapter discusses both plausible concerns and future directions so that the globally celebrated, academically marginalized and ideologically charged TESOL can endorse true internationalization as a professional community.

Introduction

TESOL programs for current or pre-service teachers, a main theme in this volume, are implemented in a limited number of private institutions in Japan, such as Temple University's Japan Campus and Kanda

University of International Studies (*The Japan Times*, 2018). This chapter conceptualizes TESOL more broadly as 'a professional community' (Canagarajah, 2016) for English language teaching professionals and interdisciplinary researchers. The TESOL domain has been growing steadily as exemplified by many research and pedagogical activities dedicated to global and regional professional communities. A major contributing factor to such growth is the global pervasiveness of English as a language associated with institutional internationalization and global competitiveness. The nexus of English skills and neoliberal transformation promotes the commodification of global talents marketable in the English-centered global economy (Shin & Park, 2016) and justifies the English divide between the bilingual elite and the monolingual nonelite (Shin & Lee, 2019). As revealed by studies on East Asian and South American international students in the Philippines and Canada, their neoliberal and West-oriented mindset interferes with their willingness to learn about non-western languages and cultures from other international students and contact with nonideal locals such as immigrants (Jang, 2018; Tavares, 2022).

Meanwhile, the competitiveness and privilege of neoliberal subjects educated in English-medium modes reconfirm the significance of English language instruction in the context of internationalization. This literature-based chapter positions itself as a critical and hopeful attempt to address challenges, limitations and affordances in English language instruction in the context of Japan's higher education, where internationalization has been ideologically and pedagogically intertwined with local and global perspectives.

Study Background

Context

The close entanglement of West-centered ideologies of internationalization and neoliberalism with native-speaker norms has produced a pervasive illusion that the acquisition of native-like English skills and western culture knowledge amounts to internationalization in school contexts. Japan has expressed its commitment to internationalizing English education and cultivating young citizens with a global mindset through their learning of English from expatriate language assistant teachers who speak English with 'contemporary standard pronunciation' (Kobayashi, 2023). The socially prevalent idealization of western native English-speaking teachers (NESTs) that accords a privilege to them manifests in the form of discrimination against other visible minority teachers (Glasgow, 2023). The dominance of Western male NESTs in Japan's English teaching contexts (Appleby, 2014; Kobayashi, 2014) has also resulted in discriminatory practices against Western female NESTs as well (Hayes, 2013; Hicks,

2013). Similar voices of marginalization were also reported in a study involving seven Japanese female university English teachers (Nagatomo, 2012) who 'experience gender isolation in the workplace', that is 'a man's world' (2012: 140).

Meanwhile, the supposedly most privileged western, predominantly male NESTs feel disempowered and commoditized, isolated from local Japanese teachers of English and other disciplines (Brown, 2019; Rivers, 2013; Whitsed & Wright, 2011). Citing Houghton and Rivers (2013), Copland *et al.* (2016: 12) argued that 'once they have joined an institution, NESTs (and non-Japanese nationals) may be subject to less favorable conditions than their "Japanese" counterparts'. Another study conducted with a broader group of 14 international faculty members of diverse ethnic and academic backgrounds in Japan's higher education (Brotherhood *et al.*, 2020) also revealed 'participants' general disillusionment with internationalization' and 'perception that hiring international faculty was a symbolic gesture' (2020: 506).

These studies consistently cast doubt on the seriousness of the Japanese higher education system's commitment to internationalization reforms, which are, in reality, assigned to international but low-ranked foreign teachers to render the power and privilege of local Japanese faculty members invulnerable to such cosmetic internationalization. Meanwhile, it remains unknown whether the tokenism of internationalization experienced by foreign teachers is observed outside liberal arts departments and language centers such as science, technology, engineering and mathematics (STEM) departments and whether the highest-ranked positioning of Japanese (male) faculty members in non-STEM programs is altered within the hierarchy of an entire institution.

Conceptual framework

Studies on the internationalization of higher education in western countries have critically and rather pessimistically argued that educational policies and practices are bound to serve the interests of governments and gatekeeping industries whose priority is to preserve the dominant social system and ideology (Tight, 2021). For example, the recruitment and representation of international students in the United States are indicative of the prevailing racial ideology and white-dominant structure, which projects the image that visible minority students are happy on campus, despite the hidden fact that their cultural backgrounds are not perceived as assets that contribute to local mainstream students, host institutions, or societies (Lee & Rice, 2007; Pippert *et al.*, 2013). Similarly, Tavares (2022) claimed that the pressing issue of Canada's labor shortage is addressed by local institutions' policy of recruiting international students who are prepared 'to fit into Canadian society, rather than to transform it' (2022: 12).

Thus, higher education's policies and practices are complicit in sustaining and legitimizing the persistent socioeconomic, racial, gender and other inequalities under the guise of individual responsibility and competitiveness (Bamberger *et al.*, 2019): Visibly '"diverse" students and faculty may likely find that their diversity (particular if it is not of an elite variety) is undervalued' because neoliberalism-framed internationalization is 'focusing on celebrating the possibility of the few who can achieve, instead of the embedded inequalities within the system' (2019: 208). 'The few who can achieve' consist of faculty members of TESOL and other liberal arts 'privileged plurilingual scholars' who can act as ideal neoliberal subjects within 'neoliberal academic institutions' and 'further accrue cultural, economic and symbolic capital from presenting and publishing while moving further away from real-world problems' (Kubota, 2016: 490). Aware of and acknowledging the limitation of academic studies and discussions within neoliberal academic institutions, this chapter aims to expand dialogue on seemingly celebratory policy discourses about English teaching for internationalization, which are inevitably embedded in the local and global issues of inequalities and hierarchies within and outside the TESOL field. (See Tavares's introduction in this volume.) By expanding its focus from language-related programs and departments familiar to the TESOL community, this chapter aims to provide a larger picture of internationalization in Japan's higher education.

'True' Internationalization Expected from STEM Research Universities

Japan's Ministry of Education has been implementing a range of internationalization projects such as Global 30, Re-inventing Japan and the Go Global Japan Project (Rose & McKinley, 2018). Most recently, the Top Global University Project was launched in 2014 'to enhance the international compatibility and competitiveness of higher education in Japan' by providing 'prioritized support of the world-class and innovative universities that lead the internationalization of Japanese universities' (MEXT, 2014: 1).

As shown in Table 3.1 and illustrated in the project's official English website (MEXT, n.d.), Japan selects a total of 37 out of 775 universities and categorizes them into types of A and B. One point to highlight here is that even though these two types are graphically shown equally as the absolute top global institutions that can 'achieve true internationalization' (MEXT, n.d.), a distinct dividing line is drawn between the two groups. Whereas type B is open to liberal arts/nonelite colleges, type A 'world-class universities' are confined to a select group of elite universities in Japan, suggesting that no other universities can be candidates. In fact, even before the implementation of the Top Global University Project, Japan's leading research universities (RU) formed a consortium called

Table 3.1 Two categories of universities in the Top Global University Project

Categories	Definition of each type	Selected institutions
Type A (Top Type)	'world-class universities that have the potential to be ranked in the top 100 of the world's universities'	Top-tier national universities (n = 11) and the two most prestigious private institutions (Keio and Waseda)
Type B (Global Traction Type)	'innovative universities that lead the internationalization of Japanese society, based on continuous improvement of their current efforts'	Liberal arts and nonelite private colleges

Source: MEXT (2014: 1) and the project's official English website (MEXT, n.d.)

'RU11' in November 2009 with the following mission statement, 'In an age of intense global competition, creation of new knowledge, technology and innovation are [*sic*] the key to maintaining a prosperous nation' and 'We strongly argue that Japan must have pre-eminent research universities in the world to survive against international competition'.[1] The participating institutions were national universities that included Hokkaido University, Tohoku University, University of Tsukuba, the University of Tokyo, Tokyo Institute of Technology, Nagoya University, Kyoto University, Osaka University, and Kyushu University and two private universities: Waseda University and Keio University.

Over the decades, science and technology have been Japan's top priority to gain and sustain global recognition as the world's major technological and economic power. According to the government's Sixth Science and Technology Basic Plan complied in 2021, science and technology 'served as the basis for Japan's recovery from the devastation of the postwar period' and 'are at the core of an increasingly intense struggle for supremacy between countries' (Government of Japan, 2021: 4–5). Since Japan is losing its competitiveness, pressure has intensified on STEM-based research universities. Faced with the reality that 'Japan is losing its presence not only among the top universities in Europe and the United States, but also among Asian universities' (2021: 69), the government anticipates that the country will lose its 'supremacy' in Asia and the world. This hampers its ambition to 'play a leading role in creating a new world order and rules' (2021: 5). Accordingly, the government's demand for STEM-based research universities is presented with a tangible goal to 'be ranked in the top 100 of the world's universities' (MEXT, 2014: 1).

Japan's revitalization as the world's major technological nation is contingent on the quality and quantity of English-related internationalization efforts implemented at STEM-based research universities. These efforts entail (1) improving the ability of local monolingual (male) STEM researchers to advance international collaborative research with well-cited scientists and produce high-impact scientific papers written in English and (2) drawing talented international students toward Japan's research universities by touting the country as 'one of the top science countries in the world' that 'provides you with unique research environments and career opportunities' (MEXT, 2016: 1). The significant role of English in STEM departments at research universities is demonstrated in English-medium instruction (EMI) classes offered at these institutions. The Education Ministry's latest survey report shows a list of undergraduate departments that allow students to earn a degree by taking only EMI classes (MEXT, 2022: 61). These include the STEM departments of Japan's top-ranked universities such as the University of Tokyo, Kyoto University and Waseda University.

An extremely limited number of studies on EMI courses offered by STEM graduate programs suggest that these courses are predominantly taught by Japanese STEM faculty members who supervise both local and international students (Shimauchi, 2012: 9) because it is 'practically, extremely difficult' to hire NESTs who specialize in STEM and have taught at the university level [original in Japanese] (Adachi, 2017: 31). One such case is Waseda University's English-based Undergraduate Program in the School of Fundamental Science and Engineering, which began in 2018. As of June 2023, its official website reports that the 34 professors and associate professors teaching the Mathematical Sciences Program in English are composed of 27 Japanese men, 3 Japanese women, 2 Western men (applied mathematics and advanced geometry) and 2 non-Japanese Asian men (mathematical statistics and probability theory) (https://www.fse.sci.waseda.ac.jp/en/faculty/ms/). The dominance of Japanese male faculty members in STEM EMI programs is in stark contrast with the promotional representation of Western (male) NESTs as the symbol of internationalization in liberal arts institutions and language centers.

Symbolic Internationalization Tolerated Outside STEM Research Universities

In contrast with the Japanese Education Ministry's explicit directives for STEM research universities, their official yet equivocal expectation for type B 'innovative universities' is to 'lead the internationalization of Japanese society, based on continuous improvement of their current efforts' (MEXT, 2014: 1). Since even the chosen few 'innovative' universities are allowed to continue 'their current efforts' to 'lead the internationalization of Japan', it is highly unlikely that the ministry expects more than 'current efforts', let alone sweeping change, from many other not-so-innovative, non-STEM institutions.

As discussed earlier, TESOL studies conducted by and with visibly and linguistically foreign (male) NESTs have shown that language centers and liberal arts programs/departments assign them a seemingly privileged but virtually peripheral role as symbols of internationalization (Brotherhood *et al.*, 2020; Brown, 2019; Rivers, 2013; Whitsed & Wright,

2011). They then argue that such symbolic internationalization is ascribed to the presence of conservative Japanese (male) faculty members who wish to be spared from the impact of internationalization. According to one of these marginalized foreign teachers, 'I feel like they just want to work peacefully as they always have and are afraid of being wrapped up in the tornado of change' (Brotherhood *et al.*, 2020: 505).

The Top Global University Project's moderate expectation of non-world-class, non-STEM universities suggests that the ministry itself does not anticipate a 'tornado of change' from liberal arts programs. Because of this, local bureaucratic administrative staff and liberal arts faculty members feel a sense of certainty that the symbolic internationalization imposed on foreign teachers would draw no criticism from inside and outside, which are, the governing boards of universities and policymakers, respectively. The ministry's low expectation of liberal arts and language programs is articulated in a notice sent by former education minister Shimomura Hakubun to presidents of national universities in 2014 – the same year the Top Global University Project was launched – that commanded them to either abolish or reorganize supposedly uncompetitive and unproductive humanities and social sciences departments to 'serve areas that better meet society's needs' as widely reported in Japan and beyond (e.g. Kingston, 2015; Traphagan, 2015). This incident was not an isolated case in Japan, as many countries invest in global research universities (i.e. type A 'world-class universities') that can serve their interests in an era of intensifying international competition. These include the UK government that suggested that universities go along with 'a huge wave of course closures in the arts, languages, humanities and social sciences, derided by the Tory government as "dead-end courses"' (Lee, 2021).

Factors Behind the Continued Existence of Liberal Arts Departments in Japan

Liberal arts departments expected to serve as contributors to STEM development

Today, many humanities departments and liberal arts programs staffed with NESTs remain in operation across Japan. Officially speaking, the latest policy statements suggest that government officials and business leaders have come to acknowledge the significance of liberal arts education within the development of 'Society 5.0'. The creation of Society 5.0, or 'a super-smart society', was proposed in the Fifth Science and Technology Basic Plan as 'an ideal form of our future society' that 'will bring wealth to the people' '[T]through an initiative merging the physical space (real world) and cyberspace by leveraging ICT to its fullest' (Government of Japan, 2015: 13). *Keidanren* (the Japan Business

Federation) proclaimed the importance of liberal arts education with the premise that Society 5.0 needs human resources that 'possess a broad educational background in ethics, philosophy, literature and history – collectively called liberal arts–' (Takamitsu, 2020). From the perspective of the Ministry of Education, the government's policy of creating Society 5.0 considers the need for liberal arts to be 'studied in common by all students' without separating them based on the traditional dichotomy 'between the humanities and sciences' called *bunri* (liberal arts [*bun*] vs. science [*ri*]) (MEXT, 2018: 5). Nonetheless, the ministry does not acknowledge the significance of the humanities as equal to that of the sciences.

Marketing Japan as 'one of the top science countries in the world' that 'provides you [STEM-major international students] with unique research environments and career opportunities' (MEXT, 2016: 1), both the government and business world situate STEM 'at the core of an increasingly intense struggle for supremacy between countries' (Government of Japan, 2021: 4–5). Japan's bid to sustain its position as a major technology power explains why the Ministry of Education is concerned that the percentage of university students majoring in humanities and social sciences (50%) is higher than that of those in science and engineering (20%), which is lower than in Germany (40%) and in Finland and South Korea (30%), and calls for more focus on science, technology, engineering, art and mathematics (STEAM) as well as design thinking (MEXT, 2018: 3). Accordingly, the government and the industrial world acknowledge the significance of humanities and social sciences knowledge on the assumption that they serve as a foundation for the cultivation of STEM – or STEAM – major human resources. In line with this, the University Division of the Central Council for Education, the Education Ministry's advisory body, submitted the following proposal to the minister in 2019:

> In an era of Society 5.0, it is demanded to expand the potential of our nation's STEM fields more than ever, discover, and provide valuable information to society in a way that it can be utilized to the maximum in terms of modelization and monetization. It is believed that this goal increases the importance of high-level editing skills and discerning eye for information which are based on a broad perspective, including historical and geographical one, gained from the knowledge of humanities and social sciences. (translated by the author, The University Division of the Central Council for Education, 2019: 47)

Nonetheless, it is highly questionable for the government and business world to expect that liberal arts departments and colleges operating across Japan can redefine their educational mission and restructure their organizations to 'expand the potential of our nation's STEM fields more than ever', considering that, as argued above, even Japan's supposedly most 'innovative' and 'top global' liberal arts institutions are allowed to continue 'their current efforts' to 'lead the internationalization of Japan' (MEXT, 2014: 1).

Liberal arts departments expected to serve dominant ideologies and interests

Despite officially describing the potential role of liberal arts education in serving STEM-oriented national interests, the government and business world have remained silent about the cosmetic internationalization schemes of reform-resistant liberal arts departments. These academic institutions feature peripherally positioned but visibly eye-catching 'international' teaching staff while segregating them from Japanese teaching and administrative staff. A case in point is Poole (2018), an insider report at one of the most prestigious private universities in the western Japan that declared its commitment to internationalization and promoted English-taught programs (ETPs). It revealed that the position and title of 'permanent administrative officer' is accorded to Japanese nationals who acknowledge that 'we lack global skills' whereas '[T]hose with globalized skills are, like the ETPs themselves, at the university periphery, far from the center of power' (2017: 101). Thus, the reality is that a Japanese-dominant and change-resistant bureaucratic administration is conducive to the preservation of the status quo in Japan's higher education institutions (HEIs) and compounds the implementation of ETPs. He pessimistically concluded that 'the bureaucratic systems in place at HEIs prioritize protocol over education and the resulting administrative process consumes precious creative energy that could better be used to implement actual innovation and pedagogy for ETPs' (2017: 105).

A fundamental question that remains unexplored is the silence among internal and external stakeholders about symbolic internationalization being left with 'international' TESOL members. One of the most significant factors behind this is the Japanese male-centered business world's resistance to globalization. While officially calling for internationally competitive global human resources, Japan's business world continues to hire a larger number of (semi)monolingual university graduates with liberal arts degrees who would not resist workplace sexism (Kobayashi, 2018b, 2021). Understandably, higher education institutions aim to achieve a 100% employment rate by producing students who can meet the demands of companies. This university-industry relation also affects international students who seek employment in Japan, including those studying at one of Japan's two most prestigious private universities (Kobayashi, 2021: 245–246). On its official English website, the university published its 'Tips and Advices for International Students doing job-hunting in Japan' which states, 'The key point here is to get used to the Japanese style of recruitment practices' and they 'should also have an excellent command of the Japanese language' 'as well as displaying good understanding of the Japanese culture and their way of thinking'.[2]

Another contributing factor to internal and external gatekeepers' implicit approval for non-STEM institutions' continuation with symbolic internationalization is the awareness among the governing boards of universities and the Ministry of Education that such a scheme is an effective means of student recruitment marketing in a Japanese-dominant society, where the learning of English and foreign languages from foreign teachers itself is conceived as an act of internationalization and the best way to work globally upon graduation (Rivers, 2013). Particularly, liberal arts programs with the names such as 'international', 'global', 'English', 'foreign language' and 'intercultural communication' have continued to be popular educational choices for many female students, a tendency observed among many other young Asian/Western women (Kobayashi, 2018a, 2020). As argued above, these programs are statistically successful in producing graduates for jobs offered by Japan's business world. Both university governing boards and policymakers care less about the mismatch between internationalization-minded, Japanese female and international job seekers and Japan's non-globalized business world that sustains Japanese male-centered work culture (Kobayashi, 2018b, 2021).

Thus, quite ironically, the factor of Japaneseness (i.e. the myth of monolingual Japanese masculinities) helps Western (male) expatriate TESOL members stay employed and included in pseudo-international, male-dominant liberal arts programs and language centers, which are popular among globally minded, young female students and cater to Japan's non-globalized businessmen's world. The TESOL domain as a whole could be critiqued in terms of the disciplinary complicity in the maintenance of the dominant ideology and practice that serve the interests of governments and gatekeeping industries (Tight, 2021).

TESOL included and excluded from the internationalization of higher education

TESOL as a professional community and its members have long been capitalizing on the global demand for English (medium) education and related research activities. In this sense, the TESOL domain is deservedly included in global education worldwide. In fact, the practice of TESOL extends beyond TESOL-familiar venues. As argued in this chapter, Japanese male faculty members assume a central role in internationalization by teaching EMI courses at STEM research departments and universities. Situated in teaching contexts with a rarity of NESTs who teach STEM EMI courses even at top-tier research universities, local STEM teachers might be teaching courses in English as the common lingua franca of science and technology unbound by native English norms (Adachi, 2017: 31–32). The presence of these nonnative English-speaking faculty members who teach content courses in English deserves much attention from the TESOL teaching and research communities, which have been contending with the globally pervasive idealization of Western NESTs.

This chapter also discussed the significance of addressing the overlooked issue of exclusion from perspectives outside the confines of TESOL-familiar contexts. One limitation of the existing literature is that it confines the issues of marginalization and symbolic internationalization to TESOL-familiar teaching contexts where different types and titles of (prospective) university faculty members are argued to be discriminated against each other: non-Japanese teachers' sense of exclusion from the dominant Japanese teaching/administrative staff (Brotherhood et al., 2020; Poole, 2018), the advantage of Western male NESTs over visible minority teachers and Western female NESTs (Appleby, 2014; Glasgow, 2023; Hayes, 2013; Hicks, 2013), and Japanese female English teachers' sense of being discriminated against the dominant group of Japanese male faculty members (Nagatomo, 2012). Taking a different approach, this chapter examined TESOL-familiar contexts within an academic hierarchy in a neoliberal era of international competition and STEM productivity because that explains why liberal arts departments and language centers have been allowed to continue their practice of symbolic internationalization.

With the importance of science and technology in Japan's and many other countries' pursuit of economic competitiveness and national security, the domain of liberal arts-oriented TESOL and its members have been positioned near the bottom of academic hierarchies not only in Japan but also elsewhere. Nonetheless, non-STEM and non-world-class institutions that provide job opportunities to TESOL members are spared from closures in this non-English-speaking Asian country because of global and local factors: (1) the existence of internationalization-oriented high school students (many of whom are female) who, similar to their Asian and Western peers, wish to major in liberal arts programs and engage in intercultural educational activities (Kobayashi, 2018a, 2020) and (2) the reform-resistant Japanese male-centered corporate world that prefers to employ domestically educated university graduates with little or no international experience (Kobayashi, 2018b, 2021). Thus, TESOL members in Japan thrive on both globally and locally pervasive ideologies, which are, (1) global ideological discourses aligned with English-fluent global talents and (2) Japanese(ness) ideologies that idealize monolingual/monocultural Japan and Japanese men. Accordingly, in contrast with the 'true' internationalization expected from Japan's world-class STEM research universities, other non-STEM and non-world-class institutions are modestly and nebulously expected to continue 'their current efforts' to 'lead the internationalization of Japan' (MEXT, 2014: 1), aware that such internationalization efforts are left with visibly 'international' expatriate TESOL faculty members positioned on the periphery.

Conclusion

What remains to be seen is how the TESOL domain and its members can contend with exclusion and symbolic internationalization from inside liberal arts departments and language centers, where they are segregated from local teaching/administrative staff, who are convinced that their lack of involvement in internationalization schemes would invite no criticism from internal and external stakeholders. One issue here is the attempt by marginalized TESOL teachers to improve their status by transforming themselves into academic researchers rather than TESOL practitioners. Indeed, more than ever, TESOL professionals and other liberal arts faculty members of neoliberal academic institutions must conduct studies and produce papers to be employed and promoted ('the more the merrier!'; Kubota, 2016: 489). This is despite the fact that such research activities are not considered as the primary contributors to a country's supremacy as a leading or emerging economy. Nonetheless, similar to any other university-based researchers, the most privileged and prominent applied linguists are those with a long list of international (i.e. English) publications that 'get cited, recycled, and propagated incessantly', who can then 'benefit from this activity in advancing our own careers' (Kubota, 2016: 489–490). This neoliberal notion of productive university faculty members legitimizes the reality that 'the gap widens between researchers and practitioners' as well as 'between those who are seen as doing intellectual work and those who are seen as doing service' (Kramsch, 2015: 458–459).

Overall, TESOL community members as well as other liberal arts researchers affiliated with neoliberal academic institutions are increasingly required to strike a delicate balance between job security and a sense of inclusion without blindly internalizing neoliberal 'ideal' work values and sustaining the globally and locally dominant ideology and system. Because ideologies are deeply entrenched in local and global communities and that the TESOL domain and its members worldwide thrive on them (e.g. global English ideology, Whiteness), an attempt to enhance and contribute to internationalization from inside TESOL-familiar teaching venues is expected to be challenging. Practically and hopefully, such an attempt should be conceived as a longitudinal challenge that requires both regional and global TESOL communities to engage in discussions about the role of globally celebrated, academically marginalized and ideologically charged TESOL as a professional community with a mission to endorse true internationalization.

Notes

(1) http://www.ru11.jp/eng/mission.html
(2) https://www.waseda.jp/inst/weekly/careercompass-en/2017/06/02/29040/

References

Adachi, K. (2017) Enhancement and faculty development of English-medium instruction in science courses [text in Japanese]. *Forum of Higher Education Research* 7, 25–34.

Appleby, R. (2014) *Men and Masculinities in Global English Language Teaching.* Palgrave Macmillan.

Bamberger, A., Morris, P. and Yemini, M. (2019) Neoliberalism, internationalisation and higher education: Connections, contradictions and alternatives. *Discourse: Studies in the Cultural Politics of Education* 40 (2), 203–216.

Brotherhood, T., Hammond, C.D. and Kim, Y. (2020) Towards an actor-centered typology of internationalization: A study of junior international faculty in Japanese universities. *Higher Education* 79 (3), 497–514.

Brown, C.A. (2019) Foreign faculty tokenism, English, and 'internationalization' in a Japanese university. *Asia Pacific Journal of Education* 39 (3), 404–416.

Canagarajah, S. (2016) TESOL as a professional community: A half-century of pedagogy, research, and theory. *TESOL Quarterly* 50 (1), 7–41.

Copland, F., Mann, S. and Garton, S. (2016) Introduction: Positions, experiences and reflections on the native speaker issue. In F. Copland, S. Garton and S. Mann (eds) *LETs and NESTs: Voices, Views and Vignettes* (pp. 5–19). British Council.

Glasgow, G.P. (ed.) (2023) *Multiculturalism, Language, and Race in English Education in Japan: Agency, Pedagogy, and Reckoning.* Candlin and Mynard ePublishing.

Government of Japan (18 December, 2015) Report on the 5th Science and Technology Basic Plan [Tentative Translation].

Government of Japan (26 March, 2021) Science, Technology, and Innovation Basic Plan [Tentative Translation]. Retrieved from https://www8.cao.go.jp/cstp/english/index.html

Hayes, B.E. (2013) Hiring criteria for Japanese university English-teaching faculty. In S.A. Houghton and D.J. Rivers (eds) *Native-Speakerism in Japan: Intergroup Dynamics in Foreign Language Education* (pp. 132–146). Multilingual Matters.

Hicks, S.K. (2013) On the (out)skirts of TESOL networks of homophily: Substantitve citizenship in Japan. In S.A. Houghton and D.J. Rivers (eds) *Native-Speakerism in Japan: Intergroup Dynamics in Foreign Language Education* (pp. 147–158). Multilingual Matters.

Houghton, S.A. and Rivers, D.J. (eds) (2013) *Native-Speakerism in Japan: Intergroup Dynamics in Foreign Language Education.* Multilingual Matters.

Jang, I.C. (2018) Legitimating the Philippines as a language learning space: Transnational Korean youth's experiences and evaluations. *Journal of Sociolinguistics* 22 (2), 216–232.

Kingston, J. (2015) Japanese university humanities and social sciences programs under attack. *Japan Focus: The Asia-Pacific Journal* 13 (39), 1–12.

Kobayashi, Y. (2014) Gender gap in the EFL classroom in East Asia. *Applied Linguistics* 35 (2), 219–223.

Kobayashi, Y. (2018a) *The Evolution of English Language Learners in Japan: Crossing Japan, the West, and South East Asia.* Routledge.

Kobayashi, Y. (2018b) The neo-liberal notion of global language skills vs. monolingual corporate culture: Co-existence or rivalry? *Journal of Multilingual and Multicultural Development* 39 (8), 729–739.

Kobayashi, Y. (ed.) (2020) *Attitudes to English Study among Japanese, Chinese and Korean Women: Motivations, Expectations and Identity.* Routledge.

Kobayashi, Y. (2021) Non-globalized ties between Japanese higher education and industry: Crafting publicity-driven calls for domestic and foreign students with global qualities. *Higher Education* 81 (2), 241–253.

Kobayashi, Y. (2023) 'Contemporary standard' English policy and pseudo-diversity among inner and outer circle assistant language teachers in Japan. *International Journal of Applied Linguistics* 33 (2), 260–274.

Kramsch, C. (2015) Applied linguistics: A theory of the practice. *Applied Linguistics* 36 (4), 454–465.
Kubota, R. (2016) The multi/plural turn, postcolonial theory, and neoliberal multiculturalism: Complicities and implications for applied linguistics. *Applied Linguistics* 37 (4), 474–494.
Lee, H. (2021) UK universities cut arts, languages, humanities and social science degrees. *World Socialist Web Site*, 8 July. https://www.wsws.org/en/articles/2021/07/09/unic-j09.html
Lee, J.J. and Rice, C. (2007) Welcome to America? International student perceptions of discrimination. *Higher Education* 53 (3), 381–409.
MEXT (September 2014) Selection for the FY 2014 Top Global University Project. https://www.mext.go.jp/b_menu/houdou/26/09/__icsFiles/afieldfile/2014/10/07/1352218_02.pdf
MEXT (19 July, 2016) Research with/in Japan. Retrieved from https://www.mext.go.jp/en/policy/science_technology/policy/title01/detail01/1304788.htm
MEXT (5 June, 2018) human resource development for society 5.0: changes to society, changes to learning (summary). Retrieved from https://www.mext.go.jp/a_menu/society/index.htm
MEXT (n.d.) TOP GLOBAL UNIVERSITY JAPAN. https://tgu.mext.go.jp/en/index.html
MEXT (23 November, 2022) Regarding the status of affairs on university education's reform in contents and others in the fiscal 2020 (Summary) [text in Japanese]. Retrieved from https://www.mext.go.jp/a_menu/koutou/daigaku/04052801/1417336_00009.htm
Nagatomo, D.H. (2012) *Exploring Japanese University English Teachers' Professional Identity*. Multilingual Matters.
Pippert, T.D., Essenburg, L.J. and Matchett, E.J. (2013) We've got minorities, yes we do: Visual representations of racial and ethnic diversity in college recruitment materials. *Journal of Marketing for Higher Education* 23 (2), 258–282.
Poole, G. (2018) Administrative impediments: How bureaucratic practices obstruct the implementation of English-taught programs in Japan. In A. Bradford and H. Brown (eds) *English-Medium Instruction in Japanese Higher Education: Policy, Challenges and Outcomes* (pp. 91–107). Multilingual Matters.
Rivers, D.J. (2013) Institutionalized native-speakerism: Voices of dissent and acts of resistance. In S.A. Houghton and D.J. Rivers (eds) *Native-Speakerism in Japan: Intergroup Dynamics in Foreign Language Education* (pp. 75–91). Multilingual Matters.
Rose, H. and McKinley, J. (2018) Japan's English-medium instruction initiatives and the globalization of higher education. *Higher Education* 75 (1), 111–129.
Shimauchi, S. (2012) Research on internationalization of higher education and EMIDP (English medium instruction degree programs) in Japan [text in Japanese]. *Journal of International Education* (18), 1–17.
Shin, H. and Joseph Park, S.-Y. (2016) Researching language and neoliberalism. *Journal of Multilingual and Multicultural Development* 37 (5), 443–452.
Shin, H. and Lee, B. (2019) 'English divide' and ELT in Korea: Towards critical ELT policy and practices. In X. Gao (ed.) *Second Handbook of English Language Teaching* (pp. 1–19). Springer International Publishing.
Takamitsu, S. (2020) Strong liberal arts education is key to success in Society 5.0. *The Japan Times*, 17 February. https://www.japantimes.co.jp/opinion/2020/02/17/commentary/japan-commentary/strong-liberal-arts-education-key-success-society-5-0/
Tavares, V. (2022) Neoliberalism, native-speakerism and the displacement of international students' languages and cultures. *Journal of Multilingual and Multicultural Development*, 1–14. https://doi.org/10.1080/01434632.2022.2084547
The Japan Times. (2018) TESOL master's program for working teachers. *The Japan Times*, 22 October. https://www.japantimes.co.jp/news/2018/10/22/national/tesol-masters-program-working-teachers/#.W9k_btczaM8

The University Division of the Central Council for Education. (2019) A vision for ideal postgraduate schools for 2040: Organizational reform measures aimed at the cultivation of human resources who can lead the society [text in Japanese]. Retrieved from http://www.mext.go.jp/component/b_menu/shingi/toushin/__icsFiles/afieldfile/2019/02/18/1412981_001r.pdf

Tight, M. (2021) Globalization and internationalization as frameworks for higher education research. *Research Papers in Education* 36 (1), 52–74.

Traphagan, J.W. (2015) The Japanese government's attack on the humanities and social sciences. *The Diplomat*, 26 September. https://thediplomat.com/2015/09/the-japanese-governments-attack-on-the-humanities-and-social-sciences/

Whitsed, C. and Wright, P. (2011) Perspectives from within: Adjunct, foreign, English-language teachers in the internationalization of Japanese universities. *Journal of Research in International Education* 10 (1), 28–45.

4 Higher Education English Teachers' Ideologies on Translanguaging: Monolingual Mindset Meets Internationalization

Md. Sadequle Islam and Sílvia Melo-Pfeifer

There have always been discussions about whether it is beneficial or detrimental to navigate across various linguistic resources in the language classroom in different linguistic contexts (mono, bi or multilingual), from primary to higher education. In this chapter, we discuss English teachers' ideologies toward translanguaging and its use in Higher Education (HE) Teaching English to Speakers of Other Languages (TESOL) classrooms in Germany. Our results from classroom observation show that, although TESOL classrooms are governed by a monolingual English-only policy frequently recalled by the teacher, translanguaging is nevertheless used as a resource in several ways both by students and teachers. Teacher interviews, however, portray a more strict and implicit exclusion and disaffirmation of the use of other languages or language varieties. This mismatch between the ideology and practice of translanguaging in HE TESOL classrooms in Germany is interpreted through the lens of internationalization of higher education institutions as a specific goal within higher education and the language policies promoted to achieve it.

Introduction

The perception of Germany as a monolingual state has been changing as it shifts from a linguistically homogenous nation to a more pluralistic society shaped by population mobilities (Sliwka, 2010). As a result, educational institutions in Germany show an increased heterogeneity among students, which ultimately fosters bi/multilingualism in education. Whenever it comes to so-called monolingual, bilingual or multilingual educational contexts, from primary to higher education (HE), the question arises regarding the use of more plural linguistic resources, and when it might be beneficial for teachers and students in the foreign language (FL) and TESOL classroom more specifically (Islam & Melo-Pfeifer, 2023). Though the debate regarding this issue is still ongoing, some authors have identified clear communicative and learning teaching purposes and learning benefits associated with pedagogical translanguaging in the HE English classroom (Chiras & Galante, 2021; García & Li, 2014).

In the context of English language classrooms in German HE institutions, issues of internationalization, population heterogeneity and multilingualism have already led to curricular, pedagogical and methodological reforms. So, while for internationalization purposes English has been reinforced, to answer to students' heterogeneity translanguaging emerged as a responsive practice. Therefore, how translanguaging in English classroom aligns with implicit or explicit language ideologies, namely around internationalization, is of interest to both educators and researchers. Yet, there is little empirical research on HE English language classrooms in Germany, and when it comes to translanguaging practices in German HE, research is scarce. In this chapter, we engage with and expand this discussion by formulating the hypothesis that teachers' ideologies on translanguaging in HE English classes may relate to HE institutions' internationalization policies rather than being bound by pedagogical concerns only.

Pedagogical Translanguaging: A Focus on Internationalization and Teacher Ideologies

Leask (2009) defines internationalization of the curriculum as 'the incorporation of an international and intercultural dimension into the content of the curriculum as well as [into] the teaching and learning arrangements and support services of a program of study' (2009: 209). In HE, in most cases, internationalization through the teaching of English and teaching in English fails to adequately reflect the idea of plurality and interculturality that goes along with demands for internationalization because it lacks the dimension of diversity (Liddicoat, 2003: 23). Internationalization of HE has legitimized the view of a monolingual teaching and learning tradition, restricting the incorporation of multicultural-multilingual skills. Marginson (1999) therefore argues that teaching English as a strategy of internationalization promotes an English-only mindset, 'a form of soft imperialism which imposes 'Western' ways of thinking, doing, and acting' (1999: 19).

Over the last few years, translanguaging has become a much-discussed scientific concept because of its transformative potential as a way to counter the pervasiveness of English in internationalized HE

(Chiras & Galante, 2021). As a theory of communication and language, translanguaging is the process of making meaning, shaping experiences and gaining understanding and knowledge by using individuals' full linguistic repertoires and other meaning-making resources (Cenoz & Gorter, 2021; García & Li, 2014). As a pedagogical practice, translanguaging can be considered 'a theoretical and instructional approach that aims at improving language and content competences in school contexts by using resources from the learner's whole linguistic repertoire and it is about activating multilingual speakers' resources so as to expand language and content learning' (Cenoz & Gorter, 2021). Pedagogical translanguaging can relate to English in a variety of ways: it can be a pedagogical approach to learn English by adding this language to students' linguistic repertoires, or as part of the semiotic repertoire used to acquire other linguistic resources (Melo-Pfeifer & Islam, forthcoming).

García (2020) reminds us that translanguaging requires more than simple support to bilingualism and multilingualism, as bilingualism – a term García uses to encompass multilingualism as well – is more likely to push back translanguaging than to support it. Kubota (2020) points out the gap between translanguaging theory (that blurs the boundaries between socially constructed languages) and the reality of monolingual gatekeeping practices. She claims that classroom practices that celebrate language diversity can remain superficial and that translanguaging needs 'to find a closer synergy with critical multiculturalism, by exploring deeper questions of linguistic and cultural inequalities in relation to associated language ideologies' (2020: 318; see also MacSwan, 2017, on why a multilingual perspective on translanguaging is needed).

Set within the German context, this chapter deals with HE English teachers' ideologies toward pedagogical translanguaging, as a practice to leverage students' multilingual repertoire, develop metalinguistic and metacognitive skills, and foster target language acquisition (Cenoz & Gorter, 2021). Research on teachers' ideologies toward translanguaging, as toward other multilingual pedagogies, is still emerging. This research trend assumes that teachers' ideologies can have an impact on their pedagogical practices (Goodman, 2022). Language ideologies are intertwined with power structures and the concept refers to 'the values, practices and beliefs associated with language use by speakers, and the discourse that constructs values and beliefs at state, institutional, national and global levels' (Blackledge, 2008). Kroskrity (2010: 192) defined language ideologies in the following terms:

> the concepts, beliefs and feelings about language structure and use which often index the political economic interests of individual speakers, ethnic and other interest groups, and nation states.

Jonsson (2017) has argued that language ideologies affect attitudes toward languages, dialects, registers, languaging and translanguaging practices;

they affect values, norms, standards, language loyalty, prestige or stigmatization, as well as language politics.

Language education and language education institutions have been controlled by monolingual ideologies for a long time. Therefore, teachers' ideologies regarding multilingualism and translanguaging are still rooted in prevalent monolingual stances toward language instruction, and multilingual pedagogies are often seen with some suspicion (Gorter & Arocena, 2020). The Second-Language Acquisition field has taken monolingual discourse for granted at least since the beginning of the 20th century with the end of the grammar-translation method and the dissemination of the direct method. The immersion model in which only the target language is used, in conjunction with the communicative language teaching (CLT) approach (Ke & Lin, 2017), became the preferred strategy. Given the linguistic power of the English language, English as a Foreign Language (EFL) classrooms foster the unspoken norm that all English teaching in an English class is expected to be monolingual (Cummins, 2007), with English of the inner circle (Kachru, 1985) being preferred over other varieties. Monolingual orientations are based on the idea that 'languages have their own unique systems and should be kept free of mixing with other languages for meaningful communication', and that 'for communication to be efficient and successful we should employ a common language with shared norms' (Canagarajah, 2013: 1).

Translanguaging works against these monolingual ideologies of homogeneity by acknowledging and valuing the diversity of linguistic resources. Language ideologies can be transformational in the sense that they can 'transform the material reality they comment on' (Woolard, 1998). This shows that translanguaging has a transformative potential in society and may thus legitimate various verbal and non-verbal repertoires as well as fluid usage of those repertoires, and could result in speakers' empowerment (Jonsson, 2017). Paulsrud and Rosén (2019) have also mentioned that, as an ideology, translanguaging challenges a monolingual bias in education by legitimizing all languages for learning and asserting learners' right to use their entire linguistic repertoires, fostering cognitive and social justice.

Goodman (2022) has contended that student teachers may be exposed during their learning path to negative perceptions toward the use of linguistic resources beyond the target language, influencing how they perceive this pedagogical resource. However, the same author argues that these negative perceptions, influenced through official language regulations and sometimes going against pedagogical evidences, can be overcome through specific instruction about the values attached to translanguaging, meaning that perceptions about translanguaging can be overcome through explicit discussion of teachers' ideologies about it.

The Empirical Study

The purpose of the present study is to investigate how teachers' ideologies toward translanguaging are reflected in German HE English classrooms. Two research questions guided the study:

- Research Question 1: To what extent do translanguaging practices relate to ideologies of internationalization?
- Research Question 2: How do teachers perceive the use of translanguaging in their English classes?

Context of Data Collection

Our research, conducted between January and June 2023 in a German university, follows a qualitative approach through a set of expert interviews. Meuser and Nagel (2009) define the expert interview as a qualitative interview based on a topical guide and focusing on the knowledge of the expert, which is broadly characterized as specific knowledge in a certain field of action.

According to the website 'My German University' (2023), 2670 BA and MA degree programs are available in English in German HE institutions for the winter 2023 semester. While absolute numbers look quite impressive, the relative percentage of English-taught programs shows a different picture. Based on recent figures provided by the German Rectors' Conference (HRK), only 17% of all MA and 3.3% of all BA programs offered in Germany are taught in English (DAAD, 2023). Apart from these English-taught programs, most of the German Universities have an Institute of English and American Studies where BA and MA courses are offered in English literature and culture. These institutes also offer English sub-degree programs (BA & MA) for future teachers of primary, secondary or vocational schools.

Over the last few decades, foreign language education programs in Germany have changed a lot, with regard to the objectives, the content, teaching principles and methods. At the university level, as the internationalization strategies are drawn up by most German universities, English as a Medium of Instruction (EMI) is offered for the international BA, MA and PhD degrees. This rapid inclusion of English in the degree programs is also perceived in the fact that even German funding organization for research and HE emphasizes the importance of English, as a tool to promote internationalization. The DAAD (Deutscher Akademischer Austauschdienst) report of 2002 emphasized the use of English and implicitly favored that language by stating that '… degree programs should contribute to the internationalization (of the curriculum) by offering courses in English' (DAAD, 2002). So, it is quite clear that English is used as a tool to internationalize German HE and enhance its prospects of competitiveness in the global market for students, scholars and researchers.

Specifically, regarding the University of Hamburg where the data collection took place, internationalization of research and teaching are at the core of the institution's linguistic policies. A document on the university's internationalization strategy (Presidium, n.d.), states that 'a special achievement of the University of Hamburg is the wide range of foreign languages offered. At the University of Hamburg, one can study around 100 languages, so that the goal of multilingual education can be realized in a special way' (our translation). While praising the teaching of these many separate languages, it is also clear that for internationalization purposes only English alongside the national language are considered: 'This offer of the Language Centre is supplemented by a specific subject language offer, which should make it easier for students, foreign as well as German students, to study in German or in English in terms of subject semantics' (n.d.: 7; our translation). The university also identifies the need to increase the offer of EMI courses as a way to enhance the attractiveness of its programs: 'Increasing attractiveness includes not only the visibility of the university, but also the studyability of the degree programs. The university management has therefore set incentives for the establishment of further English-language study programs within the framework of the target and performance agreement with the faculties' (n.d.: 9; our translation). In the same document, international experience and command of English are also considered crucial aspects in staff hiring policies.

Participants and Data Collection

We observed eight English classes from courses focusing on the four language skills and attended mostly by student teachers. After the classroom observations, four semi-structured expert interviews with the teachers of the respective courses were carried out in English. Non-probability purposive sampling has been used for the sampling and participants were chosen according to their teaching functions at the university. The classroom observation served to frame the interviews: teachers were called to comment on observed episodes which served as prompts to stimulate dialogue based on facts, whose discussion led the researchers to uncover their underlying ideologies on translanguaging pedagogies.

Among the questions asked during the interview, the following are particularly important to understand the analysis:

- Are other languages/linguistic resources used in your class?
- Can you describe a typical situation where other languages/linguistic resources are used?
- How frequently are other languages used?
- Is the use of other languages planned or spontaneous?
- How do you see the use of other languages/linguistic resources in your classroom?

Interviews were transcribed for content and discourse analysis (Brown & Yule, 1983; Coulthard, 1977). For the content analysis, the excerpts that thematize internationalization and contain discussion on the international dimension of English education were specifically considered. After the thematic selection, those excerpts were subjected to a more granular discourse analysis. In the next section, we describe how, when and why English teachers in German HE use or allow translanguaging strategies, and how they perceive the use of other languages for English learning purposes. When analyzing teachers' responses, an identification code is used (T1, T2…. T4). Table 4.1 summarizes the interviewee profiles.

Findings

The presentation of the findings is structured around the two research questions of this study.

To what extent do translanguaging practices relate to ideologies of internationalization?

Our classroom observations showed that translanguaging is quite common in HE English classes in Germany. The findings revealed that translanguaging served interpersonal and instructional purposes, as also noted in the literature. Even if they do not admit it in the interviews, teachers use translanguaging for giving examples, clarifying unfamiliar lexical items, teaching pronunciation, explaining difficult grammatical rules and clarifying unknown concepts by comparison. The analysis of teachers' interviews differs significantly from the findings of the classroom observation. It showed that teachers have mixed positions on the use of translanguaging and also that there is a mismatch between teachers' ideologies and classroom practice.

During the interview, when they were asked about the aims of English learning in HE, T1 and T2 said that the prime aim should be producing fluent and native-like English speakers. Such statements are in line with 'native-speakerism' ideology (Holliday, 2006) and promote a monolithic

Table 4.1. Profile of the participants and data collected

Identification code	Gender	Teaching experience (in years)	Experience of Teaching TESOL abroad (in years)	Interview duration	No. of interview excerpts considered for the analysis
T1	Male	6.5	6.5	50 minutes	7
T2	Female	10	8	46 minutes	8
T3	Male	7	5.5	52 minutes	5
T4	Female	2	2	55 minutes	6

understanding of English with striking similarities to the WEIRD bias. The abbreviated term WEIRD (Western, Educated, Industrialized, Rich and Democratic) was first used by Henrich *et al.* (2010), who criticize the tendency to universalize research findings from WEIRD contexts to the rest of the world, a tendency which they term the 'WEIRD bias'.

When asked about whether translanguaging/other linguistic resources can be used in English classes in HE in Germany, both T2 and T3 had similar views of not allowing other linguistic resources in the English classroom. One of the teachers [T3] opined:

> Okay, eh… other languages should not be used actually… the policies that should guide English learning here, eh… is that umm…everyone here needs to speak English, I mean, eh… exclusively English to compete internationally in the global world, right? So, it's at the top of the policy agenda… eh… it's practical in the sense that it gives you a leg up in your career in the future… [T3]

This excerpt shows a connection between the teacher's monolingual mindset ('other languages should not be used'), the role of English as an international language ('to compete internationally'), and the institution's internationalization aims ('at the top of the policy agenda'). This teacher expresses the view that English should be used exclusively as the medium of instruction and communication, with the goal of preparing individuals to compete in a global world. This mindset is rooted in the belief that English language skills will benefit students and help them compete in the global market, and eventually favor their future career thus being attached to neoliberal and capitalist ideologies. By stating this, the teacher also suggests that this monolingual English language policy is at the top of the agenda in educational institutions, because it entails pragmatic benefits ('it's practical'). These practical benefits, anchored in the idea that English proficiency can enhance employability and open international opportunities, were already present in the document mentioned above on the University of Hamburg's internationalization strategy.

How do teachers perceive the use of translanguaging in their English classes?

Like the proponents of the exclusive use of the target language (Hawks, 2001; Krashen, 1982), T2 and T3 espouse ideologies which go against the use of students' other language resources. These teachers think that the use of translanguaging does not encourage learners to use the target language in the classroom and too much use of other languages deprives learners of target language input and immersion – two pedagogical ideologies that they associate with enhanced performance leading to better language learning the extract below from one of the teachers reflects this:

> It's… I think it's usually multilingual… my classroom and the students… but I don't explicitly ask them and I also… I don't really teach bilingually.

> So, I know there are different schools of thought here, but I use the target language exclusively in my classes and I don't really see the value in this context for bilingual education... we work on your English language skills exclusively so, my ideology is -shape freedom and do not use other languages except English [T2]

Teacher T2 acknowledges that her classroom is inherently multilingual, indicating that her students bring diverse linguistic backgrounds and possibly speak languages other than English. Yet, she doesn't explicitly ask the students about it, nor does she make use of that potential linguistic diversity in her teaching. She declares explicitly adopting a monolingual approach using the target language (English) exclusively in her classes even if they seem to be aware of different pedagogical approaches and theories ('I know there are different schools of thought here'). Her use of adverbs underscores two pedagogical principles: 'explicitly', meaning that the use of other languages has to be made clear by the teacher (leaving no agency to the students: 'I don't explicitly ask them'); and 'exclusively', an adverb used twice in this excerpt to underscore the English-only policy in the classroom. We also note the use of the adverb 'really', which is used to nuance negative assertions: 'I don't really teach bilingually' and 'I don't really see the value in this context for bilingual education'. This use helps to mitigate negative attitudes toward the object being referred to.

Despite the teachers' strong advocacy for monolingualism ('I use the target language exclusively'), and several attempts to leave other linguistic resources (specifically, German) outside of the classroom, the majority language still forms a part of the classroom interactions in all the classes observed, as both students and teachers used German–English translanguaging. This is in line with prior studies, which demonstrated that multilinguals have consistently resisted monolingual English-only policies imposed in educational contexts (Makalela, 2015).

During the first part of the interview, as seen above, T2 was very strict in terms of English-only policy in the classroom. This English-only policy can be seen as part of the internationalization policy of German HE institutions (Erling & Hilgendorf, 2006). Nevertheless, during the classroom observation, we found that German–English translanguaging was common both from the teachers and between students. During the last part of the interview, when T2 was asked about her ideology on the use of other language resources in the English classroom by pointing at the instances of using German in her English class, her position conflicted with the initial comment of the exclusion of translanguaging. This conflict is highlighted by the teacher's hesitations in her discourse:

> Okay, um... it's clear from the premise of this course and the course documents that the student should speak in English... but there could be moments... um... where they [students] are not entirely sure of what they want to say, and... you know... umm... so it [translanguaging] helps them to verbalize their ideas... but it comes from the students, you

know... not from me... and... when other languages enter into the classroom, and umm... I think it can help actually to open up the space for discussion [T2]

While previously defending a monolingual pedagogical approach in her classes, T2 acknowledges that translanguaging does occur and it can be helpful. The teacher recognizes the contradiction between the official policies ('the premise of this course') and the expectation from the institution that students should use only English, as well as the inevitability of translanguaging. This inevitability is communicated by creating a sort of shared professional positionality with the interviewer (also an English teacher), by pausing between arguments with a rhetorical 'you know'. Such use of 'you know' might suggest the expression of a corporate stance rather than a personal view. The teacher notes that students may find it challenging to express ideas in English, leading to translanguaging. She highlights that students often resort to using other languages but she avoids being perceived as accomplices to this 'pedagogical abnormality'. The teacher therefore rejects any responsibility for translanguaging, emphasizing that it originates from students ('not from me'), suggesting a lack of control over its occurrence and even a lack of agency in exploring its affordances.

Another teacher [T4] claims to follow an English-only policy and insists students do the same, even during after-class informal communication. According to T4, translanguaging comes exclusively from the students because they are occasionally unable to express their ideas. However, when asked if the use of translanguaging in the classroom is planned or spontaneous, T4 mentions several instances where she has used translanguaging:

I plan it beforehand... because what we do also involves teaching critical thinking skills... ahh... sometimes German expressions are employed in academic context... ahh... also... in academia, we use a lot of words that have Latin derivations...today during one of my classes, I used those... I also plan a sentence or maybe a paragraph in German to show them, look, this is what German is like [T4]

In this statement, the teacher explains that her approach to translanguaging is intentional ('I plan it beforehand'), which seems to contradict previous statements attributing responsibility for translanguaging exclusively to students. T4 mentions the planned use of several languages to enhance the learning experience and develop critical thinking skills. T4 acknowledges that German expressions are sometimes used in academic contexts, and justifies the use of translanguaging with the existence of difficult linguistic content such as 'words that have Latin derivations'.

T1 and T3 expressed a more flexible attitude toward translanguaging in the English classroom. Yet, despite this, they often explicitly reproached students for translanguaging with their peers, urging them to repeat content in English, which created a constant dilemma for the teachers. T3 suggested that since German and English share etymological connections, translanguaging could be used, but this approach may still exclude other parts of students' linguistic repertoires. The teachers acknowledged a diverse learner group in German HE English classrooms, mainly German L1 speakers, but also speakers of many other languages (either foreign or heritage languages). He justified translanguaging as a tool for comparing English and German, aiming to enhance students' language learning. T1 stated:

> Yeah… sometimes it's easier to translanguage than it is to describe something in one language… and yeah, I think that the more you get them [students] to reflect on the difference [between German and English], the better language learners they become. Some things are not translatable easily, and that's part of language learning. And that's important, and that's why you have to have both languages if you can… like I think it's enriching if it's used in a… targeted way [T1]

During T1's classroom observation the students were found to talk occasionally with one another mostly in German and drew on a variety of linguistic resources, such as when they checked one other's answers or spoke about topics unrelated to the exercises. However, if noticed by the teacher, the students were often reprimanded for using linguistic resources other than English, which contradicts T1's flexible ideology on translanguaging. There is therefore a mismatch between the teacher's ideology (using translanguaging in a 'targeted way') and classroom practice. This mismatch fits the findings of Ganuza and Hedman (2017) as they showed how translanguaging can be the *de facto* practice in the classroom despite explicit monolingual ideology. However, the monolingual stance (English-only) may have been reinforced by the observer's presence, as he might have been seen as a symbol of teaching practices exposing English-only hegemony or institutional policing, as well as the extent to which the presence may have caused the teachers to emphasize the drawbacks of using translanguaging in English class more forcefully than they otherwise would have.

Discussion

The findings presented above suggest the topic of translanguaging faces teachers with a dilemma regarding its use as a pedagogy in HE. Attempting to answer our research questions ('To what extent do translanguaging practices connect to ideologies of internationalization?' and 'How do teachers perceive the use of translanguaging in their TESOL classes?') based on the reported findings remains hazardous, which shows the complexity of teachers' beliefs in terms of (mis)matches between declared assumptions and pedagogical practices.

On the one hand, some teachers prioritize monolingualism in English as a means to prepare students for success in an increasingly interconnected and globalized world. This underscores how teachers often tend to see the practical and career-related advantages associated with English language proficiency. In fact, both using and not using translanguaging in HE English classes can be justified by neoliberal (and institutional) ideologies anchored in the international status of English. Teachers who do not prioritize the use of diverse languages in their classroom believe in the value of exclusively using English. When other linguistic resources are referred to only German is mentioned, meaning that where translanguaging exists it encompasses only the use of the target and majority languages and leaving other linguistic resources aside. On the other hand, other teachers highlight a more flexible approach to language use in the classroom. While the English course's content and principles emphasizes English use, some teachers recognize the value of translanguaging as a means to facilitate communication and promote open discussions, particularly when it is initiated by students.

As we also saw, some teachers explicitly reject using translanguaging even though it was observed in the classroom, while others accept it even while censoring its use during their classes. Thus, rejection or acceptance of translanguaging do not correlate with its presence or absence in the classroom. During the classroom observation some teachers allowed translanguaging (at times they initiated translanguaging themselves), whereas in the interviews with the researcher those teachers still showed a firm opposition to its use. At the same time, other teachers didn't allow students to translanguage (not even with their peers), but during the interview those same teachers showed a flexible ideology toward the use of other linguistic resources. This mismatch and ambiguity between ideology and practice, and the puzzling stance of teachers can be seen as the results of multiple discourses at play. One of those discourses refers to the internationalization process in German HE, which in fact undermines plurilingual competences by encouraging a generally exclusive, monolingual and monocultural outlook of Englishization.

Conclusion

Recent decades have seen a sharp rise in internationalization in many areas of society, including education. In Germany, English is one of the main tools for this internationalization, with aim of making German HE internationally competitive. Teaching English as the first foreign language in German schools reinforces the process of internationalization of German HE institutions based on competences in that language (Erling & Hilgendorf, 2006). This wave of 'Englishization' in German HE has also influenced English classrooms, where a pervasive monolingual mindset appears to meet the need to internationalize both the institution and its student population. Internationalization of the institution is thus (paradoxically) conceived in terms of monolingualization, which highlights an interplay loop between individuals and institutions' ideologies over time.

The empirical analyses showed that other languages or linguistic resources of the students were still used during classroom interactions in all the observed classes, and this despite teachers' strong support for monolingualism and frequent attempts to keep other languages (most often German) out of their English classroom. Teachers' exclusion of German or other linguistic resources is largely consistent with what has been reported in previous research, which frames classroom practice as a de facto monolingual and hegemonic process (Cots *et al.*, 2014; Phillipson, 2006). The findings of this study reveal how translanguaging can be a *de facto* practice in the classroom despite the teacher's explicit monolingual ideology. This is consistent with previous findings from Ganuza and Hedman (2017) and Choudhury (2017). Our findings show that teachers' ideology regarding the aim of English language learning in Germany is in line with the universalizing and totalizing attempts associated to the WEIRD bias (Melo-Pfeifer & Islam, forthcoming), emphasizing the development of native-like English speakers to meet the perceived needs of internationalization. Such a stance also suggests that teachers' and their institutions' ideologies about translanguaging might be aligned, a perspective that deserves further (empirical) research.

Translanguaging and the inclusion of students' linguistic repertoires is often challenged by the traditional monolingual norm and monolingual bias toward internationalization. The 'English-only' monolingual policy in HE English classes may even prevent the 'internationalization in Education' which should be 'a process of integrating an international, intercultural or global dimension into the purpose, functions or delivery of post-secondary education' (Knight, 2003: 2–3). Excluding other languages or linguistic resources in the English language classroom – or leaving space for German only as an assumed common L1 – can be seen as an attempt to limit linguistic diversity and multilingualism, which runs counter to learners' linguistic security and equity in education and might therefore even become an obstacle to institutions' internationalization prospects. To analyze the alignment of language teaching staff and institutional ideologies on translanguaging and internationalization, it would be important to carry out further research with teacher of other languages in the same HE institution and to compare the same tendency across national and institutional borders.

References

Blackledge, A. (2008) Language ecology and language ideology. In A. Creese, P. Martin and N. Hornberger (eds) *Encyclopedia of Language and Education. Vol. 9: Ecology of Language* (pp. 27–40). Springer.

Brown, G. and Yule, G. (1983) *Discourse Analysis*. Cambridge University Press.
Canagarajah, A.S. (2013) *Translingual Practice: Global Englishes and Cosmopolitan Relations*. Routledge.
Cenoz, J. and Gorter, D. (2021) *Pedagogical Translanguaging*. Cambridge University Press.
Chiras, M. and Galante, A. (2021) Policy and pedagogical reform in higher education: Embracing multilingualism. In K. Raza, C. Coombe and D. Reynolds (eds) *Policy Development in TESOL and Multilingualism: Past, Present and The Way Forward* (pp. 13–24). Springer. https://doi.org/10.1007/978-981-16-3603-5_2
Choudhury, R. (2017) What my schoolteachers failed to tell me about translanguaging. In M. Borjian (ed.) *Language and Globalization: An Autoethnographic Approach* (pp. 103–114). Routledge.
Cots, J.M., Llurda, E. and Garrett, P. (2014) Language policies and practices in the internationalisation of higher education on the European margins: An introduction. *Journal of Multilingual and Multicultural Development* 35 (4), 311–317. https://doi.org/10.1080/01434632.2013.874430
Coulthard, M. (1977) *An Introduction to Discourse Analysis*. Longman.
Cummins, J. (2007) Rethinking monolingual instructional strategies in multilingual classrooms. *Canadian Journal of Applied Linguistics* 10, 221–240.
Deutscher Akademischer Austauschdienst (DAAD) (2002) *Internationale Studiengänge (Master-Plus und Auslandsorientierte Studiengänge): Zahlen und Fakten*. DAAD.
Deutsche Akademischer Austauschdienst (DAAD) (2023) Higher education compass. Courses of study in Germany. https://www.daad.de/en/study-and-research-in-germany/courses-of-study-in-germany/all-studyprogrammes-in-germany/
Erling, E.J. and Hilgendorf, S.K. (2006) Language policies in the context of German higher education. *Language Policy* 5 (3), 267–293.
FMKS (2014) FMKS: Bilinguale Kitas in Deutschland. https://www.fmks.eu/files/fmks/download/B%C3%BCcher/fmks_Bilinguale%20Kitas%20Studie2014_Langassung.pdf
Ganuza, N. and Hedman, C. (2017) Ideology vs. practice: Is there a space for pedagogical translanguaging in mother tongue instruction? In B. Paulsrud, J. Rosén, B. Straszer and Å. Wedin (eds) *New Perspectives on Translanguaging and Education* (pp. 208–226). Multilingual Matters.
García, O. (2020) Singularity, complexities and contradictions: A commentary about translanguaging, social justice, and education. In J.A. Panagiotopoulou, L. Rosen and J. Strzykala (eds) *Inclusion, Education and Translanguaging. Inklusion und Bildung in Migrationsgesellschaften* (pp. 11–20). Springer.
García, O. and Li, W. (2014) *Translanguaging: Language, Bilingualism and Education*. Palgrave MacMillan.
Goodman, B. (2022) Shifting beliefs and practices on translanguaging in an online master's programme. *Journal of Multilingual Theories and Practices* 3 (1), 1–6. https://doi.org/10.1558/jmtp.21042
Gorter, D. and Arocena, E. (2020) Teachers' beliefs about multilingualism in a course on translanguaging. *System* 92, 102272. https://doi.org/10.1016/j.system.2020.102272
Hawks, P. (2001) Making distinctions: A discussion of the use of the mother tongue in the foreign language classroom. *Hwa Kang Journal of TEFL* 7 (1), 47–55.
Henrich, J., Heine, S.J. and Norenzayan, A. (2010) The weirdest people in the world? *The Behavioral and Brain Sciences* 33 (2–3), 61–135. https://doi.org/10.1017/S0140525X0999152X
Holliday, A. (2006) Native-speakerism. *ELT Journal* 60 (4), 385–387.
Islam, M.S. and Melo-Pfeifer, S. (2023) 'Bangla helps learners to get the gist better'– Translanguaging in post-colonial English as a foreign language classes in higher

education in Bangladesh. In K. Raza, D. Reynolds and C. Coombe (eds) *Handbook of Multilingual TESOL in Practice* (pp. 71–83). Springer.
Jonsson, C. (2017) Translanguaging and ideology: Moving away from a monolingual norm. In B. Paulsrud, J. Rosén, B. Straszer and Å. Wedin (eds) *New Perspectives on Translanguaging and Education* (pp. 20–37). Multilingual Matters.
Kachru, B. (1985) Standards, codification and sociolinguistic realism: The English language in the outer circle. In R. Quirk and H.G. Widdowson (eds) *English in The World: Teaching and Learning the Language and Literatures* (pp. 11–30). Cambridge University Press.
Ke, I.C. and Lin, S. (2017) A translanguaging approach to TESOL in Taiwan. *English Teaching and Learning* 41 (1), 33–61. https://doi.org/10.6330/ETL.2017.41.1.02
Knight, J. (2003) Updated internationalization definition. *International Higher Education* 33, 2–3.
Krashen, S. (1982) *Principles and Practice in Second Language Acquisition*. Pergamon.
Kroskrity, P.V. (2010) Language ideologies: Evolving perspectives. In J. Jaspers, J. Östman and J. Verschueren (eds) *Society and Language Use (Handbook of Pragmatics Highlights (HoPH)* (pp. 192–211). John Benjamins Publishing Company.
Kubota, R. (2020) Promoting and problematizing multi/plural approaches in language pedagogy. In S.M.C. Lau and S. Van Viegen (eds) *Plurilingual Pedagogies: Creative and Critical Endeavors for Equitable Language (in) Education* (pp. 303–321). Springer.
Leask, B. (2009) Using formal and informal curricula to improve interactions between home and international students. *Journal of Studies in International Education* 13, 205–221.
Liddicoat, A. (2003) Internationalisation as a concept in higher education: Perspectives from policy. In A. Liddicoat, S. Eisenchlas and S. Trevaskes (eds) *Australian Perspectives on Internationalising Education* (pp. 13–26). Language Australia.
Lin, X. and Yang, C. (2020) Language ISSUE in German higher education internationalization: Ideologies, management and practices for English-medium instruction. *International Journal of English Linguistics* 10 (6), 16–29.
MacSwan, J. (2017) A multilingual perspective on translanguaging. *American Educational Research Journal* 54 (1), 167–201. https://doi.org/10.3102/0002831216683935.
Makalela, L. (2015) Moving out of linguistic boxes: The effects of translanguaging strategies for multilingual classrooms. *Language and Education* 29 (3), 200–217.
Marginson, S. (1999) After globalization: Emerging politics of education. *Journal of Education Policy* 14 (1), 19–31. https://doi.org/10.1080/026809399286477
Melo-Pfeifer, S. and Islam, M.S. (Forthcoming) A research agenda for English as an international language, social justice education and multilingual pedagogies. In N. Galloway and A.F. Selvi (eds) *The Routledge Handbook of Teaching English as an International Language*. Routledge.
Meuser, M. and Nagel, U. (2009) The expert interview and changes in knowledge production. In A. Bogner, B. Littig and W. Menz (eds) *Interviewing Experts* (pp. 17–42). Palgrave Macmillan.
My German University. (2023) Study finder. https://www.mygermanuniversity.com/study finder?p=1andpp=25andsort=application_deadlineanddir=ASC
Paulsrud, B. and Rosén, J. (2019) Translanguaging and language ideologies in education: Northern and Southern perspectives. In S. Brunn and R. Kehrein (eds) *Handbook of the Changing World Language Map* (pp. 3533–3547). Springer.
Phillipson, R. (2006) English, a cuckoo in the European higher education nest of languages? *European Journal of English Studies* 10 (1), 13–32.
Präsidium der Universität Hamburg (n.d.) *Internationalisierungsstrategie des Präsidiums der Universität Hamburg*. Universität Hamburg. https://www.uni-hamburg.de/internationales/download/internationalisierungsstrategie-uhh-praesidium.pdf.

Sliwka, A. (2010) From homogeneity to diversity in German education. In OECD (ed.) *Educating Teachers for Diversity: Meeting the Challenge, Educational Research and Innovation* (pp. 205–216). OECD.

Woolard, K.A. (1998) Introduction: Language ideology as a field of inquiry. In K.A. Woolard, B. Schieffelin and P.V. Kroskrity (eds) *Language Ideologies: Practice and Theory* (pp. 3–47). Oxford University Press.

Part 2

Identifying Trends, Knowledges and Skills to Support Internationalization

5 Harnessing Teacher Identity for Globalization and Internationalization of TESOL Curricula

Manfred Man-fat Wu

Internationalization of Teaching English to Speakers of Other Languages (TESOL) teacher education curricula informed by globalization has created demands for teacher educators to develop and possess a unique make-up of their teacher identity to nurture future-ready teachers. Analyses and syntheses of literature to date related to globalization, language teaching identity and internationalization of TESOL teacher education indicate that to enact an internationalized curriculum, teacher educators are encouraged to possess dispositions that embrace diverse perspectives on culture and language when it comes to English. Another mission for internationalized TESOL teacher education is to produce teachers who are equipped with relevant pedagogical knowledge and skills on global citizenship. Among the elements in global citizenship, morality, more specifically duty to others and its actualization, is an essential trait for both TESOL educators and student teachers (Bowman, 2010; Tsang *et al.*, 2021). Identity of teacher educators are advised to be infused with respect for personhood possessing rights on a global scale (Starkey, 2023). To achieve the above aims, it is suggested that teacher training curricula include the following elements: personal reflections on the roles of self as teachers and the English language in the internationalized curricula, and updating the TESOL teacher education curricula in the context of internationalization.

Introduction

Internationalization[1] of university caused by ever-intensifying and ever-expanding globalization (Turner & Robson, 2008), 'the processes by virtue of which the sovereign nation states intermingle and interweave through transnational actors' (Roldán, 2018), has been influencing students and educators in the higher education sector in various aspects. Baker and Fang (2022) remarked that internationalization of higher education is diverse and multilayered in nature, and these two features equally apply to TESOL education. One example is that there has been a rapid increase in the number of English medium instruction (EMI) programs offered by universities worldwide (see Baker & Fang, 2022), which augments the need for TESOL teachers and educators. This massive-scale trend has intensified the need for internationalization of the TESOL teacher education curricula, so that future higher education TESOL teachers can produce learners who can achieve academically in EMI programs. It has been found that learners' self-perceived English proficiency was positively related to their levels of participation and interactions with others in intercultural activities (Tsang & Yuan, 2022; Tsang et al., 2023; see also Baker & Fang, 2022). This means that self-perceived English proficiency influences the extent to which an individual practices globalization. Another example is the standardization of the curriculum (Cross, 2020). With the expansion of internationalized programs to an unprecedented extent, there is a strong need for benchmarking programs, including of the TESOL teacher education curricula, for both the competitiveness of programs on a global scale and for the academic and career developments of students (which very often involve international experiences). Kamyab and Raby (2023) highlighted that there are unintended consequences of internationalization of higher education, but they are largely under-researched.

There are several benefits of internationalization of TESOL teacher education curricula. Firstly, the English classroom can be seen as an ideal niche for global identity development, especially global citizenship (Reynolds et al., 2020). This means that the teaching of the English language, unlike subjects such as mathematics, can enable learners to be aware of and to appreciate the fact that they are a member of the global community that possesses diverse cultures. After completing TESOL teacher education, future teachers of English will be able to equip the future generations to thrive in a growing globalized world, both in their personal and career lives. This is because teacher education curricula harnessed with elements for nurturing global identity can equip future teachers with the attitude, knowledge and skills to foster their students' positive development of global identity. Therefore, to make the fullest use of the benefits of language education they received, learners need to have a global perspective. This means that one important aim for teacher training is the development of a global perspective.

Contemporary post-structural identity is characterized by fluidity and flexibility (Choi, 2018; Cross, 2020; Lee & Canagarajah, 2019b), and is cognitive, social, emotional, ideological and historical (Barkhuizen, 2017). Internationalization of TESOL teacher education curricula has the aim of producing TESOL future teachers who embrace diversity in terms of value, culture and knowledge. Globalization exerts influences on the concept of personhood within society ideologically (Gledhill, 2004). Internationalization of TESOL teacher education, if planned and implemented properly, can meet the need for the changing concept of personhood, as it has been consistently found that the self-identity of teachers (i.e. the beliefs, attitudes, values and commitment an individual holds toward being a teacher which are negotiated through experience over time) influences their pedagogy (see Richards, 2021) and their perceptions on students (e.g. Reeves, 2018). Understanding language teacher identity has been suggested to contribute to social justice and challenge social oppression (Kayi-Aydar, 2019). In sum, internationalized TESOL curricula need to pay due attention to teacher identity, including that of TESOL teacher educators.

While research on learner identity in the TESOL discipline has a long history and has become a branch in TESOL research (see Norton, 2021), it was only recently that researchers began to pay attention to the identity of language teachers (De Costa & Green-Eneix, 2021; Sadeghi & Bahari, 2022; Yazan, 2018; Yazan & Lindahl, 2020b). Two recent examples are that Yazan and Lindahl (2020b) have devoted an edited volume and Karpava (2023) a handbook on language teacher identity. Despite the sudden surge in the amount of research on language teacher identity (see Barkhuizen, 2019; Yazan & Lindahl, 2020a; Yazan & Rudolph, 2020a), how teacher identity needs to be updated to meet the demands of globalization has seldom been on the agenda of researchers. Research in this area has instead focused on aspects such as methodology (Yazan, 2018), descriptions on the characteristics of TESOL teacher educators (Barkhuizen, 2021), identity constructions and negotiations (Torres-Rocha, 2023), language choices of pre-service teachers (Gelfuso, 2017) and teacher attrition (Ayar, 2023). The synthesis of reflections of 18 applied linguists in 15 countries (Ng & Cheung, 2022) indicates that language teacher identity is influenced by not only professional, but also cultural and societal discourses on a global level. Other than the above, no other major research or discussion on globalization and TESOL teacher identity has been made.

Feng and Kim (2022) expressed that research on the pernicious effects of globalization on teacher identity has been overlooked. Another reason for the need to pay attention to how globalization influences the identity of TESOL educators is that globalization has augmented the role of English teaching as a tool for social justice (Kayi-Aydar, 2019). This implies that the identity of TESOL teachers has become increasingly more important, especially in terms of values and morality. Given the increasing extent of internationalization of TESOL curricula caused by globalization and the lack of attention given to how globalization influences teacher identity, this chapter proposes qualities for TESOL teacher educators to be able to meet the demands of globalization. This is achieved through analyzing and synthesizing relevant literature on the topics of internationalization of higher education and TESOL teacher education identity. In the next section, the proposed qualities will be introduced. This will be followed by suggestions for fostering the proposed qualities.

The Demand for Updating Teacher Identity for Internationalization

Professional identity of TESOL teacher educators formed in their teacher education training is no longer adequate for meeting the emerging demands brought by globalization (both as teacher educators and teachers), as globalization has substantially altered how language learning takes place (Richards, 2022; Starkey, 2023). There is an urgent need to address this issue because a large part of language teacher identity is formed through teacher training (Yazan & Lindahl, 2020a). In this section, the elements proposed for internationalized TESOL teacher education curricula in terms of the identity of teacher educators will be explored.

Intercultural communication competence

Internationalized TESOL teacher education curricula are suggested to be infused with intercultural communicative competence (ICC) (Heggernes, 2021). This chapter argues that ICC constitutes a significant part of the identity of TESOL teacher educators. This is especially true with the increasing diversity of learners who will be teachers owing to globalization. More and more studies have indicated the significance of the effectiveness of strategies on ICC in resolving miscommunication in multilingual classrooms (see Matsumoto, 2018).

Tajeddin and Ghaffaryan (2020) conducted empirical research on language teachers' intercultural identity in Iran. Quantitative results indicated that teachers possess the capacity for ICC, concluding there is a need to expand the intercultural identity of language teachers in Iran. In her empirical study, Matsumoto (2018) found that it was the identity of teachers as being multilingual rather than their status as a non-native speaker of English that enabled teachers to resolve miscommunication with students. Baker (2011a, 2011b) advocates the empirically supported concept of intercultural awareness, which includes behaviors and skills for negotiating and mediating communications grounded on different cultures.

The existence of privilege for native-speaking (NS) and the marginalization of non-native-speaking (NNS) English teachers are still two core perennial issues in TESOL (e.g. Fang, 2020; see also Yazan & Rudolph, 2020b). The undesirable outcomes of adopting a dichotomous NS/NNS perspective and the positive outcomes of adopting a multilingual/translingual perspective have been documented (see Feng & Kim, 2022). There have been calls for moving beyond the dichotomous NS and NNS classification of TESOL teachers (e.g. Lee & Canagarajah, 2019b; Matsumoto, 2018; Richards, 2021; Yazan & Rudolph, 2020a) and adopting alternative perspectives. Lee and Canagarajah (2019a, 2019b) recommended a translingual perspective, and there have been calls for reflection and paradigm shift among teachers and teacher educators (e.g. Ng & Cheung, 2022). Yazan and Rudolph (2020a) call for critical attention to the experiences of non-native English-speaking teachers, which is under-theorized.

Given the above forces and conflicts caused by globalization, one essential element to be incorporated into the internationalized curriculum is ICC. Sensitivity to cultural and contextual, including social, political and linguistic influences, is treated in this chapter as an essential part of internationalized teacher educators' personal and professional identities, given the fluidity of transnational movements and the advancement of electronic communication and entertainment technology (Giddens, 2006; Tarozzi & Torres, 2016).

Global citizenship

Increasing interactions among individuals and cultures across the globe place demands for global citizenship to avoid conflicts and confusion on the part of learners. With the increasing awareness of the powerful influences of globalization, more teacher training programs around the world include the dimension of global citizenship (Estellés & Fischman, 2020). Despite its significance as a core dimension of teacher identity, the roles of global citizenship in English teaching and teacher identity have seldom been researched. Recently there have been scattered discussions on this area, for example, in the form of conference discussions (e.g. Madya *et al.*, 2018) and edited books (e.g. Lütge *et al.*, 2023). Yemini *et al.* (2019) pointed out the gap between how global citizenship education is perceived by theorists and implemented in teacher training.

A global perspective is recommended for internationalization of teacher education curricula. To interact effectively with individuals from other parts of the globe, it is encouraged that learners be informed about the concept of global citizenship. This is particularly true for English student teachers, given that English has been enjoying the status of lingua franca (e.g. Jenkins, 2012), meaning that English is a common vehicle of communication by native speakers of different languages. The need for linkages among nations was particularly evident during the Covid-19 pandemic (Baker & Fang, 2022). In addition to being recognized as a lingua franca, the English language is also adopted as a means for world peace, civil society and democracy (Lu & Corbett, 2014). These elements are advised to be incorporated into the identity of TESOL teacher educators.

Focusing on teacher educators of various disciplines, Mairi *et al.* (2023) identified that the participants went through different paths in their journey of understanding global citizenship education and multilingual competence. This finding reveals the fluidity and malleability of teacher identity. Given the diversity of experiences, Mairi *et al.* (2023) recommended ample time, resources and opportunities be provided in the development and implementation of curriculum for global citizenship education and multilingual competence. The authors also recommended taking into consideration individual differences of learners, including TESOL teacher educators. In another study by Villegas *et al.* (2020), it was found that student teacher identity construction in second language teaching took place over time without any fixed patterns and routes. This finding concurs with the fluidity, malleability and 'negotiativeness' of teacher identity concluded by Mairi *et al.* (2023), Sadeghi and Bahari (2022), as well as Ng and Cheung (2022). Consequently, identity work is one practical way to foster global citizenship.

It has been pointed out that the lack of awareness, knowledge and pedagogical competence of TESOL teachers in promoting global citizenship are major hurdles for global citizenship education (see Wu, 2020). Prejudices and biased views such as that learners need a native-level English proficiency for global citizenship are a threat to the existence of local identities (Cavanagh, 2020). This chapter contends that these issues be infused as parts of their identity by ensuring that their values are free from native-speakerism and other forms of biases, as value is a key dimension of self-identity. However, there has been a lack of systematic inclusion of global citizenship education across the teacher education curriculum and settings internationally (Mairi *et al.*, 2023).

Morality on a global scale

Internationalization of TESOL teacher education curricula inevitably results in conflicting values and ethics as diverse cultures are taken into consideration in the design of curricula. Byram and Wagner (2018) prescribed TESOL as a field to assume moral and ethical responsibilities for sustainability on the global scale and to connect English to the local and global communities (Byram *et al.*, 2017). Morality on a global scale needs to be problematized because the neo-liberal ideas on the global connections being owned by elites are at odds with the value of equality and justice of globalization (De Costa *et al.*, 2021). There is a need for respect of personhood regardless of ethnicity, gender, age, religion, i.e. human rights (Starkey, 2023), and this value is recommended to be an integral part of identity for teacher educators.

An earlier discussion by Coldron and Smith (1999) explored how social space, or the relations an individual has with others, is related to how teachers construct their professional identities. Their conclusion is that the craft tradition (which views teaching as a set of techniques), the scientific tradition (which views teaching as a science that can be replicated), the moral tradition (with teaching involving moral judgments) and the artistic tradition (which involves teachers' subjective meanings and feelings) affect teachers' trajectory in the development of their professional identity. Of particular relevance to the focus of this chapter is the moral tradition, that there is a strong need for morality in the globalized world.

Morality of TESOL teacher educators has to be coupled with its actualization (Wu, 2024). Human rights, or more specifically cosmopolitan right and hospitality right, and the respect for personhood put to practice enable English learning to exert a positive influence on a global scale.

Practical Recommendations for TESOL Teacher Educators

One unique characteristic of teacher identity is that its development is multifaceted in nature (Gee, 2017). Therefore, a multipronged approach covering its various dimensions is proposed in this chapter. The details are given below.

Reflection

Reflective practices in different forms and the ability for reflection have always been highly recommended in teacher training (e.g. Barkhuizen, 2017; Dragas, 2019; Farrell, 2019; Mann & Walsh, 2017; Ng & Cheung, 2022). Through reflective practices, TESOL teacher educators can enhance their understanding of the different aspects of the teacher education they offer, especially in the context of the internationalization of TESOL curricula. Neokleous and Krulatz (2020) advocated the idea of reflective teachers for TESOL teacher educators, given the interceptive nature and fluidity of teacher identity in the globalized era. De Costa (2022) as well as Ng and Cheung (2022) reiterated the importance of teacher reflexivity, among teacher emotion, teacher agency and beliefs, as the core elements of language teacher identity.

TESOL teacher educators' competence to critically evaluate one's own and other cultures, i.e. critical cultural awareness (Kramsch, 2023), is an essential quality that an internationalized TESOL teacher education curricula to aim at. Open-mindedness, an element advocated by UNESCO (2014), and a critical perspective are two suggestions participants of Mairi *et al.*'s (2023) provided for promotion of global citizenship education.

TESOL teacher educators are advised to raise their awareness on how personal history influences teachers' attitudes, their own language learning identity and the approaches they adopt, as it has been consistently found that personal history exerts significant influence on learner identity (see Sadeghi & Bahari, 2022; Tsang & Yuan, 2022; Tsang *et al.*, 2023).

Lee and Canagarajah (2019a) identified that critical thinking and reflection are two dispositional qualities for learners to develop an open disposition towards diversity. A translingual perspective equips learners to negotiate differences across languages. Cross (2020) also highlighted the role of the language teacher as learner, meaning that teachers update themselves on an ongoing basis. This is especially true that identity is being negotiated through experience constantly (Richards, 2021). These proposals can be equally applied to TESOL teacher educators. An essential step for positive teacher identity development is self-reflection. Tajeddin and Ghaffaryan (2020) reported empirical evidence for the extreme opposite orientation among Iranian English language teachers: anti-cultural-globalization and pro-cultural-globalization as part of their teacher identity. Therefore, personal reflection and critical thinking are desirable elements in teacher training for TESOL teacher educators to foster a healthy identity development of English language teachers.

Regarding the implementation of reflection especially for identity construction of pre-service language teachers, Yuan and Mak (2018) provided evidence for the effectiveness of integrated and interactive tasks involving collaborative lesson planning, group consultation, microteaching and video reflection.

Updating the TESOL teacher education curricula for internationalization

There is a high degree of standardization in the provision of consumer products and services under globalization because of a global market consisting of diverse cultures (Giddens, 2006). Education is no exception, and internationalization of TESOL teacher education curricula will result in standardized content for learners of diverse backgrounds, which is achieved through benchmarking of coursework materials, teacher training, accreditation (Cross, 2020; see Cavanagh, 2020; see Kamyab & Raby, 2023) and tests (Reeves, 2018). Internationalization of higher education also gave rise to innovations and the establishment of bodies such as national consortium and government-endorsed public and private institutions which increase revenue and visibility (see Kamyab & Raby, 2023). However, standardization means that the individual subjectivity and personal needs of learners will tend to be neglected (McNamara, 2019; Reeves, 2018) and the differences between cultures will become narrow, leading to homogenization in terms of culture (Galloway & Rose, 2015; Holborrow, 2006), as well as education and language policies (Benson, 2006) among nations. Facing these trends, Cross (2020) calls for a heightening of critical awareness on the global language teaching landscape in language teacher training. Educators of future TESOL teachers are advised to inform student teachers on how internationalization of TESOL teacher education curricula influences the learning of student teachers, what qualities in terms of professional identity are advocated and to make adjustment to their curricula. This is especially true since past experience and teacher education are important sources of teacher identity (Richards, 2021).

Compared to local curricula, internationalized curricula tend to place less emphasis on local culture (Demuth, 2018). Globalization also creates resistance and reactive feelings for some cultures, which may give rise to nationalism (Mallinson, 2021). This is especially true that internationalization of higher education has been criticized as over-relying on the English language, which creates tensions for the local or native identity of learners (see Cavanagh, 2020), including that of TESOL teacher educators. Advancements in communication technology exert considerable influences on identity particularly through imagined communities (Pavlenko & Norton, 2007), and this area has been attracting attentions by researchers (Wargo & De Costa, 2017).

Universities are appealed to reflect on the potential of ICC as part of the of formal and out-of-class curricula (Tsang *et al.*, 2023), especially for student teachers of English. An example they provided is the 'learning beyond the classroom model' (see Tsang *et al.*, 2023). Butler (2011) stressed the importance of developing 'communities of learning outside the classroom' (2011: 50). These suggestions are applicable for nurturing the identity of TESOL teacher educators.

The English as a Lingua Franca (ELF) perspective is also advocated by Baker and Fang (2022) as an element to be incorporated into the internationalized curricula. Based on the ELF perspective, Blair (2015) argues that sociolinguistics, pragmatics, global Englishes, critical evaluation of theory and literature on ELT and TESOL, and regular challenging of key constructs and assumptions, such as nativeness, be included in teacher training. Dewey (2012), again from an ELF perspective, offered several suggestions for enhancements in curricula for language teacher education, which are equally valid for the training of TESOL educators. His list of suggestions included highlighting the particular environment and sociocultural context in which English(es) will be used, increasing exposure to the diverse ways in which English is used globally, engaging with student teachers in critical classroom discussions about globalization and growing diversity of English, paying less attention to English as a native language and focusing on communicative strategies.

Another suggestion offered in this chapter is that room be made for learners (i.e. TESOL teacher educators) to express their voices in different types of curricula (Choi, 2018; Lee & Canagarajah, 2019a). This is essential for negotiation among multiple languages and is especially true for the 'negotiating nature' of language teacher identity (Kennedy, 2020). As pointed out by Yazan and Lindahl (2020a), teachers' identity work involves ongoing engagement with revisiting, reconstruction and rewriting of past experiences. Knowledge and skills are of equal importance, and many approaches, models, guidelines which take into consideration both local and international contexts are available (Yazan & Lindahl, 2020b).

Conclusion

Internationalization of TESOL teacher education curricula has created the demand for identity of teacher educators to be comprehensive, diversity embracing, fluid, flexible for the design and implementation of internationalized TESOL teacher educator curricula. The conclusion of this chapter is that in addition to knowledge and skills as part of teacher identity for overcoming the challenges caused by internationalization of TESOL teacher education curricula, morality, awareness and ICC are equally, if not more, important parts of their personal traits. There is always resistance to change, and the internationalization of higher education curricula is no exception (Hammond & Radjai, 2022).

An area which highly influences the formation and maintenance of self-identity especially in terms of second language is government policies and responses to language. As remarked by Choi (2018), even if learners are in an environment which they can negotiate their identity freely in an autonomous manner, negative influences of the macro environment may not allow identity negotiation to take place properly. As stated by Yazan and Rudolph (2020a: 10):

> [t]hrough a postmodern and poststructural lens, apprehending the negotiation of identity – of positioning and being positioned – involves attending to individuals' contextualized, local-global, negotiations of linguistic, cultural, ethnic, socioeconomic, religious, political, educational, geographical, professional, and gender-related discourses, and of fluid privilege-marginalization.

Note

(1) According to Knight (2008), internationalization of higher education is 'the process of integrating an international, intercultural or global dimension into the purpose, functions or delivery of HE at the institutional and national levels' (2008: 21).

References

Ayar, Z. (2023) The driving forces behind teacher attrition and its multifaceted face in language teaching: A scoping review of the articles from 2000 to 2020. In S. Karpava (ed.) *Handbook of Research on Language Teacher Identity* (pp. 510–328). IGI Global. https:// doi.org/10.4018/978-1-6684-7275-0.ch017

Baker, W. (2011a) From cultural awareness to intercultural awareness: Culture in ELT. *ELT Journal* 66 (1), 62–70. https://doi.org/10.1093/elt/ccr017

Baker, W. (2011b) Intercultural awareness: Modelling an understanding of cultures in intercultural communication through English as a lingua franca. *Language and Intercultural Communication* 11 (3), 197–214. https://doi.org/10.1080/14708477.201 1.577779

Baker, W. and Fang, F. (2022) Intercultural citizenship and the internationalisation of higher education: The role of English language teaching. *Journal of English as a Lingua Franca* 11 (1), 63–75. https://doi.org/10.1515/jelf-2022-2067

Barkhuizen, G. (ed.) (2017) *Reflections on Language Teacher Identity Research*. Routledge.
Barkhuizen, G. (2021) *Language Teacher Educator Identity*. Cambridge University Press.
Benson, P. (2006) Autonomy in language teaching and learning. *Language Teaching* 40, 21–40. https://doi.org/10.1017/S0261444806003958
Blair, A. (2015) Evolving a post-native, multilingual model for ELF-aware teacher education. In Y. Bayyurt and S. Akan (eds) *Current Perspective on Pedagogy for English as a Lingua Franca* (pp. 89–101). Walter de Gruyter.
Bowman, N.A. (2010) Assessing learning and development among diverse college students. *New Directions for Institutional Research* 145, 53–71. https://doi.org/10.1002/ir.322
Butler, Y.G. (2011) The implementation of communicative and task-based language teaching in the Asia-pacific region. *Annual Review of Applied Linguistics* 31, 36–57. https://doi.org/10.1017/S0267190511000122
Byram, M. and Wagner, M. (2018) Making a difference: Language teaching for intercultural and international dialogue. *Foreign Language Annals* 51, 140–151.
Byram, M., Golubeva, I., Han, H. and Wagner, M. (2017) *From Principles to Practice in Education for Intercultural Citizenship*. Multilingual Matters.
Cavanagh, C. (2020) The role of English in global citizenship. *Journal of Global Citizenship and Equity Education* 7 (1), 1–23. https://doi.org/10.13140/RG.2.2.21671.60328
Choi, L.J. (2018) Embracing identities in second language learning: Current status and future directions. *Problems of Education in the 21st Century* 76 (6), 800–815.
Coldron, J. and Smith, R. (1999) Active location in teachers' construction of their professional identities. *Journal of Curriculum Studies* 31 (6), 711–726.
Cross, R. (2020) The 'subject' of Freeman and Johnson's reconceived knowledge base of second language teacher education. *Language Teaching Research* 24 (1), 37–48. https://doi.org/10.1177/1362168818777521
De Costa, P.I. (2022) Afterword: Second language teacher identity and more. In K. Sadeghi and F. Ghaderi (eds) *Theory and Practice in Second Language Teacher Identity* (pp. 309–312). Springer. https://doi.org/10.1007/978-3-031-13161-5
De Costa, P.I. and Green-Eneix, C. (2021) Identity in SLA and second language teacher education. In H. Mohebbi and C. Coombe (eds) *Research Questions in Language Education and Applied Linguistics* (pp. 537–541). Springer Nature. https://doi.org/10.1007/978-3-030-79143-8_94
De Costa, P.I., Green-Eneix, C. and Li, W. (2021) Embracing diversity, inclusion, equity and access in EMI-TNHE: Towards a social justice-centered reframing of English language teaching. *RELC Journal* 52 (2), 227–235. https://doi.org/10.1177/00336882211018540
Demuth, C. (2018) Liberalism's all-inclusive promise of freedom and its illiberal effects: A critique of the concept of globalization. In C. Roldán, D. Brauer and J. Rohbeck (eds) *Philosophy of Globalization* (pp. 63–77). Walter de Gruyter.
Dewey, M. (2012) Towards a post-normative approach: Learning the pedagogy of ELF. *Journal of English as a Lingua Franca* 1 (1), 141–170. https://doi.org/10.1515/jelf-2012-0007
Dragas, T. (2019) Embedding reflective practice in an INSET course. In S. Walsh and S. Mann (eds) *The Routledge Handbook of English Language Teacher Education* (pp. 138–154). Routledge.
Estellés, M. and Fischman, G. (2020) Who needs global citizenship education? A review of the literature on teacher education. *Journal of Teacher Education* 72 (2), 1–14. https://doi.org/10.1177/0022487120920254
Fang, F. (2020) Glocalization, English as a lingua franca and ELT: Reconceptualizing identity and models for ELT in China. In B. Yazan and N. Rudolph (eds) *Criticality,*

Teacher Identity, and (In)Equity in English Language Teaching (pp. 23–39). Springer Nature. https://doi.org/10.1007/978-3-319-72920-6_2

Farrell, T.S.C. (2019) Reflective practice in L2 teacher education. In S. Walsh and S. Mann (eds) *The Routledge Handbook of English Language Teacher Education* (pp. 38–51). Routledge.

Feng, M. and Kim, H.K. (2022) EFL teachers' spatial construction of linguistic identities for sustainable development in globalization. *Sustainability* 14, 4532. https://doi.org/10.3390/su14084532

Galloway, N. and Rose, H. (2015) *Introducing Global Englishes*. Routledge.

Gee, J.P. (2017) Identity and diversity in today's world. *Multicultural Education Review* 9 (2), 83–92. https://doi.org/10.1080/2005615X.2017.1312216

Gelfuso, A. (2017) Facilitating the development of preservice teachers' pedagogical content knowledge of literacy and agentic identities: Examining a teacher educator's intentional language choices during video-mediated reflection. *Teaching and Teacher Education* 66, 33–46. http://dx.doi.org/10.1016/j.tate.2017.03.012

Giddens, A. (2006) Modernity and self-identity: Tribulations of the self. In A. Jaworski and N. Coupland (eds) *The Discourse Reader* (pp. 415–427). Routledge.

Gledhill, J. (2004) Neoliberalism. In D. Nugent and J. Vincent (eds) *A Companion to the Anthropology of Politics* (pp. 332–348). Blackwell Publishing.

Hammond, C.D. and Radjai, L. (2022) Internationalization of curriculum in Japanese higher education: Blockers and enablers in English-medium instruction classrooms in the era of COVID-19. *Higher Education Forum* 19, 87–107. https://doi.org/10.15027/52117

Heggernes, S.L. (2021) A critical review of the role of texts in fostering intercultural communicative competence in the English language classroom. *Educational Research Review* 33, 100390. https://doi.org/10.1016/j.edurev.2021.100390

Holborrow, M. (2006) Ideology and language: Interconnections between neo-liberalism and English. In J. Edge (ed.) *(Re-)locating TESOL in an Age of Empire* (pp. 84–103). Palgrave Macmillan. https://doi.org/10.1057/9781137029423_5.

Jenkins, J. (2012) English as a lingua franca from the classroom to the classroom. *ELT Journal* 66 (4), 486–494. https://doi.org/10.1093/elt/ccs040

Kamyab, S. and Raby, R.L. (2023) Introduction. In S. Kamyab and R.L. Raby (eds) *Unintended Consequences of Internationalization in Higher Education: Comparative International Perspectives on the Impacts of Policy and Practice* (pp. xxvii–xxxiii). Routledge.

Karpava, S. (ed.) (2023) *Handbook of Research On Language Teacher Identity*. IGI Global. https:// doi.org/10.4018/978-1-6684-7275-0

Kayi-Aydar, H. (2019) Language teacher identity. *Language Teaching* 52 (3), 281–295.

Kennedy, L.M. (2020) At the dinner table: Preservice EFL teachers' identity negotiations and resources. In B. Yazan and K. Lindahl (eds) *Language Teacher Identity in TESOL: Teacher Education and Practice as Identity Work* (pp. 46–62). Routledge.

Knight, J. (2008) *Higher Education in Turmoil: The Changing World of Internationalization*. Sense Publishers.

Kramsch, C. (2023) Re-imagining foreign language education in a post- COVID-19 world. In C. Lütge, T. Merse and P. Rauschert (eds) *Global Citizenship in Foreign Language Education: Concepts, Practices, Connections* (pp. 15–40). Routledge. https://doi.org/10.4324/9781003183839-3

Lee, E. and Canagarajah, A.S. (2019a) The connection between transcultural dispositions and translingual practices. *Journal of Multicultural Discourses* 14, 14–28. https://doi.org/10.1080/17447143.2018.1501375

Lee, E. and Canagarajah, A.S. (2019b) Beyond native and nonnative: Translingual dispositions for more inclusive teacher identity in language and literacy education. *Journal of Language, Identity and Education* 18 (6), 352–363. https://doi.org/10.1080/15348458.2019.1674148

Lu, P. and Corbett, J. (2014) An intercultural approach to second language education and citizenship. In J. Jackson (ed.) *Routledge Handbook of Language and Intercultural Communication* (pp. 325–339). Routledge.

Lütge, C., Merse, T. and Rauschert, P. (eds) (2023) *Global Citizenship in Foreign Language Education: Concepts, Practices, Connections*. Routledge.

Madya, S., Hamied, F.A., Renandya, W.A., Coombe, C. and Basthomi, Y. (eds) (2018) *ELT in Asia in the Digital Era: Global Citizenship and Identity*. Routledge.

Mairi, S., Gruber, J., Mercer, S., Schartner, A., Ybema, J., Young, T. and van der Meer, C. (2023) Teacher educators' perspectives on global citizenship education and multilingual competences. *Journal of Multilingual and Multicultural Development*. https://doi.org/10.1080/01434632.2023.2170388

Mallinson, W. (2021) *Guicciardini, Geopolitics and Geohistory: Understanding Interstate Relations*. Palgrave Macmillan. https://doi.org/10.1007/978-3-030-76537-8_7

Mann, S. and Walsh, S. (2017) *Reflective Practice in English Language Teaching: Research-Based Principles and Practices*. Routledge.

Matsumoto, Y. (2018) Teachers' identities as 'non-native' speakers: Do they matter in English as a lingua franca interactions? In B. Yazan and N. Rudolph (eds) *Criticality, Teacher Identity, and (In)Equity in English Language Teaching* (pp. 57–80). Springer Nature. https://doi.org/10.1007/978-3-319-72920-6_9

McNamara, T. (2019) *Language and Subjectivity*. Cambridge University Press.

Neokleous, G. and Krulatz, A. (2020) Intercepting and fluid identities: From reflective teacher educators to reflective teachers. In B. Yazan and K. Lindahl (eds) *Language Teacher Identity in TESOL Teacher Education and Practice as Identity Work* (pp. 231–249). Routledge.

Ng, C.H. and Cheung, Y.L. (2022) Second language teacher identity: A synthesis of reflections from applied linguists. In K. Sadeghi and F. Ghaderi (eds) *Theory and Practice in Second Language Teacher Identity* (pp. 59–74). Springer. https://doi.org/10.1007/978-3-031-13161-5_5

Norton, B. (2021) Identity in language learning and teaching. In H. Mohebbi and C. Coombe (eds) *Research Questions in Language Education and Applied Linguistics* (pp. 81–85). Springer. https://doi.org/10.1007/978-3-030-79143-8_15

Pavlenko, A. and Norton, B. (2007) Imagined communities, identity, and English language learning. In J. Cummins and C. Davison (eds) *International Handbook of English Language Teaching* (pp. 669–680). Springer. https://doi.org/10.1007/978-0-387-46301-8_43

Reeves, J. (2018) Teacher identity work in neoliberal schooling spaces. *Teaching and Teacher Education* 72, 98–106. https://doi.org/10.1016/j.tate.2018.03.002

Reynolds, R., Macqueen, S. and Ferguson-Patrick, K. (2020) Active citizenship in a global world: Opportunities in the Australian curriculum. *Curriculum Perspectives* 40 (1), 63–73. https://doi.org/10.1007/s41297-019-00084-2

Richards, J.C. (2021) Teacher, learner and student-teacher identity in TESOL. *RELC Journal* 54 (1), 252–266. https://doi.org/10.1177/0033688221991308

Richards, J.C. (2022) Foreword. In K. Sadeghi and F. Ghaderi (eds) *Theory and Practice in Second Language Teacher Identity* (pp. vii–ix). Springer.

Roldán, C. (2018) The thinning and deformation of ethical and political concepts in the era of globalization. In C. Roldán D. Brauer and J. Rohbeck (eds) *Philosophy of Globalization* (pp. 109–122). Walter de Gruyter.

Sadeghi, K. and Bahari, A. (2022) Second language teacher identity: A systematic review. In K. Sadeghi and F. Ghaderi (eds) *Theory and Practice in Second Language Teacher Identity* (pp. 11–30). Springer. https://doi.org/10.1007/978-3-031-13161-5_2

Starkey, H. (2023) Challenges to global citizenship education: Nationalism and cosmopolitanism. In C. Lütge, T. Merse and P. Rauschert (eds) *Global Citizenship in Foreign Language Education: Concepts, Practices, Connections* (pp. 63–78). Routledge. https://doi.org/10.4324/9781003183839-5

Tajeddin, Z. and Ghaffaryan, S. (2020) Language teachers' intercultural identity in the critical context of cultural globalization and its metaphoric realization. *Journal of Intercultural Communication Research* 49 (3), 263–281. https://doi.org/10.1080/17475759.2020.1754884

Tarozzi, M. and Torrres, C.A. (2016) *Global Citizenship Education and the Crises of Multiculturalism: Comparative Perspectives.* Bloomsbury Academic. https://doi.org/10.5040/9781474236003

Torres-Rocha, J.C. (2023) English language teacher educators' critical professional identity constructions and negotiations. *Language and Intercultural Communication* 23 (1), 53–68. https://doi.org/10.1080/14708477.2023.2166058

Tsang, A. and Yuan, R. (2022) Examining home and international students' awareness of, attitudes towards and participation in intercultural activities on campus. *Journal of Studies in International Education* 26 (3), 390–409. https://doi.org/10.1177/1028315321990741

Tsang, A., Yang, M. and Yuan, R. (2021) The relationships between participation in intercultural activities on campus, whole-person development, and academic achievement: A mixed-methods study. *Journal of Multilingual and Multicultural Development.* http://dx.doi.org/10.1080/01434632.2021.1963121

Tsang, A., Aubrey, S. and Yuan, R. (2023) Multiculturalism and multilingualism in higher education: Intercultural activity participation and opportunities for language learning. *International Journal of Multilingualism.* https://doi.org/10.1080/14790718.2022.2164769

Turner, Y. and Robson, S. (2008) *Internationalizing the University.* Continuum.

UNESCO (2014) *Global Citizenship Education: Preparing Learners for the Challenges of the 21st Century.* https://unesdoc.unesco.org/ark:/48223/pf0000227729

Villegas, D.F.M., Varona, W.H. and Sánchez A.G. (2020) Student teachers' identity construction: A socially-constructed narrative in a second language teacher education program. *Teaching and Teacher Education* 91, 103055.

Wargo, J.M. and De Costa, P.I. (2017) Tracing academic literacies across contemporary literacy sponsorscapes: Mobilities, ideologies, identities, and technologies. *London Review of Education* 15 (1), 101–114.

Wu, M.M. (2020) Second language teaching for global citizenship. *Globalisation, Societies and Education* 18 (3), 330–342. http://doi.org/10.1080/14767724.2019.1693349

Wu, M.M. (2024) *Globalisation and Second Language Identity: Opportunities, Challenges and the Importance of Morality.* Springer Nature.

Yazan, B. (2018) A conceptual framework to understand language teacher identities. *Journal of Second Language Teacher Identities* 1 (1), 22–48. http://doi.org/10.1558/slte.24908

Yazan, B. and Lindahl, K. (2020a) Language teacher learning and practice as identity work: An overview of the field and this volume. In B. Yazan and K. Lindahl (eds) *Language Teacher Identity in TESOL: Teacher Education and Practice as Identity Work* (pp. 1–10). Routledge.

Yazan, B. and Lindahl, K. (eds) (2020b) *Language Teacher Identity in TESOL: Teacher Education and Practice as Identity Work.* Routledge.

Yazan, B. and Rudolph, N. (2020a) Introduction: Apprehending identity, experience, and (in)equity through and beyond binaries. In B. Yazan and N. Rudolph (eds) *Criticality, Teacher Identity, and (In)Equity in English Language Teaching* (pp. 1–19). Springer Nature. https://doi.org/10.1007/978-3-319-72920-6_1

Yazan, B. and Rudolph, N. (eds) (2020b) *Criticality, Teacher Identity, and (In)Equity in English Language Teaching* (pp. 1–19). Springer Nature. https://doi.org/10.1007/978-3-319-72920-6_1

Yemini, M., Tibbitts, F. and Goren, H. (2019) Trends and caveats: Review of literature on global citizenship education in teacher training. *Teaching and Teacher Education* 77, 77–89. https://doi.org/10.1016/j.tate.2018.09.014

Yuan, R. and Mak, P. (2018) Reflective learning and identity construction in practice, discourse and activity: Experiences of pre-service language teachers in Hong Kong. *Teaching and Teacher Education* 74, 205–214. https://doi.org/10.1016/j.tate.2018.05.009

6 Internationalizing TESOL Teacher Education by Connecting Global and Local Practices from a 'Teacher Agency' Perspective

Zhenjie Weng

This chapter considers how the increased mobility of English language teachers around the world has helped to reveal some of the weaknesses of Teaching English to Speakers of Other Languages (TESOL) teacher education curricula when preparing international teacher candidates. A global–local disconnection has been a long-lasting problem in TESOL. One proposed solution to the disconnection is to provide more context-specific elective courses to the increasingly diverse teacher populations. However, with the complexity and uncertainty embedded in the increased mobility of teachers, those context-specific courses might not always be helpful. This chapter therefore introduces a conceptual tool, namely teacher agency (TA), which also serves as a critical lens, that TESOL teacher candidates can draw upon for their future practice regardless of the location of their workplace. Through reviewing literature that unpacks the current issues in internationalizing TESOL teacher education and demonstrating how TA as a conceptual tool can be used to address the issues, the author emphasizes the need to integrate TA in TESOL teacher education to prepare teacher candidates to be agents of change in their local contexts.

Introduction

English language teaching (ELT), being a global phenomenon, has played a crucial role in creating and expanding formal opportunities for

English language learners to enhance their proficiency (Sadeghi & Richards, 2021). As the number of English language learners and users continues to rise worldwide, the start of English language learning at progressively younger ages has become prevalent among learners in countries like China (Li, 2020). Owing to this influence, there exists a substantial global demand for English language teachers (Faez & Karas, 2019; Sun *et al.*, 2020; Weng & McGuire, 2021), resulting in a heightened mobility of English language teachers. The flow of English language teachers involves native English-speaking teachers (NESTs) who venture to English as a Foreign Language (EFL) settings (such as South Korea, Japan and China) to teach (Cinnamon, 2021; Guo *et al.*, 2019; Nelson, 1998). For example, The Japan Exchange and Teaching Program, the English Program in South Korea, the Native English Teacher Scheme in Hong Kong and the Foreign English Teachers Recruitment Project in Taiwan collectively demonstrate the recruitment of NESTs as exemplary English language instructors (Guo *et al.*, 2019). At the same time, non-native English-speaking teachers (NNESTs) also travel to native English-speaking countries (e.g. US, UK, New Zealand, Australia and Canada) for TESOL teacher education or professional development (Faez & Karas, 2019; Stapleton & Shao, 2018). In this regard, the diversity of teacher population, including pre-service and in-service TESOL teachers with transnational identities, highlights a range of unique needs in TESOL teacher education and professional development (Carrier, 2003).

This increased mobility of English language teachers around the world has revealed some weaknesses of TESOL teacher education curricula when preparing the rapidly growing body of teacher population (Carrier, 2003; Govardhan *et al.*, 1999). Numerous studies (e.g. Ilieva & Ravindran, 2018) have revealed the problematic issues embedded in current TESOL teacher education. The global–local disconnection has been identified as one of the concerns (Liu, 1998; Sun *et al.*, 2020). For example, Ilieva and Ravindran (2018) found that in a MATESOL program in a Canadian university, the international teacher candidates criticized native speakerism, promoted multilingualism in practice and reconstructed their identity as future agents of change; however, after returning to their home country, most of them were unable to actualize their reconstructed identity owing to restricted contextual factors, indicating the gap between global pedagogical approaches and local instructional realities. To enhance the effectiveness of TESOL teacher education programs and contribute to the refinement of strategies that balance global best practices with the unique needs of diverse educational environments, one proposed solution to the global–local disconnection is to offer more context-specific elective courses to the increasingly diverse teacher populations (Stapleton & Shao, 2018). Given the intricate and unpredictable nature of the growing mobility among teacher populations, it could be impractical to consistently provide context-specific courses that effectively address the diverse needs of every teacher.

Therefore, in this chapter, an introduction is provided to a conceptual tool referred to as TA. This tool serves a dual purpose by also serving as a critical lens, one that TESOL teacher candidates can deliberately and purposefully leverage to engage in reflective processes concerning their teaching methodologies and simultaneously undertake comprehensive analyses of the intricate teaching contexts in which they find themselves. This, in turn, equips them with the capacity to respond to their teaching circumstances in a proactive and agentive manner. Their response further demonstrates an increased level of control and influence over their instructional practices and the challenges posed by their unique teaching situations. Through reviewing literature that unpacks the current issues in internationalizing TESOL teacher education and demonstrating how TA as a conceptual tool can be used to address the issues, this chapter provides important insights on connecting TA with the internationalization of TESOL teacher education in response to globalization and increased mobility of TESOL teachers.

Overview of Internationalizing TESOL Teacher Education

TESOL teacher education exists as a distinct field within the realm of education, encompassing various programs, courses and initiatives that aim to prepare individuals to become effective TESOL educators. As the TESOL teacher population becomes more mobile, there is a growing need to internationalize TESOL teacher education to accommodate their diverse needs. However, early work (Carrier, 2003; Liu, 1998; Nelson, 1998; Richards, 1987) on TESOL teacher education has criticized the issues and dilemma in its curriculum design and assessment. For example, according to Nelson (1998), less than half of TESOL masters' degree programs in the US taught a course in or related to intercultural communication in their programs, in other words,

> Without a course that increases both students' self-awareness and their awareness of other cultures, TESOL graduates are more likely to enter into intercultural teaching situations from an ethnocentric perspective, evaluating (often negatively) what they experience in terms of their own culture. (Nelson, 1998: 27)

Teachers without the adequate training are not likely to be effective in intercultural communication, and this could exert an adverse impact on training TESOL teachers who might teach across different contexts domestically and/or internationally. In another study, Carrier (2003) revealed the lack of relevance of Western-based TESOL programs for transnational teacher candidates who came to the programs to learn how to teach English effectively and later return to their countries with the 'better' knowledge and skills. The TESOL programs were criticized for not adequately recognizing and addressing the diverse needs and interests of the teacher candidates in key areas, which include 'contextually responsive teacher education content, training for success in a different school culture, competing with native English-speaking teacher trainees (NSs), promoting self-confidence and encouraging contributions by NNS teacher trainees to the field of English language teaching' (Carrier, 2003: 242). To internationalize the TESOL teacher education, Carrier (2003) proposed an introductory course that covered the aforementioned key areas. However, as she emphasized, this course was only an initiative to ensure the entire curriculum responsive to the transnational teacher trainees in Western-based TESOL programs.

Dogancay-Aktuna (2006) further pointed out the scarcity of TESOL teacher education courses that deal with the sociocultural and political context of TESOL particularly considering the globalization of teaching English as an international language. She therefore proposed three areas of inquiry that should be integrated into existing TESOL teacher education curricula, two of which are 'discussion of crosscultural variation in language teaching and learning and tools for investigating this variation' and 'examination of the sociopolitical factors surrounding the teaching of English as an international language' (2006: 278). The two areas of inquiry are closely related to teachers' awareness of diverse cultural backgrounds and contextual factors influencing their teaching practices and relevant to preparing TESOL teachers who teach abroad. Dogancay-Aktuna (2006) claimed that:

> our goal is not for teachers to learn lists of items about different cultures, which would indeed lead to stereotyping, but to become more sensitive to the cultural diversity in teaching and learning experiences that students bring to the classroom. (2006: 284)

In line with Nelson (1998), Dogancay-Aktuna (2006) supported the integration of intercultural communication into TESOL programs, ensuring TESOL teachers are well prepared for teaching in diverse linguistic and cultural contexts and conducive to the internationalization of TESOL teacher education. More recently, Sun *et al.* (2020) asserted the necessity for TESOL programs to re-examine English learning and teaching through *transnational lens*. They proposed that:

> TESOL teacher educators and curriculum developers should aim to nurture teachers' capacity for analysing the demands of new contexts of teaching with transnational students, and making more socioculturally informed pedagogical decisions. (2020: 37–38)

TESOL teachers are now expected to cultivate reflective and analytical skills for recognizing and discerning contextual factors, such as sociocultural and political influences, that may impact their effective implementation of pedagogies within specific contexts. Resonating with some other scholars (Liu, 1999; Park, 2012), Sun *et al.* (2020) further suggested that TESOL teacher educators can collaborate with international student teachers to pinpoint aspects of the program curriculum that might not be applicable to their local teaching situations, and TESOL teacher educators could then modify the educational content to align with the students' academic and career requirements. This approach could work if a TESOL program has a stable constituent of student population. Otherwise, it would pose a challenging task to the program as they have to constantly modify their curriculum, which could lead to a series of issues; for example, logistical and financial burden. One specific need Sun et al. (2020) proposed was for more culturally responsive pedagogies to increase student teachers' understandings of immigrant or refugee students' unique situations. This proposal is more for those who stay domestically to teach TESOL courses. For individuals who plan to return to their home country after completing TESOL training abroad, Sun et al. (2020) supported the ideas presented by Faez and Valeo (2012).

This support pertained to the effective integration and adept execution of the practicum component within TESOL programs. The integration of a well-structured practicum experience is seen as an invaluable means of equipping prospective TESOL teachers with practical skills and strategies that transcend theory, allowing them to bridge the gap between the pedagogical knowledge acquired in their coursework and the actual realities they will face in their teaching careers. By immersing themselves in hands-on teaching experiences, TESOL teachers gain insight into the nuances and intricacies of language instruction that are often elusive within the confines of a classroom. Such integration can significantly enhance teachers' readiness for the diverse contexts they may encounter and assist them in aligning their expectations with real-world situations. Additionally, in line with the perspective of Stapleton and Shao (2018), offering tailored electives designed for specific teaching environments was considered advantageous for students preparing to teach in a variety of settings.

These suggestions are undoubtedly contributing to TESOL teacher education facing a tremendous impact of transnationalism on TESOL teacher education and making TESOL teacher education more applicable in preparing TESOL teachers to teaching internationally. Nevertheless, there are constraints to these recommendations. For example, the specific contexts for practicum in Western-based TESOL programs are very likely to be different from transnational teachers' targeted teaching contexts. Also, electives are unable to be exhaustive and meet all students' needs. Weng and McGuire (2021), in their study, further suggested TESOL teacher education programs to provide student teachers 'different contexts of teaching for practicum or have the chance to compare and contrast the transnational impact of different contexts on their way of teaching as a development of expertise' (2021: 330). They proposed that exposing student teachers to different case studies of transnational teachers could help the students be aware of potential problems they may encounter.

Drawing from the preceding discussion, it is evident that TESOL teacher education has been undergoing a significant change in its curriculum, a process of internationalization. This evolution represents a departure from a monolingual ideology toward the adoption of a transnational epistemology (You, 2020). Considering the evolving landscape where TESOL teacher education confronts the formidable challenge of accommodating the diverse needs of students, this shift in epistemological orientation necessitates an urgent need to renovate both its curriculum and assessment methodologies. However, amid the various course suggestions and recommendations discussed thus far, a notable absence emerges: the absence of a sustainable approach, with an international dimension, aimed at nurturing and perpetuating the proactive capacity of transnational TESOL teachers to engage in reflective introspection and astute analysis of their specific teaching contexts. This capacity, which forms the bedrock of their ability to make informed pedagogical decisions and adapt their teaching methods, remains inadequately addressed.

Furthermore, it is crucial to recognize that the proposed course suggestions seem primarily tailored to consider NNEST candidates within Western-based TESOL teacher education programs. Yet, in the broader landscape of TESOL, the mobility of TESOL teachers transcends these boundaries, encompassing NESTs who embark on journeys to teach in EFL settings as their deliberate career choice. This additional facet underscores the need for a more inclusive and comprehensive approach to curriculum development and teacher training within the TESOL domain. The approach acknowledges the unique challenges and opportunities faced by both NNESTs and NESTs as they navigate the globalized world of English language education.

Challenges Transnational Teachers Face

Liu's (1998) observations shed light on a compelling aspect of the experiences of international students who undergo teacher training in North America, Britain and Australia. These students, while acquiring valuable skills and knowledge in these Western educational contexts, often encounter a significant challenge upon returning to their home countries. The predicament they face extends beyond the mere need to adapt their methods and techniques to their local teaching context. Instead, they grapple with a deeper conflict arising from the clash between the innovative ideas they have acquired abroad, and the entrenched, traditional approaches followed by local professionals in their home country. This conundrum forces these international students to undertake a process of readjustment in their instructional methods, and it frequently leads to the (re)construction of their teacher identities upon their return home. This negotiation process is intricate and demands a keen awareness of agency, as these transnational teachers must navigate the constraints of their local educational environment strategically.

Interestingly, while much research has explored the experiences and professional identity construction of NNESTs who return to their countries for teaching, there has been comparably less attention given to the experiences of NESTs. NESTs, who are often seen privileged in the ELT job market owing to their native speaker status (Cinnamon, 2021; Weng, 2022; Weng & McGuire, 2021; Weng *et al.*, 2023), also contend with unique challenges. For NESTs, the prestige associated with native speakerism is often accompanied by feelings of not belonging within their teaching communities. This sense of being an outsider can lead to a lack of agency and a profound confusion about their status as teaching professionals (Cinnamon, 2021). The seemingly advantageous position of NESTs in the ELT world comes with its own set of complexities and struggles, highlighting the need for a more nuanced understanding of their experiences and the dynamics of identity construction in the global context of English language education.

Cinnamon (2021) stated that NESTs with prior teaching experiences and training were still challenged to construct their professional identities in the Korean context because 'practices in the Korean education system often contradict what teachers have learned and practiced in other contexts' (Cinnamon, 2021: 85). Drawing upon the reviewed research, she suggested that 'it may be beneficial for experienced teachers to also receive formal training and professional development to adapt their professional practices specifically to a Korean context' (Cinnamon, 2021: 85–86). Further, it was found that NESTs in Korean education context were often perceived as 'fun teachers', threatening their professional identity construction (Cinnamon, 2021: 86). Indeed, NESTs in EFL contexts were often seen as 'replaceable parts', 'distanced other' or 'commercial assets', rather than as skilled educators in their host institutions (Howard, 2019: 1487). These challenges that NESTs faced while teaching abroad have not been explored in-depth in TESOL teacher education, a neglected area that could further inform and urge the internationalization of TESOL teacher education.

In another study, Weng (2022) explored a NEST's journey into the world of TESOL teaching in China. The NEST, Nathan, took an unexpected turn when he embarked on a teaching assignment in China. While he had undergone cultural training in preparation for his international teaching experience, he soon found himself facing unexpected challenges and emotions in the classroom. One of the key areas that tested his teaching expertise was the task of instructing students in letter writing, a common teaching component in EFL settings. Letter writing, a seemingly straightforward aspect of language instruction, proved to be a complex and unfamiliar territory for Nathan. This was particularly true because he had not previously encountered or taught a curriculum solely centered on letter writing at a college level in the US. The absence of prior experience in this specific context left him feeling powerless and disheartened, as he grappled with the nuances of guiding students through this skill. To adapt and enhance the course material, Nathan decided to introduce additional exercises involving free writing. He believed that encouraging students to express themselves freely through writing could be a valuable approach. However, this attempt proved to be more challenging than anticipated, primarily owing to the unfamiliarity of free writing within the Chinese student context.

Nathan's experiences in China highlight the complexity and adaptability required of TESOL teachers working in transnational settings. The study also proves that TESOL transnational teachers, including both NESTs and NNESTs, face challenges in their teaching even though the hardships they experience could be different. Nathan's study indicates that even with cultural training, teachers may encounter unexpected obstacles and struggles when faced with unfamiliar curriculum components or teaching approaches. This underscores the importance of ongoing professional development and cultural sensitivity for TESOL teachers working in diverse and cross-cultural environments. Nathan's journey ultimately serves as a reminder of a sustaining approach to maintain their proactive capability to reflect and analyze their teaching and the situated context so that to better negotiate their professional identities and agency in local contexts.

In a word, the literature suggests that internationalizing TESOL teacher education involves not only imparting cross-cultural knowledge and providing diverse practicum experiences, but also fostering critical analysis of contextual factors. To advance this process, TESOL teachers need a reliable toolkit to navigate diverse teaching situations and maintain their motivation for professional development.

Teacher Agency as a Conceptual Tool

In this chapter, I introduce the conceptual framework of TA. TA allows TESOL teacher candidates to intentionally and purposefully examine their teaching methods through engaging in reflective processes concerning their teaching approaches and, at the same time, conducting in-depth analyses of the complex teaching environments they encounter. By utilizing this framework, teacher candidates can become better equipped to respond proactively and assertively to the specific circumstances they face in their teaching roles. Being aware of their agency in teaching can empower them to exercise a higher degree of control and influence over their instructional practices and effectively address the challenges inherent to their unique teaching situations (Kim *et al.*, 2022).

In the field of education, teacher agency has gained substantial popularity in the past decade owing to an increased recognition of its pivotal role in driving educational change (Chisholm *et al.*, 2019; Tao & Gao, 2017). Recent discussions have further underscored that teacher agency manifests when teachers within schools exert influence, make decisions and adopt positions that impact both their work and their professional identity (Eteläpelto *et al.*, 2013: 61), highlighting its vital contribution to the intricate processes of professional growth – encompassing the formation of professional practices and identities (Vähäsantanen *et al.*, 2017: 517). Scholars (e.g. Kira & Balkin, 2014; Vähäsantanen, 2015) have explicitly highlighted that when conflicts or tensions arise between professional identities and work practices, teachers can engage in agentic endeavors spanning from preserving to reshaping their professional identity, thereby empowering them within their workplace. Hence, the significance of nurturing teachers' capacity for autonomous and agentic actions cannot be overstated (Eteläpelto *et al.*, 2013). Given its notable significance as discussed earlier, TA has been explored as a fundamental concept within teacher education (e.g. Eteläpelto *et al.*, 2013) and professional development contexts (e.g. Insulander *et al.*, 2019).

In language education, Kayi-Aydar (2019) defined language TA as 'a language teacher's intentional authority to make choices and act accordingly in his or her local context' (2019: 15). Particularly in EFL context, studies (e.g. Glasgow, 2016; Hamid & Nguyen, 2016) have shown that teachers do not always accept top-down policies whole-heartedly. Factors such as teachers' pedagogical skills, language proficiency, institutional support and student needs might drive teachers' actions to resist, challenge and criticize policies, dominant discourses and norms (Weng *et al.*, 2019). Toom *et al.* (2015) also conveyed that teacher agency can be manifested in actions in line with those. In ESL contexts, few studies (e.g. Trickett *et al.*, 2012) have shown teachers as advocates of education equality for their marginalized ESL students.

More importantly, in language teacher education, TA has been closely related to teacher identity, which:

> should be placed at the center of LTE [Language teacher education] programs to help teacher candidates critically explore their own identity categories and how these categories intersect, develop their capacity to exercise agency in their roles as teachers, and bridge the gaps between their learning experiences inside LTE program classes and those in their teaching practice outside the LTE classroom. (Fairley, 2020: 1038)

Based on the review of literature (Weng, 2023), tensions, including but not limited to structural constraints (e.g. Bowen *et al.*, 2021; Warren & Ward, 2021); conflicts between personal professional value and that in the broader community or of other stakeholders (e.g. Ishihara *et al.*, 2018; Liao, 2017); curricular reform or educational change (e.g. Ashton, 2022; Tan *et al.*, 2022); emotion rules (e.g. Miller & Gkonou, 2018; Yuan & Lee, 2016); and conflicts between idealized and actual teaching (e.g. Gao & Cui, 2022; Huang, 2021) are factors known to push teachers to negotiate and exercise their agency in their teaching and in reconstructing their professional identities. Being aware of these tensions and understanding how to strategically navigate them through agency allows for a shift in their identity construction and teaching practices. The global–local disconnection that TESOL transnational teachers experience is one type of tension as captured in Ilieva and Ravindran (2018). One way to strategically navigate the tensions is through enacting different forms of agency, including individual, collective, critical, self-initiated, opportunistic, positive and/or negative agency.

TESOL teacher candidates, being aware of their agency, through reflecting on their teaching, could better realize the limitations in their knowledge as well as skills, and the constraints in their teaching contexts. Subsequently, these teacher candidates could follow up by exercising different types of agency to expand their knowledge, skills and capabilities in navigating challenges that transnational TESOL teachers tend to face while teaching abroad or after returning to their home country. Particularly, for the global and local disconnection, by being aware of their agency, the transnational teachers could reflect on the gap and proactively look for support or analyze their situated context to react to the challenges they encounter, e.g. through reflecting on and analyzing the alignment between their imagined and actual professional identities. More importantly, they need to take agentive actions in negotiating the tensions and conflicts to readjust their instructional practices.

Connecting Teacher Agency with the Internationalization of TESOL Teacher Education

Extending upon the preceding discussion, I would like to advance the concept of TA, recognizing it not merely as a peripheral notion but rather as an indispensable cornerstone upon which effective and adaptable pedagogy is constructed. Although Yazan (2019) has proposed a teacher-identity oriented TESOL teacher education, the notion of TA should transcend the realms of passive acknowledgment and permeate the very fabric of teachers' professional lives, prompting them not only to recognize its existence but to actively employ it as a potent tool for addressing the intricate challenges presented by the dynamic interplay of global and local educational dynamics. Employing TA can also nurture teachers' own growth and development through continuous reflection and purposeful engagement with the diverse teaching scenarios they encounter.

The integration of TA into the broader landscape of TESOL teacher education implies a profound process that bestows teachers with the agency to assume proactive roles in their ongoing professional evolution and the decision-making processes inherent to their teaching careers. In other words, connecting TA as a conceptual tool with the internationalization of TESOL teacher education empowers TESOL teachers to take ownership of their professional development while preparing them to teach in diverse global contexts. This approach can enhance the quality of teacher education and produce more culturally sensitive and adaptable TESOL teachers. In light of this, I wish to propose a series of practical recommendations for TESOL teacher education programs to consider and adopt. The chief recommendation among all is the inclusion of a dedicated and comprehensive course solely devoted to the exploration and cultivation of TA. Such a course, I argue, should not merely stand as an ancillary component within the existing curriculum but instead serve as a fundamental pillar, equipping teachers with the knowledge, skills and mindset necessary to not only recognize their agency but, more crucially, to harness and channel it effectively. With the effort, this course can enhance TESOL teachers' pedagogical efficacy and adaptability in the face of the diverse and ever-evolving educational landscapes they encounter.

In addition to the suggested courses (e.g. cross-cultural and culturally responsive courses and practicum) by other scholars, the course on TA, as a vital component of TESOL teacher education, could be strategically positioned throughout the program as one of the culminating experiences. This intention is to prepare teacher candidates to experience their increased agency in navigating the multifaceted challenges that lie ahead in their future teaching careers. This deliberate placement serves the purpose of ensuring that teachers progressively acquire a foundational understanding of TESOL principles and pedagogical practices. The assurance allows them to critically draw upon this knowledge as a scaffold upon which they can construct and implement their agency-driven strategies and approaches when confronted with the intricacies of diverse and dynamic teaching contexts that they are likely to encounter during their professional journeys.

This multifaceted course consists of several key components, each meticulously designed to foster a holistic appreciation of TA and its transformative potential:

- Ecological Definition of TA: At the core of this course, teacher candidates can delve into an ecological definition of teacher agency, exploring not only the individual elements of agency but also its intricate interplay with the broader educational and sociocultural ecosystems. This foundational component will empower teachers to view agency as a dynamic and context-dependent phenomenon, deeply rooted in the complex web of constant recontextualization of knowledge and skills across international/domestic teaching contexts.
- Interconnection of Teacher Identity and Agency (see e.g. Eteläpelto *et al.*, 2013; Tavares, 2023): Another critical facet of the course revolves around the intrinsic interconnection between teacher identity and TA. It is imperative for teacher candidates to grasp how their personal beliefs, values and self-perceptions as educators are inextricably intertwined with their capacity to enact agency effectively. This

segment of the course can illuminate how one's sense of self as a teacher informs their agency and, conversely, how agency can shape and redefine their professional identity aligned with their mobility across contexts.

- Examination of Transnational Teachers' Agency (see e.g. Loo *et al.*, 2017): To provide a broader perspective, the course can include a diverse range of readings and case studies that illuminate how transnational teachers, often operating in culturally and linguistically diverse settings, enact their agency within their unique situated contexts. These readings can encompass a multitude of circumstances and challenges, showcasing the adaptability and versatility of TA in diverse teaching environments. In particular, the cases are used to critically demonstrate how transnational teachers can reflect and recontextualize their knowledge, skills and perceptions in the local context.
- Implementation of Action Research Projects: Another essential component of a TA-oriented course is to empower teachers with a comprehensive understanding of action research design and methodology. By equipping TESOL teacher candidates with these essential tools, the course prepares them for addressing challenges and tensions that may arise in their future teaching endeavors. Teachers will be able to confidently plan, execute and assess action research projects within their own classrooms to inform their teaching timely.
- Exploration of Different Forms of Agency (see e.g. Lai *et al.*, 2016): The course could demonstrate how the various forms TA can be manifested in teaching to tackle tensions, e.g. the global–local disconnection, in teaching. This includes but is not limited to pedagogical agency (the ability to make informed instructional decisions), advocacy agency (the capacity to advocate for students' needs and rights) and sociopolitical agency (the potential to effect change within broader educational and societal systems). By examining these diverse forms of agency, teacher candidates can develop a holistic toolkit to draw upon in their professional practice.

Incorporating these multifaceted components into the course design, as part of the internationalizing process of TESOL teacher education, will not only enrich teacher candidates' understanding of TA but also equip them with the knowledge, skills and critical perspectives necessary to become proactive, adaptable and empowered teachers capable of addressing the intricate challenges they will encounter throughout their teaching careers.

Conclusion

This chapter underscores the vital role of TA in addressing the global–local disconnection in the process of internationalizing TESOL teacher education. It focuses on preparing teachers to be adaptable and proactive in diverse teaching contexts. The chapter begins by examining the global landscape of ELT and the challenges faced by transnational teachers. It then delves into the critical need to rectify the global–local disjunction within TESOL teacher education. This involves scrutinizing the existing curriculum, often failing to align with the realities of teaching. Furthermore, the chapter introduces the concept of TA as a potential solution. TA is presented not as an auxiliary tool but as a powerful instrument for bridging the existing gap. It empowers TESOL teacher candidates to navigate their teaching methodologies proactively and analyze complex teaching environments comprehensively. TA's profound connection to teacher identity is explored to demonstrate how teachers can proactively shape their professional identities and teaching practices to meet the dynamic demands of their teaching situations. Ultimately, the chapter advocates for the integration of TA as a central element in further advancing the internationalization of TESOL teacher education. It proposes a dedicated course that immerses teacher candidates in the dimensions of TA, including its ecological definition, its connection with teacher identity, insights into transnational teachers' agency, and an exploration of the various forms it can manifest. In summary, this chapter advocates greater internationalization of TESOL teacher education by highlighting the crucial role of TA in shaping proactive, adaptable professionals prepared to excel in diverse international and/or domestic teaching contexts.

References

Ashton, K. (2022) Language teacher agency in emergency online teaching. *System* 105, 102713. https://doi.org/10.1016/j.system.2021.102713

Bowen, N.E.J.A., Satienchayakorn, N., Teedaaksornsakul, M. and Thomas, N. (2021) Legitimising teacher identity: Investment and agency from an ecological perspective. *Teaching and Teacher Education* 108, 103519. https://doi.org/10.1016/j.tate.2021.103519

Carrier, K.A. (2003) NNS teacher trainees in Western-based TESOL programs. *ELT journal* 57 (3), 242–250.

Chisholm, J.S., Alford, J., Halliday, L.M. and Cox, F.M. (2019) Teacher agency in English language arts teaching: A scoping review of the literature. *English Teaching: Practice and Critique* 18 (2), 124–152. https://doi.org/10.1108/ETPC-05-2019-0080

Cinnamon, A. (2021) The native English-speaking teacher as an agent and a professional: A reflection on current research and paths forward. *Korea TESOL* 16 (2), 77. https://www.koreatesol.org/sites/default/files/pdf_publications/KTJ16-2web.pdf#page=87

Dogancay-Aktuna, S. (2006) Expanding the socio-cultural knowledge base of TESOL teacher education. *Language, Culture and Curriculum* 19 (3), 278–295. https://doi.org/10.1080/07908310608668768

Eteläpelto, A., Vähäsantanen, K., Hökkä, P. and Paloniemi, S. (2013) What is agency? Conceptualizing professional agency at work. *Educational Research Review* 10, 45–65. https://doi.org/10.1016/j.edurev.2013.05.001

Faez, F. and Valeo, A. (2012) TESOL teacher education: Novice teachers' perceptions of their preparedness and efficacy in the classroom. *TESOL Quarterly* 46 (3), 450–471.

Faez, F. and Karas, M. (2019) Language proficiency development of Non-Native English-Speaking Teachers (NNESTs) in an MA TESOL program: A case study. *TESL-EJ* 22 (4), 1–16. https://files.eric.ed.gov/fulltext/EJ1204612.pdf

Fairley, M.J. (2020) Conceptualizing language teacher education centered on language teacher identity development: A competencies-based approach and practical applications. *TESOL Quarterly* 54 (4), 1037–1064. https://doi.org/10.1002/tesq.568

Fu, Y. and Weng, Z. (2023) Examining ESL and bilingual teachers' agency after NCLB: Expanding the ecological perspective. *International Multilingual Research Journal*. https://doi.org/10.1080/19313152.2023.220109

Gao, Y. and Cui, Y. (2022) English as a foreign language teachers' pedagogical beliefs about teacher roles and their agentic actions amid and after COVID-19: A case study. *RELC Journal*. https://doi.org/10.1177/00336882221074110

Glasgow, G.P. (2016) Policy, agency, and the (non) native teacher: 'English classes in English' in Japan's high schools. In P.C.L. Ng and E.F. Boucher-Yip (eds) *Teacher Agency and Policy Response in English Language Teaching* (pp. 58–74). Routledge.

Govardhan, A.K., Nayar, B. and Sheorey, R. (1999) Do U.S. MATESOL programs prepare students to teach abroad? *TESOL Quarterly* 33 (1), 114. https://doi.org/10.2307/3588194

Guo, X., Chen, G. and Sun, Y. (2019) An ethical analysis of native-speaking English teachers' identity construction in a mainland China university. *Journal of Multilingual and Multicultural Development*. https://doi.org/10.1080/01434632.2019.1684502

Hamid, M.O. and Nguyen, H.T.M. (2016) Globalization, English language policy, and teacher agency: Focus on Asia. *International Education Journal: Comparative Perspectives* 15 (1), 26–43. https://files.eric.ed.gov/fulltext/EJ1099019.pdf

Howard, N.J. (2019) Constructing professional identities: Native English-speaking teachers in South Korea. *The Qualitative Report* 24 (7), 1478–1510.

Huang, J. (2021) Sustainability of professional development: A longitudinal case study of an early career ESL teacher's agency and identity. *Sustainability* 13 (16), 9025. https://doi.org/10.3390/su13169025

Ilieva, R. and Ravindran, A. (2018) Agency in the making: Experiences of international graduates of a TESOL program. *System* 79, 7–18. https://www.sciencedirect.com/science/article/pii/S0346251X17305699

Insulander, E., Brehmer, D. and Ryve, A. (2019) Teacher agency in professional development programmes – A case study of professional development material and collegial discussion. *Learning, Culture and Social Interaction* 23, 100330. https://doi.org/10.1016/j.lcsi.2019.100330

Ishihara, N., Carroll, S.K., Mahler, D. and Russo, A. (2018) Finding a niche in teaching English in Japan: Translingual practice and teacher agency. *System* 79, 81–90. https://doi.org/10.1016/j.system.2018.06.006

Kayi-Aydar, H. (2019) A language teacher's agency in the development of her professional identities: A narrative case study. *Journal of Latinos and Education* 18 (1), 4–18. https://doi.org/10.1080/15348431.2017.1406360

Kim, G.J.Y., Zhu, J. and Weng, Z. (2022) Collaborative autoethnography in examining online teaching during the pandemic: From a 'teacher agency' perspective. *Teaching in Higher Education*. https://doi.org/10.1080/13562517.2022.2078959

Kira, M. and Balkin, D.B. (2014) Interactions between work and identities: Thriving, withering, or redefining the self? *Human Resource Management Review* 24 (2), 131–143. https://doi.org/10.1016/j.hrmr.2013.10.001

Lai, C., Li, Z. and Gong, Y. (2016) Teacher agency and professional learning in cross-cultural teaching contexts: Accounts of Chinese teachers from international schools in Hong Kong. *Teaching and Teacher Education* 54, 12–21. https://doi.org/10.1016/j.tate.2015.11.007

Li, Z. (2020) English education in China: An evolutionary perspective. *People's Daily* 27 April. http://en.people.cn/n3/2020/0427/c90000-9684652.html

Liao, P.C. (2017) Taiwan-educated teachers of English: Their linguistic capital, agency, and perspectives on their identities as legitimate English teachers. *Taiwan Journal of TESOL* 14 (2), 5–35. https://eric.ed.gov/?id=EJ1171166

Liu, D. (1998) Ethnocentrism in TESOL: Teacher education and the neglected needs of international TESOL students. *ELT Journal* 52, 3–10. https://doi.org/10.1093/elt/52.1.3

Liu, D. (1999) Training non-native TESOL students: Challenges for TESOL teacher education in the West. In G. Braine (ed.) *Non-Native Educators in English Language Teaching* (pp. 197–210). Routledge.

Loo, D.B., Trakulkasemsuk, W. and Zilli, P.J. (2017) Examining narratives of conflict and agency: Insights into non-local English teacher identity. *Journal of Asia TEFL* 14 (2), 292.

Miller, E.R. and Gkonou, C. (2018) Language teacher agency, emotion labor and emotional rewards in tertiary-level English language programs. *System* 79, 49–59. https://doi.org/10.1016/j.system.2018.03.002

Nelson, G.L. (1998) Intercultural communication and related courses taught in TESOL masters' degree programs. *International Journal of Intercultural Relations* 22 (1), 17–33. https://doi.org/10.1016/S0147-1767 (97)00032-1

Park, G. (2012) 'I am never afraid of being recognized as an NNES': One teacher's journey in claiming and embracing her nonnative-speaker identity. *TESOL Quarterly* 46, 127–151. https://doi.org/10.1002/tesq.4

Richards, J.C. (1987) The dilemma of teacher education in TESOL. *TESOL Quarterly* 21 (2), 209–226. https://doi.org/10.2307/3586732

Sadeghi, K. and Richards, J.C. (2021) Professional development among English language teachers: Challenges and recommendations for practice. *Heliyon* 7 (9). https://doi.org/10.1016/j.heliyon.2021.e08053

Stapleton, P. and Shao, Q. (2018) A worldwide survey of MATESOL programs in 2014: Patterns and perspectives. *Language Teaching Research* 22 (1), 10–28. https://doi.org/10.1177/1362168816659681

Sun, X., Zhang, W. and Cheung, Y.L. (2020) Researching transnationalism and TESOL teacher education: Critical review and outlook. In O.Z. Barnawi and A. Ahmed (eds) *TESOL Teacher Education in a Transnational World* (pp. 28–48). Routledge.

Tan, H., Zhao, K. and Dervin, F. (2022) Experiences of and preparedness for intercultural teacherhood in higher education: Non-specialist English teachers' positioning, agency and sense of legitimacy in China. *Language and Intercultural Communication* 22 (1), 68–84. https://doi.org/10.1080/14708477.2021.1988631

Tao, J. and Gao, X. (2017) Teacher agency and identity commitment in curricular reform. *Teaching and Teacher Education* 63, 346–355. https://doi.org/10.1016/j.tate.2017.01.010

Tavares, V. (2023) Teaching two languages: Navigating dual identity experiences. *Pedagogies: An International Journal* 18 (3), 497–518. https://doi.org/10.1080/1554480X.2022.2065996

Toom, A., Pyhältö, K. and Rust, F.O.C. (2015) Teachers' professional agency in contradictory times. *Teachers and Teaching* 21 (6), 615–623. https://doi.org/10.1080/13540602.2015.1044334

Trickett, E.J., Rukhotskiy, E., Jeong, A., Genkova, A., Oberoi, A., Weinstein, T. and Delgado, Y. (2012) 'The kids are terrific: It's the job that's tough': The ELL teacher role in an urban context. *Teaching and Teacher Education* 28 (2), 283–292. https://doi.org/10.1016/j.tate.2011.10.005

Vähäsantanen, K. (2015) Professional agency in the stream of change: Understanding educational change and teachers' professional identities. *Teaching and Teacher Education* 47, 1–12. https://doi.org/10.1016/j.tate.2014.11.006

Vähäsantanen, K., Hökkä, P., Paloniemi, S., Herranen, S. and Eteläpelto, A. (2017) Professional learning and agency in an identity coaching programme. *Professional Development in Education* 43 (4), 514–536. https://doi.org/10.1080/19415257.2016.1231131

Warren, A.N. and Ward, N.A. (2021) Negotiating the limits of teacher agency: Constructed constraints vs. capacity to act in preservice teachers' descriptions of teaching emergent bilingual learners. *Critical Discourse Studies*. https://doi.org/10.1080/17405904.2021.1999289

Weng, Z. (2022) From EFL to ESL: Nonlinear development of teacher identity and expertise across contexts. In C. Poteau, C. Winkle and B. Khoshnevisan (eds) *Nurturing Inclusivity, Equity, and Social Responsibility in English Language Teaching* (pp. 107–120). Routledge. https://doi.org/10.4324/9781003202356-9

Weng, Z. (2023) A systematic review on teacher identity agency in language teaching. Unpublished manuscript, Duke Kunshan University.

Weng, Z. and McGuire, M. (2021) Developing teaching expertise through transnational experience: Implications for TESOL teacher education. In A. Ahmed and O. Barnawi (eds) *Mobility of Knowledge, Practice and Pedagogy in TESOL Teacher Education: Implications for Transnational Contexts* (pp. 311–330). Palgrave Macmillan. https://doi.org/10.1007/978-3-030-64140-5

Weng, Z., Zhu, J.Y. and Kim, G. (2019) English language teacher agency in classroom-based empirical studies: A research synthesis. *TESOL International Journal* 14 (1), 40–64. https://files.eric.ed.gov/fulltext/EJ1244103.pdf

Weng, Z., Troyan, F., Fernandez, L. and McGuire, M. (2023) Examining language teacher identity and intersectionality across instructional contexts through the experience of perezhivanie. *TESOL Quarterly*. https://doi.org/10.1002/tesq.3237

Yazan, B. (2019) Toward identity-oriented teacher education: Critical autoethnographic narrative. *TESOL Journal* 10 (1), e00388. https://doi.org/10.1002/tesj.388

You, X. (2020) Transnationalism and education: Epistemological and theoretical exercises. In O.Z. Barnawi and A. Ahmed (eds) *TESOL Teacher Education in a Transnational World* (pp. 13–27). Routledge.

Yuan, R. and Lee, I. (2016) 'I need to be strong and competent': A narrative inquiry of a student-teacher's emotions and identities in teaching practicum. *Teachers and Teaching* 22 (7), 819–841. https://doi.org/10.1080/13540602.2016.1185819

7 Approaches and Practices for Intercultural Knowledge Development in Internationalizing TESOL Teacher Programs: An Overview of the Field

Chiew Hong Ng, Yin Ling Cheung and Weiyu Zhang

Teaching English to Speakers of Other Languages (TESOL) teachers have to develop students' global and intercultural competences to cultivate cross-cultural understanding. Although there is no lack of research on intercultural knowledge development, there is scant systematic research on intercultural knowledge development in internationalizing TESOL teacher programs in terms of these research questions: (1) What are the approaches and practices for intercultural knowledge development in internationalizing TESOL teacher programs? (2) What are the factors that facilitate or hinder teachers' intercultural knowledge development in the TESOL classrooms? Searches were conducted in Scopus databases using the following combination of keywords: 'TESOL', 'teacher program', 'internationalizing' and 'intercultural' to result in 853 English-medium research articles between 2000 to 2023. After careful reading and analyzing the retained 72 articles in full, we included 30 for review. The chapter highlights for researchers, teacher educators, pre-service and in-service teachers in TESOL how intercultural knowledge development in internationalizing TESOL teacher programs can be approached through English medium education (EME), program development, curriculum and syllabus design, courses and practices such as use of projects. The studies have also highlighted more facilitating than hindering factors.

Introduction

With English as a global language or English as lingua franca (ELF) to foster intercultural understanding, an intercultural approach to English language teaching in English as Foreign Language (EFL) education (Corbett, 2003; Liddicoat *et al.*, 2003) has emerged connecting study of culture to language learning. English is used in many different cultural contexts and developing intercultural communicative competence (ICC) is an important part of learning a foreign language. TESOL teachers can cultivate students' global and intercultural competences for cross-cultural understanding beyond national boundaries (Sinagatullin, 2019) by incorporating the principles of intercultural pedagogy into the teaching and learning process. This involves developing students' intercultural competence which includes 'historical and current information, processes and practices related to social groups and individuals, along with comparative perspectives and knowledge of the cross-cultural learning process' (Czerwionkaa *et al.*, 2015: 81). For Smolcic and Katunich (2017), 'developing intercultural competence within teachers is a multifaceted and dynamic endeavor' (2017: 56).

Leask (2009) defines the internationalization of the curriculum as 'the incorporation of an international and intercultural dimension into the content of the curriculum as well as [into] the teaching and learning arrangements and support services of a program of study' (2009: 209). This is because 'curriculum changes ... may affect teachers' pedagogical values and beliefs, their understanding of the nature of language or second language learning, or their classroom practices and uses of teaching materials' (Richards & Rodgers, 2001: 246). The term curriculum can refer to an overall plan or course design (Richards, 2013) and dimensions of a curriculum involve syllabus, methodology, process, learning outcomes, input and output (Richards, 2013). To Byram (2003), an intercultural approach can draw upon linguistics, ethnography, sociolinguistics, psychology, anthropology, register and genre analysis, critical discourse analysis and literary, media and cultural studies. According to Richards and Rodgers (2001), a teaching approach refers to 'a set of core teaching and learning principles together with a body of classroom practices that are derived from them' (2001: vii). For instance, Godwin-Jones (2019) talks about telecollaboration as an approach to developing intercultural communication competence.

While there is no lack of research on intercultural knowledge development, there is scant systematic research on intercultural knowledge development in internationalizing TESOL teacher programs in terms of the practices and methods for intercultural knowledge development in internationalizing TESOL teacher programs, as well as the elements that promote or impede teachers' intercultural knowledge development in the TESOL classrooms.

Methodology

The present study involves systematic review in terms of formulating research question(s) and describing methods for literature searching, screening, inclusion and exclusion criteria, data extraction and analysis (Wright *et al.*, 2007).

Research questions

Research question 1: What are the approaches and practices for intercultural knowledge development in internationalizing TESOL teacher programs?

Research question 2: What are the factors that facilitate or hinder teachers' intercultural knowledge development in the TESOL classrooms?

Inclusion and exclusion criteria

Only research items written in English language published in English-medium journals from 2000 to 2023 related to approaches and practices for intercultural knowledge development in internationalizing TESOL teacher programs were included. Papers were excluded if (1) the focus was on first language (L1) and (2) theoretical or conceptual papers.

Data collection and analysis

The papers in this study were identified by conducting a systematic search of the literature of the digital resources in the University library. The databases used were Scopus, Web of Science and Google Scholar. The search was conducted using a combination of the following terms: 'TESOL', 'teacher program', 'internationalizing' and 'intercultural'. From the initial search, we retrieved 853 papers based on titles. The abstracts of the papers were scrutinized to shortlist 72 papers. Closer reading led us to select 30 articles for synthesis based on the inclusion and exclusion criteria and relevance to the research focus. The 30 articles were read in detail for content analysis and coded in terms of: (1) approaches and practices for intercultural knowledge development in internationalizing TESOL teacher programs; (2) factors that facilitate or hinder teachers' intercultural knowledge development in the TESOL classrooms. Approaches and practices were coded as approaches, approaches in terms of program/curriculum/ syllabus/course, specified practices and projects (see Table 7.1) and factors that facilitate, hinder or facilitate and hinder (see Table 7.2).

Findings

The findings for the 30 studies are presented in terms of the two research questions.

Table 7.1 Approaches and practices for intercultural knowledge development

Classification	Studies	Total
Approaches	Baker and Fang (2021) Baker and Fang (2022) Cushner and Chang (2015) Gómez (2012) Orduna-Nocito and Sánchez-García (2022) Sobre (2017) Yang (2017) Yücel and Yavuz (2019)	8
Approaches in terms of program/ curriculum/ syllabus/course	Algouzi and Elkhiar (2021) Banat et al. (2021) Bodis (2020) Han (2016) Liu (2022) Papadopoulou et al. (2022) Petosi and Karras (2020) Tavassoli and Ghamoush (2023) Yılmaz and Özkan (2016)	9
Specified practices to teach intercultural knowledge	Bal and Savas (2022) Cheng (2012) Eren (2022a) Gilmore et al. (2020)	4
Projects	Bayyurt and Yalçın (2022) Dai (2019) Eren (2022b) Krajka (2019) Kurek and Müller-Hartmann (2018) Loranc-Paszylk et al. (2021) Mak and Kennedy (2012) Tanghe and Park (2016) Üzüm et al. (2020)	9

Research question 1: What are the approaches and practices for intercultural knowledge development in internationalizing TESOL teacher programs?

There were eight studies for intercultural knowledge development in internationalizing TESOL teacher programs approached through EME and specified approaches, and nine through program development, curriculum and syllabus design and course offered. In the 13 studies about practices, four had stated specific practices to teach intercultural knowledge while nine were about the specific practice of using projects (see Table 7.1).

Approaches

In terms of EME, the language for internationalization of higher education institutes (HEIs) and intercultural citizenships is often English, or ELF. Through questionnaires of 223 international students, interviews and focus groups of 43 about developing intercultural citizenship in EME, Baker and Fang (2022) found the majority of students expressed positive

Table 7.2 Factors that facilitate or hinder teachers' intercultural knowledge development in the TESOL classrooms

Factors that facilitate	Factors that hinder	Factors that facilitate and hinder
Algouzi and Elkhiar (2021)	Baker and Fang (2021)	Banat *et al.* (2021)
Baker and Fang (2022)	Bayyurt and Yalçın (2022)	Tavassoli and
Bal and Savas (2022)	Cheng (2012)	Ghamoush (2023)
Bodis (2020)	Cushner and Chang (2015)	
Dai (2019)	Kurek and Müller-Hartmann	
Eren (2022a)	(2018)	
Eren (2022b)	Orduna-Nocito and Śanchez-	
Gilmore *et al.* (2020)	García (2022)	
Gómez (2012)	Yılmaz and Özkan (2016)	
Han (2016)		
Krajka (2019)		
Liu (2022)		
Loranc-Paszylk *et al.* (2021)		
Mak and Kennedy (2012)		
Papadopoulou *et al.* (2022)		
Petosi and Karras (2020)		
Sobre (2017)		
Tanghe and Park (2016)		
Üzüm *et al.* (2020)		
Yang (2017)		
Yücel and Yavuz (2019)		
21	7	2

attitudes to intercultural citizenship in relation to experiences of other cultures and countries, as well as their ability to use English as the *de facto* language for intercultural communication and connections. Baker and Fang (2021) found intercultural citizenship was generally positively perceived and strongly linked to English for study abroad for university students from China, Japan and Thailand though development of intercultural citizenship was uneven during study abroad. Orduna-Nocito and Śanchez-García (2022) analyzed the (mis)alignment between English as medium of instruction (EMI) language policies and teachers' practices as reported by 28 lecturers in 10 HEIs across Europe in an online teacher education program to highlight the need for content courses to be more international and intercultural.

In terms of specific approaches, given the large number of international students studying in Australia, Yang (2017) proposed an intercultural communication competence approach for TESOL teachers in multicultural Australia. This is because teachers must have second language knowledge and demonstrate ability to manage intercultural verbal communicative skills and styles, intercultural nonverbal communicative style and sensitivity. Engagement in social co-construction of intercultural identity through teacher–stakeholder interaction has a positive impact on teachers themselves and their students, particularly those with a refugee background. Yücel and Yavuz (2019) indicated the importance of raising pre-service English language teachers' awareness of different approaches to interculturality in terms of these eight themes: improved interpretation and reflection skills, interculturality from theory to practice, peer collaboration, awareness of the importance of intercultural topics in language education, the relationship between course and teaching effectiveness, and process of making intercultural activities applicable in language classroom. Sobre's (2017) critical intercultural communication pedagogy (CICP) across diverse populations involves didactic, experiential and reflexive approaches to learning through teaching critical intercultural issues across diverse populations. Cushner and Chang (2015) measured intercultural competence through the Intercultural Development Inventory regarding the approach of overseas student teaching experience to suggest that overseas student teaching alone without addressing intercultural growth was insufficient to change intercultural competence. Gómez (2012) has proposed the inclusion of authentic literary texts for the teaching of Literature in EFL to develop ICC through four constructivist approaches – The Socio-constructivist Pedagogical Model, Inquiry-based Approach Dialogic Approach (Bakhtin, 1984), Transactional Approach (Rosenblatt, 1995) and Content-based Approach (Schcolnik & Kol, 2006).

Program/curriculum/syllabus/course

In terms of programs, curriculum and syllabus, Papadopoulou *et al.* (2022) used a case study to explore the language views and attitudes of graduates of a Hellenic Open University Master's international program entitled 'Language Education for Refugees and Migrants' (LRM). They found the majority of participants developed confidence, appropriate skills, knowledge, and attitudes and different approaches and methods to manage the challenges of multicultural settings after completing the program. Banat *et al.* (2021) proposed an intercultural competence–oriented approach to internationalizing writing program through a linked course model curriculum that pairs international and domestic students in separate second language – specific and mainstream first-year writing (FYW) classes. Bodis (2020) identified relevant aspects of intercultural competence (e.g. awareness, behavior) to integrate into course curricula in a tailored way and provided examples for task development to address various levels of cognitive engagement. Algouzi and Elkhiar (2021) showed how intercultural awareness can be developed through an ethnographic-based intercultural syllabus at Najran University in the Kingdom of Saudi Arabia.

In terms of courses, in developing an EFL undergraduate Intercultural Communication course, Liu (2022) formulated a model to integrate English-major students' personal experiences with pedagogical activities in a university located in northeastern China. Petosi and Karras (2020) investigated the beliefs and attitudes of 62 EFL teachers teaching English for ICC course in the Greek EFL state classroom with regards to incorporating ICC in their classroom. Tavassoli and Ghamoushi (2023) investigated 50 Iranian EFL teachers' cognition, attitude and practice in teaching ICC to find the majority were cognizant of the importance of teaching ICC. Han (2016) argued that the intercultural Australian postgraduate TESOL classrooms allowed for communication-based learner-centered Western academic values and Korean teacher-led constructivism encounters to interplay in meaning negotiation processes. Yılmaz and Özkan (2016) examined intercultural awareness regarding ownership of English and cultural integration in English language classes. The findings revealed that while both 45 instructors and 92 students were aware of the importance of intercultural awareness in English language teaching, it was not from a thorough intercultural point of view.

Practices

For the four studies highlighting specific practices for intercultural knowledge development, practices regarding intercultural language teaching for 30 EFL schoolteachers had to do with conveying information about target cultures and class discussions (Bal & Savas, 2022). Cheng (2012) found for five Taiwanese EFL teachers in HEIs of technology, textbooks dominated, lecturing occupied most of the class time and discussion with students was rare. Eren (2022a) examined 265 EFL teacher (pre-service and in-service) participants to find translanguaging as a motivational practice, as well as the use of technology in multilingual classrooms in helping teachers cope with intercultural tensions. Gilmore *et al.* (2020) reported the practice of intercultural dialogue of meaning making in literacy by lecturers in early childhood education (ECE) pre-service teacher education across Australia, New Zealand and Sweden in looking at 30 examples from 'high' to 'low' exemplars of ECE students' literacy assessment.

Projects

Nine studies looked specifically at the use of projects as practice for intercultural knowledge development in internationalizing TESOL teacher programs. There were three studies involving telecollaborative projects. Drawing upon Byram's (1997) ICC model, Üzüm *et al.* (2020) examined 48 teacher trainees' interculturality through a telecollaborative project between two teacher training classes from Turkey and the USA. Tanghe and Park (2016) developed the international collaborative project (ICP) facilitated by two teacher-educators in South Korea and the United States as an alternative pedagogical and curricular approach to develop intercultural competence and promote internationalization in teacher education. Bayyurt and Yalçın (2022) reported studies on intercultural telecollaboration projects involving cultural exchange between students in pre-/in-service teacher education programs in Turkey and abroad.

Three studies focused on the benefits of projects for both instructors and students. Mak and Kennedy (2012) devised and piloted Internationalizing the Student Experience Project as a teaching innovation to improve the intercultural awareness of instructors, and their domestic and international students studying English language (from culturally and linguistically diverse backgrounds and who may still lack the confidence and social skills to participate in group discussions). Krajka (2019) described 48 graduate Polish students of English using selected telecollaborative activities in Teaching English as an International Language (TEIL) course to teach second language acquisition, multilingualism, foreign language teaching methodology and raise intercultural awareness. Eren's (2022b) 57 pre-service EFL teachers took part in an eight-week telecollaboration project with four instructors from European universities to find intercultural development manifested through their '(a) intercultural adjustment, (b) culture-specific identity orientations, (c) gender socialization and (d) culture and technology interplay' (2022b: 1).

Three studies highlighted how projects with technology-mediated learning environments could enhance intercultural knowledge. In terms of Online Intercultural Exchanges (OIEs) for teacher training, defined as 'internet-based intercultural exchanges between groups of learners of different cultural/national backgrounds set up in an institutional blended-learning context' (Helm & Guth, 2010: 273), Kurek and Müller-Hartmann (2018) had EFL MA students (31 German teacher trainees and 22 Polish) use English as a lingua franca design and evaluate technology-mediated tasks for prospective telecollaborative learners in primary/secondary education. Dai (2019) described how the intercultural knowledge was enhanced in a technology-enabled learning environment – videoconferencing – for an undergraduate course participated by three groups of students (prescreened to ensure the conversational proficiency in English), who were globally distributed in the US, Mainland China and Taiwan. To build capacity for 21st-century digital English language teaching (ELT) practices, 16 participants from universities in the United States and Poland teaching English as a second or foreign language met weekly in cross-cultural teams for virtual exchanges via Zoom videoconferences to discuss cultural topics and subsequently reflected on their collaborative, interactive experience facilitated through the use of video-recorded interactions with other teacher candidates (Loranc-Paszylk *et al.*, 2021).

Research question 2: What are the factors that facilitate or hinder teachers' intercultural knowledge development in the TESOL classrooms?

Findings for the 30 studies were classified in terms of factors that facilitate or hinder teachers' intercultural knowledge development (see Table 7.2) and presented in terms of approaches and practices.

Factors that facilitate teachers' intercultural knowledge development in the TESOL classrooms
Approaches

In terms of EME as facilitating teachers' intercultural knowledge development in the TESOL classrooms, according to Baker and Fang (2022) language teaching is an ideal site for the implementation of intercultural citizenship education as ELT and English for Academic Purpose (EAP) prepare and support international study and EMI programs. Baker and Fang (2022) talk about using these approaches: online, or teletandem, intercultural exchanges with language learners in other parts of the world (O'Dowd, 2011) and intercultural group work projects involving mini-ethnographies to explore linguistic cultural complexity in local communities (Byram *et al.*, 2017; Porto *et al.*, 2018) and 'other' communities.

For specific approaches to enable teachers to facilitate intercultural knowledge development, for ICC competence approach, Yang (2017) has suggested TESOL teachers learn an additional language or improve their additional language literacy to foster intercultural responsiveness and use of culturally appropriate teaching and learning materials with culturally diverse students in classroom. Yücel and Yavuz (2019) highlight the use of different approaches to facilitate intercultural training in English language pre-service teacher education: microteaching to think critically about intercultural topics, integrating intercultural elements into English lessons and peer collaboration. Teachers using CICP as a process-based learning curriculum can assist students to understand both micro-level intercultural interactions and systemic, macro-level power structures (Sobre, 2017). Gómez (2012) suggests teachers use multicultural literature to help learners to understand and communicate cross-culturally with other communities.

Program/curriculum/syllabus/course

In terms of program curriculum /syllabus/course facilitating intercultural knowledge development in the TESOL classrooms, to develop cognitive intercultural competence such as cultural self-awareness and sociolinguistic awareness (Deardorff, 2006), teachers can use these interventions – 'the multicultural reader, classroom discussions about cultural themes, cross-cultural teamwork, and introspective reflection' (Banat *et al.*, 2021: 12). Papadopoulou *et al.* (2022) talk about participants highlighting their improvement through Master's international program entitled 'Language Education for Refugees and Migrants' (LRM) when teachers showed empathy toward students of different cultural orientations, adopted more inclusive communicational class environments, culturally relevant pedagogies and created material to suit the specific linguistic needs of their students. To integrate intercultural competence in course curricula, Bodis (2020) advocates using Deardorff's (2006) model to identify knowledge (self-awareness, deep cultural knowledge, sociolinguistic awareness) and skills (listening, observing, evaluating, analyzing, interpreting, relating) and using pedagogical principles such as scaffolding of skills and concepts in task design. For ethnographic-based intercultural syllabus, Algouzi and Elkhiar (2021) suggest using Corbett's (2003) ethnographic methodology for communicating appropriately with other cultural groups and analytical understanding of systems of meanings through ELF.

In Liu's (2022) ICC course, reflecting on personal experiences with peers and the teacher enhanced students' awareness of stereotyping, prejudice and bias in communication with other cultures. Petosi and Karras (2020) found in teaching English for Intercultural Communication, Byram's (1997) model helped teachers understand the concept of ICC. To teachers, the most important objective was to develop students' positive, open and tolerant attitudes toward foreign culture because students' attitudes could be affected through cultural teaching as 87% of students indicated being open and tolerant of foreigners when surveyed. In teaching ICC, Tavassoli and Ghamoush (2023) too concluded EFL teachers' positive attitudes toward teaching cultural issues helped students learn a foreign language. Han (2016) believed the intercultural Australian postgraduate TESOL classrooms could give lecturers and program coordinators in intercultural TESOL courses ideas for a curriculum responsive to international needs in terms of interactive identity (trans)formation for students with multiple identities in their intercultural situation.

Practices

In terms of specific practices, Bal and Savas (2022) suggest more training opportunities for middle and high school teachers through sessions to help teachers see language and culture connections from multiple perspectives while boosting both teachers' and students' EIL. To Eren (2022a) translanguaging in language classrooms as a multilingual pedagogy for bi/multilingual students in both plurilingual and pluricultural contexts could facilitate the intercultural learning process by motivating students and helping them resolve potential intercultural tensions. Gilmore *et al.* (2020) see Sorrells' (2006) intercultural praxis model as offering an approach to view international teacher education through intercultural dialogue of meaning making in literacy.

Projects

Teachers' intercultural knowledge development in the TESOL classrooms can be facilitated through projects. Tanghe and Park (2016) talk about ICP as increasing 'intercultural experiences and engagement with various teaching contexts, facilitating reflection on the uniqueness of individual teaching contexts' (2016: 12). According to Mak and Kennedy (2012), the Internationalizing the Student Experience Project was an approach to support internationalization in improving the intercultural capability of higher education instructors and students through cultural experiential learning tools, such as EXCELL Alliance Building and Cultural Mapping. Eren (2022b) sees telecollaboration as enabling participants to assess how instructors across different cultures perceive the same topics to challenge their established opinions and it should be integrated into the wider teaching curriculum on intercultural pedagogy. Krajka's (2019) intercultural teacher training with telecollaborative activities facilitated language awareness in TEIL and enhancement of intercultural teaching competence to increase the global dimension of teacher training. To Üzüm *et al.* (2020), the telecollaborative project afforded the teacher trainees intercultural learning corresponding to five components of Byram's (1997) ICC development model: awareness of heterogeneity in their own culture, critical cultural awareness, skills of interpreting and relating and skills of discovery and interaction. Loranc-Paszylk *et al.* (2021) found virtual exchanges via Zoom video conferences helped teachers create communities of practice. To Dai (2019), comparative reflection approach for the intercultural knowledge construction through videoconferencing enhanced intercultural education in quality and equity, interactive and collaborative reflection and 'created a "glocal" learning experience [involving]… locally situated task engagement and globally expanded intercultural exchange' (2019: 9).

Factors that hinder teachers' intercultural knowledge development in the TESOL classrooms
Approaches

In terms of factors hindering teachers' intercultural knowledge development in the TESOL classrooms in EME, according to Orduna-Nocito and Sanchez-García (2022), lecturers were concerned about what and how to assess intercultural competence in EMI courses as official documents provided no guidance. They opined that content courses had to be more international and intercultural. The participants in the study by Baker and Fang (2021) about EMI programs in international university abroad perceived the link between English use and the development of intercultural citizenship negatively. The absence of formal education in intercultural citizenship or intercultural interaction meant they were left to develop their intercultural knowledge, skills and identities on their own which resulted in differing levels of development or no development.

In terms of factors hindering teachers' intercultural knowledge development in the TESOL classrooms for specific approaches, Cushner and Chang (2015) found students teaching overseas did not develop intercultural competence significantly as intercultural gains are not acquired through just living and teaching in an overseas environment.

Program/curriculum/syllabus/course

In terms of factors hindering teachers' intercultural knowledge development in the TESOL classrooms in terms of program/curriculum/syllabus/course, the formative assessment data from reflective writing from Banat et al. (2021) highlighted the need for developing indicators of intercultural competence in the cognition, affect and behavior domains and steps for writing an intercultural reflection to enable critical evaluation for meaningful learning in recounting an intercultural experience. Tavassoli and Ghamoush (2023) found most of the teachers' intercultural teaching practices were limited to what course-book material offered. In looking at intercultural awareness regarding ownership of English and cultural integration in English language classes, Yılmaz and Özkan (2016) talk about the need to develop an intercultural curriculum, textbook and teacher training programs to enhance intercultural awareness in the English language teaching and learning process.

Practices and projects

In terms of specific practices, to Cheng (2012), there is the need to help teachers and students deal with IC in the field of EFL/ESL education as merely relying on textbooks could hinder EFL teachers. For factors hindering teachers' intercultural knowledge development in the TESOL classrooms for projects, according to Kurek and Müller-Hartmann (2018), in teacher-training OIEs, instructors may not always succeed in spotting and responding to all of the problems immediately as they could be affected by institutional constraints. Bayyurt and Yalçın (2022) advocate raising English language teachers' intercultural citizenship awareness and integrating global citizenship into in-service teacher education seminars, workshops and material development.

In summary, there were more studies highlighting factors that facilitate (21) than factors that hinder (7) and two highlighting both factors.

Discussion of Findings

Approaches for intercultural knowledge development in internationalizing TESOL teacher programs have been looked at through EME and specific approaches (8). For the eight studies for intercultural knowledge development through EME, English is perceived as the *de facto* language for ICC and the cultivation of intercultural citizenship. In terms of intercultural knowledge development through program development, curriculum and syllabus design, and courses offered, the study has shown how teacher and teachers educators can develop intercultural international program (Papadopoulou et al., 2022), integrate intercultural competence into course curricula (Bodis, 2020), use ethnographic-based intercultural syllabus (Algouzi & Elkhiar, 2021), teach English for Intercultural Communication courses (Petosi & Karras, 2020) and ICC in class (Han,

2016; Tavassoli & Ghamoush, 2023; Yılmaz and Özkan, 2016). The 13 studies looking at specific practices (4) and using projects (9) involved conveying information about target cultures and class discussions (Bal & Savas, 2022), lecturing (Cheng, 2012), translanguaging (Eren, 2022a) and projects such as OIEs and intercultural telecollaboration projects.

Twenty-one studies have highlighted factors that facilitate, seven factors that hinder and two both factors. Intercultural knowledge for TESOL teachers can be facilitated by them learning an additional language or improving their additional language literacy and intercultural training in English language pre-service teachers education. Teachers can use CICP or multicultural literature to facilitate intercultural knowledge development too. In terms of program curriculum/syllabus/course to facilitate intercultural knowledge development, teachers are to show empathy for students of different cultural orientations and have positive attitudes toward teaching cultural issues. They can consider adopting Deardorff's (2006) model, Byram's (1997) model, Corbett's (2003) ethnographic methodology, Sorrells' (2006) intercultural praxis model and culturally relevant pedagogies. These practices can facilitate intercultural knowledge development in the TESOL classrooms by teachers: translanguaging in language classrooms as a multilingual pedagogy, ICP, telecollaborative activities, virtual exchanges or videoconferencing.

Seven studies highlighted these as hindering factors for intercultural knowledge development in the TESOL classrooms: the absence of formal education in intercultural citizenship in international university abroad, the lack of intercultural curriculum, textbook and teacher training programs (seminars, workshops) to enhance intercultural awareness in English language teaching and learning process.

Teaching Implications and Recommendations for Future Directions in Research

TESOL teachers can consider these specific approaches for their teaching besides teaching ICC through English in courses or in class: Sobre's (2017) CICP, teaching of Literature in EFL to develop ICC through four constructivist approaches, an intercultural competence-oriented approach to internationalizing writing program (Banat *et al.*, 2021), and integrating students' personal experiences into EFL undergraduate ICC course (Liu, 2022). In terms of practice, translanguaging in language classrooms can be a multilingual pedagogy.

TESOL teacher educators can consider adopting these for teaching or research: intercultural communication competence approach and practices for TESOL teachers (Yang, 2017), raising pre-service English language teachers' awareness of different approaches to interculturality (Yücel & Yavuz, 2019), the practice of intercultural dialogue of meaning making in literacy in ECE (Gilmore *et al.*, 2020), Internationalizing the

Student Experience Project (Mak & Kennedy, 2012), OIEs and intercultural telecollaboration projects involving cultural exchanges between students in pre-/in-service teacher education programs (e.g. Bayyurt & Yalçın, 2022).

Conclusion

This chapter looks at TESOL curricula of teacher candidates and teacher educators to develop international and intercultural knowledge as internationalization practices to advance global and ethical citizenship. It has surfaced eight studies for intercultural knowledge development in internationalizing TESOL teacher programs approached through EME and specified approaches, nine through program development, curriculum and syllabus design, and course offered and 13 studies about specific practices (four) and use of projects (nine). There were more studies highlighting factors that facilitate (21) than factors that hinder (7) and two highlighting both factors showing the positive impact of intercultural knowledge development in internationalizing TESOL. Educators and researchers can consider employing for teaching and conducting research diverse approaches and practices highlighted in the study such as EME, intercultural international program, integrating intercultural competence into course curricula and syllabus, English for Intercultural Communication courses, translanguaging and using projects such as OIEs and intercultural telecollaboration projects.

References

Algouzi, S. and Elkhiar, A. (2021) An ethnographic approach to developing intercultural awareness: A case study of EFL learners at Najran University. *Theory and Practice in Language Studies* 11 (7), 788–797.

Baker, W. and Fang, F. (2021) 'So maybe I'm a global citizen': Developing intercultural citizenship in English medium education. *Language, Culture and Curriculum* 34 (1), 1–17.

Baker, W. and Fang, F. (2022) Intercultural citizenship and the internationalisation of higher education: The role of English language teaching. *JELF* 11 (1), 63–75.

Bakhtin, M. (1984) *Problems of Dostoevsky's Poetics* (ed. and trans. C. Emerson). The University of Minnesota Press.

Bal, N.G. and Savas, P. (2022) Intercultural language teaching and learning: Teachers' perspectives and practices. *Participatory Educational Research* 9 (6), 268–285.

Banat, H., Sims, R., Tran, P., Panahi, P. and Dilger, B. (2021) Developing intercultural competence through a linked course model curriculum: Mainstream and L2-specific first-year writing. *TESOL Journal*.

Bayyurt, Y. and Yalçın, Ş. (2022) Intercultural citizenship and pre-service teacher education. *JELF* 11 (1), 105–115.

Bodis, A. (2020) Integrating intercultural competence in course curricula in a tailored way. *English Australia Journal* 36 (1), 26–38.

Byram, M. (1997) *Teaching and Assessing Intercultural Communicative Competence.* Multilingual Matters.

Byram, M. (2003) On Being 'Bicultural' and 'Intercultural'. In G. Alred, M. Byram and M. Fleming (eds) *Intercultural Experience and Education* (pp. 50–66). Multilingual Matters.

Byram, M., Golubeva, I., Han, H. and Wagner, M. (eds) (2017) *From Principles to Practice in Education for Intercultural Citizenship*. Multilingual Matters.

Cheng, C.-M. (2012) The influence of college EFL teachers' understandings of intercultural competence on their self-reported pedagogical practices in Taiwan. *English Teaching: Practice and Critique* 11 (1), 164–182.

Corbett, J. (2003) *An Intercultural Approach to English Language Teaching*. Multilingual Matters.

Cushner, K. and Chang, S.-C. (2015) Developing intercultural competence through overseas student teaching: Checking our assumptions. *Intercultural Education* 26 (3), 165–178.

Czerwionkaa, L., Artamonovaa, T. and Barbosaa, M. (2015) Intercultural knowledge development: Evidence from student interviews during short-term study abroad. *International Journal of Intercultural Relations* 49, 80–99.

Dai, Y. (2019) Situating videoconferencing in a connected class toward intercultural knowledge development: A comparative reflection approach. *The Internet and Higher Education* 41, 1–10.

Deardorff, D.K. (2006) Identification and assessment of intercultural competence as a student outcome of internationalization. *Journal of Studies in International Education* 10 (3), 241–266.

Eren, Ö. (2022a) Towards multilingual turn in language classes: Plurilingual awareness as an indicator of intercultural communicative competence. *International Journal of Multilingualism,* 1–19.

Eren, Ö. (2022b) Negotiating pre-service EFL teachers' identity orientations through telecollaboration. *Innovation in Language Learning and Teaching,* 1–16.

Gilmore, G., Margrain, V. and Mellgren, E. (2020) Intercultural literacy dialogue: International assessment moderation in early childhood teacher education. *Intercultural Education* 31 (2), 208–227.

Godwin-Jones, R. (2019) Telecollaboration as an approach to developing intercultural communication competence. *Language Learning and Technology* 23 (3), 8–28.

Gómez, L.F.R. (2012) Fostering intercultural communicative competence through reading authentic literary texts in an advanced Colombian EFL classroom: A constructivist perspective. *PROFILE* 14 (1), 49–66.

Han, I. (2016) Four Korean teacher learners' academic experiences in an Australian TESOL programme and disclosure of their multiple identities. *English Teaching: Practice and Critique* 15 (1), 129–154.

Helm, F. and Guth, S. (2010) The multifarious goals of telecollaboration 2.0: Theoretical and practical implications. In S. Guth and F. Helm (eds) *Telecollaboration 2.0: Language, Literacy and Intercultural Learning in the 21st Century* (pp. 69–106). Peter Lang.

Krajka, J. (2019) Electronic appearances in teil instruction – Expanding intercultural teacher training with telecollaborative activities. *ROCZNIKI HUMANISTYCZNE LXVII,* 65–81.

Kurek, M. and Müller-Hartmann, A. (2018) 'I feel more confident now' – Modelling teaching presence in teacher-training online intercultural exchanges. *The European Journal of Applied Linguistics and TEFL* 7 (2), 157–177.

Leask, B. (2009) Using formal and informal curricula to improve interactions between home and international students. *Journal of Studies in International Education* 13, 205–221.

Liddicoat, A., Papademetre, L., Scarino, A. and Kohler, M. (2003) *Report on Intercultural Language Learning*. The Commonwealth Department of Education, Science and Training.

Liu, Y. (2022) Developing students' intercultural communicative competence through threads of personal experiences: A reflective approach. *Chinese Journal of Applied Linguistics* 45 (3), 433–444.

Loranc-Paszylk, B., Hilliker, S.M. and Lenkaitis, C.A. (2021) Virtual exchanges in language teacher education: Facilitating reflection on teaching practice through the use of video. *TESOL Journal* 12 (3), 1–15.

Mak, A.S. and Kennedy, M. (2012) Internationalising the student experience: Preparing instructors to embed intercultural skills in the curriculum. *Innovative Higher Education* 37, 323–334.

O'Dowd, R. (2011) Online foreign language interaction: Moving from the periphery to the core of foreign language education? *Language Teaching* 44 (3), 368–380.

Orduna-Nocito, E. and Sánchez-García, D. (2022) Aligning higher education language policies with lecturers' views on EMI practices: A comparative study of ten European Universities. *System* 104, 1–14.

Papadopoulou, K., Palaiologou, N. and Karanikola, Z. (2022) Insights into teachers' intercultural and global competence within multicultural educational settings. *Educational Sciences* 12 (502), 1–18.

Petosi, E. and Karras, I. (2020) Intercultural communicative competence: Are Greek EFL teachers ready? *European Journal of Applied Linguistics* 8 (1), 1–21.

Porto, M., Houghton, S.A. and Byram, M. (2018) Intercultural citizenship in the (foreign) language classroom. *Language Teaching Research* 22 (5), 484–498.

Richards, J.C. (2013) Curriculum approaches in language teaching: Forward, central, and backward design. *RELC Journal* 44 (1), 5–33.

Richards, J.C. and Rodgers, T.S. (2001) *Approaches and Methods in Language Teaching*. Cambridge University Press.

Rosenblatt, L.M. (1995) *Literature as Exploration* (5th edn). The Modern Language Association.

Schcolnik, M. and Kol, S. (2006) Constructivism in theory and in practice. *English Teaching Forum* 4, 12–20.

Sinagatullin, I.M. (2019) Developing preservice elementary teachers' global competence. *International Journal of Educational Reform* 28, 48–62.

Smolcic, E. and Katunich, J. (2017) Teachers crossing borders: A review of the research into cultural immersion field experience for teachers. *Teaching and Teacher Education* 62, 47–59.

Sobre, M.S. (2017) Developing the critical intercultural class-space: Theoretical implications and pragmatic applications of critical intercultural communication pedagogy. *Intercultural Education* 28 (1), 39–59.

Sorrells, K. (2016) *Intercultural Communication, Globalization and Social Justice* (2nd edn). Sage.

Tanghe, S. and Park, G. (2016) 'Build[ing] something which alone we could not have done': International collaborative teaching and learning in language teacher education. *System* 57, 1–13.

Tavassoli, K. and Ghamoushi, M. (2023) Exploring Iranian EFL teachers' cognition, attitude, and practice in teaching intercultural issues. *Interchange* 54, 173–201.

Üzüm, B., Akayoglu, S. and Yazan, Y. (2020) Using telecollaboration to promote intercultural competence in teacher training classrooms in Turkey and the USA. *ReCALL* 32 (2), 162–177.

Wright, R.W., Brand, R.A., Dunn, W. and Spindler, K.P. (2007) How to write a systematic review. *Clinical Orthopaedics and Related Research* 455, 23–29.

Yang, P. (2017) Developing TESOL teacher intercultural identity: An intercultural communication competence approach. *TESOL Journal* 9, 525–541.

Yılmaz, B. and Özkan, Y. (2016) An investigation into English language instructors' and students' intercultural awareness. *The Qualitative Report* 21 (10), 1932–1959.

Yücel, N. and Yavuz, A. (2019) Rethinking intercultural training in teacher training. *Journal of Intercultural Communication* 51, 1–12.

Part 3

Exploring the Potential of Study Abroad and Virtual Exchange Experiences in TESOL

8 The Value of Virtual Exchange in Internationalizing the TESOL Curriculum: Centering Global Competencies

Zuzana Tomaš and Anna Slatinská

This chapter examines the value of virtual exchanges (VEs) for Teaching English to Speakers of Other Languages (TESOL) teacher candidates in the ESL and EFL contexts. VEs engage two groups of students from different cultural contexts in collaborating online, often on a shared product. Recent scholarship on VEs has shown a variety of benefits for teachers, including increased confidence to teach, improved ability working in multicultural settings, enhanced global competence, digital literacy and problem-solving skills. To add to this important body of research, the authors explore teacher candidates' perceived value of VEs, the nature of pedagogical products developed during the VE and self-reported changes in the teacher candidates' global competence. Specifically, teacher candidates worked together to co-create free online English books aimed at newcomer learners (e.g. an Afghan English learner in Michigan, a Ukrainian refugee in Slovakia) as per requests of teachers in both contexts. Teacher candidates from the two universities then used the ebooks in Zoom-based lessons with actual English learners in Slovakia. After describing the program, the authors discuss implications of using globally centered VEs in the TESOL curriculum.

Introduction

With the advance of technology and the recent global pandemic, the virtual exchange (VE hereinafter) approach has become an increasingly popular innovation in TESOL programs' internationalization initiatives. Given its rising popularity and potential for internationalizing TESOL curriculum, this chapter outlines VEs and their related benefits, especially in the area of global competencies. We describe two successful VE programs that effectively engaged TESOL pre-service teachers (PSTs hereinafter) in Slovakia and the midwestern United States, demonstrating how these projects nurtured the development of PSTs' global competencies.

Virtual Exchanges as Tools for Internationalizing TESOL Curriculum

Despite some trepidation around terminology associated with online, intercultural exchanges, increasingly, the term virtual exchange (VE) has been adopted in scholarship and by funding agencies (O'Dowd, 2022). VEs are conceived as a mechanism for 'engag[ing] learners in sustained online collaborative learning and interaction with partners from different cultural backgrounds as part of their study programmes and under the guidance of teachers or trained facilitators' (O'Dowd, 2022: 11). Initially, VEs were employed almost exclusively in foreign language education, but are now common across the disciplines as a way of internationalizing curriculum (for more details on impact of VEs across the curriculum, see O'Dowd, 2020, 2022).

In the context of TESOL teacher education, engaging in VEs has had multiple benefits for PSTs. VEs have been shown to improve PSTs' ability to work in multicultural settings (Jaramillo Cherrez & Gleason, 2022), enhance their digital literacy and use of technology (Rets *et al.*, 2020) and develop problem-solving skills (Lenkaitis & Loranc, 2021). On the practical level, VEs are also appealing because they bypass prohibitive expenses associated with other internationalization efforts such as study abroad, international practicum or mobility programs. Arguably, one of the most significant benefits of VEs from the standpoint of internationalizing TESOL curriculum is their potential to develop PSTs' global competencies, which results from their active participation in collaborative, globally-relevant projects (e.g. Lin, 2021).

Centering Global Competencies in Virtual Exchange Programs

Global competence has been broadly defined as 'the comprehensive capability to live, communicate, and work in a multiculturally interconnected world' (Kang *et al.*, 2018). In education a commonly accepted definition conceives global competence as 'the capacity to examine local, global and intercultural issues; to understand and appreciate the perspectives and worldviews of others; to engage in open, appropriate and effective interactions with people from different cultures; and to act for collective well-being and sustainable development' (Asia Society/OECD 2018: 5).

Global competence comprises knowledge, skills, attitudes and values that are seen as integral to any profession that involves working within culturally and linguistically diverse contexts, which makes this concept particularly relevant to TESOL. Indeed, TESOL scholarship has increasingly examined the potential of developing PSTs' global competencies alongside TESOL content and pedagogy, including in the VE context (e.g. Kopish & Marques, 2020; Lenkaitis & Laranc, 2021; Syahrin et al., 2023).

After analyzing several models of global competencies in VE scholarship and education, we arrived at five domains of global competencies outlined in Table 8.1. Domains 2, 3, 4 and 5 have been adapted from a frequently cited framework developed by Boix Mansilla and Jackson (2011). Domain 1 was adapted from the Global Learning Value Rubric developed by the Association of American Colleges and Universities (2014). We chose to include this domain because we believe that self-awareness of one's background, identity and citizenship is a foundation upon which we can build the other global competencies.

Table 8.1 Adapted domains of global competencies

Domains of Global Competencies	Description of Global Competencies in TESOL Teacher Education
1. Deepening personal, local and global self-awareness and identity	Exploring one's identity as a local and global citizen, examining how certain influences from one's own background (e.g. values, upbringing, class status, etc.) and access to knowledge, rights, resources and technology impacts individuals' and society's educational outcomes and quality of life overall
2. Investigating the world	Examining differences and connections between values and worldviews (e.g. materialistic accumulation, individualism), power structures and systems (e.g. in education, government, industry) across cultures, and using credible sources to ask deep questions and form informed and compelling arguments
3. Recognizing perspectives	Recognizing that people's personal backgrounds and cultural, economic, historical and social realities affect their perspectives, perceptions and actions, seeking to act with empathy and commitment to avoid ethnocentric attitudes and stereotypes
4. Communicating effectively	Understanding that backgrounds affect communication, relating to diverse people by initiating and sustaining positive interactions, using available linguistic repertoires and effective communication strategies across various media
5. Taking action	Taking personal and/or collective action to address a locally or globally relevant, ethical, social and/or environmental challenge and reflect on the impact of the intervention, having self-efficacy to organize, positively influence and speak up for others.

Methodology

Although the positive impact of VEs has been effectively documented (O'Dowd, 2022) and global competencies are viewed as integral in the

TESOL curriculum, we acknowledge the critiques around global competency measures (e.g. Engel *et al.*, 2019). Partly owing to these critiques and partly owing to the relatively exploratory nature of our VEs, we have chosen to employ action research methodology, following similarly scaled, action research studies of PSTs' global competencies (e.g. Arndt *et al.*, 2021; Ramos *et al.*, 2021; and Syahrin *et al.*, 2023). Action research is well-suited for pragmatically oriented educators whose goal is to continually assess and improve their practice with the view of supporting students to achieve high academic outcomes (Burns, 2010). This methodological choice was also well aligned with the reality of our VE programs – we were direct participants who not only collected and analyzed PSTs' data, but we also critically examined our own practice and engaged in meaning-making.

In line with action research methodology, we did not rely only on self-reported data, and instead, we triangulated data sources from PSTs' early, mid and post-VE individual reflections, multimodal team reflections, instructional deliverables that included ebooks, lesson plans, lesson video recordings, slides, activities and worksheets. We also considered anonymous program evaluation surveys by PSTs and participating English learners. Finally, we took careful observation notes and kept journals on our perceptions about PSTs' practices, attitudes and any changes related to global competencies that we noticed throughout the programs. The following research questions guided our work:

- To what extent does VE participation help TESOL PSTs develop identities as educators of global competencies?
- In what domains of global competencies do TESOL PSTs engage with global competencies during a VE?
- In what ways do TESOL PSTs enact pedagogy centered on global competencies in a VE project?

Participants and Context

A total of 97 PSTs participated in our two VEs, 63 from a university in Slovakia and 34 from a mid-western University. The first VE project was implemented in 2022 and involved PSTs in learning about refugee-background learners and producing ebooks with language exercises for newcomers (e.g. an Afghan refugee-status newcomer in Michigan, a Ukrainian refugee-status newcomer in Slovakia) per requests of local teachers looking for more culturally and linguistically responsive materials for teaching these populations. All of the books adapted a Google Slides book template, making it easy to share the final product with teachers and learners.[1]

The second VE project was implemented in 2023. Phase 1 of this project involved teacher candidates in learning about dimensions of well-being and critically reflecting on their own well-being and well-being of the communities they belong to and considering larger global implications. Phase 2 of the project involved teams of PSTs taking turns teaching online lessons in each area of well-being to secondary English learners. Finally, PSTs considered learner feedback, and produced a multimodal team reflection in which they highlighted global competencies in their lessons, elaborated on possible action projects in their area that they could develop with their own future students, and shared thoughts about their co-teaching experiences.

Data Collection and Analysis

To analyze the collected data combined across sites, we met to code 10% of the collected reflections, lessons, lesson delivery and group meeting transcripts for alignment with the identified domains of global competencies. We then worked independently to code the rest of the data and met to compare and discuss our analysis, primarily in instances where multiple codes were applicable.

Findings

Research question 1: *To what extent does participation in a VE help TESOL PSTs develop identities as educators of global competencies?*

All but three participating PSTs appeared to either fully or partially embrace their identity as global skills educators, many crediting the VE program and referring to a variety of benefits for themselves and their students, as per PSTs' reflective assignment and evaluation excerpts below:

'This was the first time that I have viewed myself as a global skills educator. This can help learners see things and possible problems in the world from different points of view, it helps them to respect others' feelings, opinions and beliefs.'

'I see myself as a global skills educator and I hope to help my future students develop important skills for living and working in this world that is connected in many ways.'

'It will allow me to inspire them [future students] to become good global citizens.'

'Learning about global competencies is important because it helps students learn about important global issues and helps them be more educated and tolerant people.'

'..knowing about the world around us improves critical thinking.'

PSTs who expressed some hesitation around their global educator identity saw this area as 'important', 'an added value', or said that they 'want to work on this'. However, they tended to continue to think of themselves as lacking in sufficient confidence, skills or both. Typical responses by these PSTs included statements that suggested that they are 'not there yet', that they were 'partly', 'not fully', or 'not 100% confident' as global skills educators, and that they needed 'to get better at this', 'have a lot of things to learn and improve' and 'need more practice and experience'. Despite some reluctance to fully embrace this identity, many of these PSTs expressed commitment to work toward a classroom that incorporates global competencies and saw benefits to doing so:

> 'I am unsure of how I will go about it but would like to be able to educate my future students in a way that is open and gives them a view of the world outside of their own.'

Of the various VE activities and resources aimed at fostering PSTs' global competencies, as well as pedagogical practices, the '3Ys Global Thinking Routine' (Boix Mansilla *et al.*, 2017) was often mentioned as particularly helpful and something that PSTs felt comfortable incorporating into their own teaching practice. This practical strategy that prompts students to examine an issue from a personal, local and global lens, appears to be a powerful pedagogical entryway into global competencies. In addition to this global thinking routine, incorporation of critical readings during the initial knowledge deepening phase of the VE, and of course, the immersive, collaborative VE experience itself have contributed to the PSTs' developing identities as global educators who can teach global competencies alongside their subject area and/or English as an additional language.

Three PSTs (one US-based and two Slovak) explicitly stated that they did not yet view themselves as educators whose identity extended into global competencies. One PST from the US said her reason lay in 'not hav[ing] enough experience with other cultures and communities outside the United States' but that 'this could change' if she were to gain more experience working with diverse students. One Slovak PST lamented 'At the moment, I am not sure whether I am able to educate anyone in anything, let alone global skills'. Although lacking confidence could be a possible explanation for the two Slovak PSTs, it is also possible that they have never fully intended to pursue a teaching profession post-graduation; many Slovak graduates from the English program have traditionally chosen to work in other industries.

Research question 2: *In what domains of global competencies do TESOL PSTs engage with global competencies during a VE?*

PSTs who participated in our VE projects engaged, to varied degrees of intensity, with all of the five domains of global competencies outlined in Table 8.1. An early VE assignment was designed to *deepen their global self-awareness and identity* (Domain 1) by guiding them to reflect on their identities as local and global citizens and the various influences that have had an impact on their behaviors and beliefs systems. After reflecting individually in writing, PSTs were invited to read over the summary points of their teammates' reflections. They also engaged in a conversation around implicit biases in education and were guided to interrogate their privilege in the context of working with students from refugee-background or marginalized minority groups. Several PSTs demonstrated self-awareness of their privilege as it relates to identity, frequently expressing empathy toward marginalized populations as is illustrated in the two quotes below:

'For some people, it's hard to socialize. They become excluded from groups. In Slovakia and my community, racism is noticeable. We have communities living at the edge of town, somewhat excluded from society – the gypsies. They live in poverty, and most people tend to avoid them. It is because of many stereotypes and their behaviour in various situations which then results in a lack of empathy from our community. This hinders meaningful relationships with them. We had classmates from these communities in our primary schools, and we often excluded them from our activities, games etc.'

'I think that people of different ethnicities, disabled people, or marginalized communities have the most problems. We live in Eastern Europe and the mentality of a lot of people here is disturbing.'

Many Slovak PSTs juxtaposed their identity as forward-thinking individuals who had empathy for others against other citizens whom they perceived as 'conservative' or 'hypocritical' in their attitudes toward marginalized groups and/or immigrants.

'It is really important to help others, in my village there are a few refugees who try to live with us in peace. But I think a lot of people are afraid of refugees not only from Ukraine. Because Slovakia is a little bit of a conservative country in accepting other nationalities and ethnicities.'

'Slovakia is a rather conservative country which can be seen in the way we react for example to the refugee situation or anything that doesn't fit the mold of ideals that are found in mainstream society. It creates backlash and a sense of anger, especially in the younger generation.'

The participating PSTs engaged in *investigating the world beyond their own environment* (Domain 2) in different ways. First, they did so on the basis of conversations with international peers while working in their teams. Some of these conversational opportunities were structured, but often, PSTs gained insights into areas more organically. For example, after one group talked about the costs of higher education in the US, one Slovak PST shared his negative feelings about the lack of equity in the US education system while problematizing this access for the minorities living in Slovakia.

'However bad it might be in Slovakia, at least we somewhat start with equal opportunity unlike in the US. In Slovakia, as long as you do not come from the poorest marginalized communities, you can earn a degree in a high-paying job and be more or less set. The state will cover the expenses of the opportunity that is given to you.'

A US-based teacher in the group was surprised at the number of young professionals who leave the country in search of better opportunities:

'I learned so much about the issue with Slovakian professionals and scholars benefiting from free university education only to use their degree in another country.'

Teacher candidates also investigated the world by completing preselected readings. In the case of the first VE, PSTs learned about the issues affecting people with refugee status and in the case of the second VE, PSTs deepened their knowledge of the various dimensions of well-being across cultural contexts. Encountering information that they may have found shocking and being able to discuss it with peers from both local and global contexts was perceived positively. For example, the PSTs from the US university were surprised to learn that their nation, at that time, only awarded around 11,000 visas for refugees per year. Slovak PSTs related the topic of refugees to what they knew and read about the influx of Ukrainians, following the invasion by Russia. PSTs from both groups also appreciated the various facts they learned about local and global well-being trends, many referring to the information as 'shocking', 'thought-provoking' and 'informative'.

The third domain of global competencies – *recognition of perspectives* – was encouraged from the beginning of the project where PSTs in each team read each other's initial reflection on personal influences and upbringing and the impact they had on their beliefs systems. PSTs also explored their own and peers' strengths and weaknesses by using a personality test and discussed how different thinking and working preferences impact group members and how they can be patient and empathetic when working collaboratively. In addition to learning more about perspectives of others, in a few powerful instances, PSTs gained a deeper insight into their own perspectives as can be seen in one US-based PST's reflective excerpt below:

'There was a moment when my group mates and I were forced to think deeper on our perspectives about the world. We were discussing some of the worries we had about going into the teaching field and I said, 'Well, there's the whole school shootings thing, haha'. As soon as I said that, I could tell that both of the Slovak students became extremely uncomfortable. I then realized just how normalized this was to me owing to my nationality and the reality of teaching and attending school in the US. The possibility of a school shooting is something that has lived with me since first grade (I remember my first active shooter drill), and I know the same is true for the majority of people my age. I assume Slovakia does not have an issue with school shootings, so they have the luxury of not seriously having to think about that.'

The communicative nature of VEs ensures an alignment with the fourth domain of global competencies – *Communicating ideas*. Both native and non-native English-speaking PSTs were challenged to communicate across various media and with three generations-their peers, professors and elementary and secondary learners. Although an overwhelming majority of PSTs were positive about the authentic opportunities to communicate across global contexts, a few expressed frustration with their communication style or reacted to their peers or learners:

> 'I see my biggest weaknesses in that, sometimes when I started talking, I did not let others interrupt my monologue and to express their thoughts. I just wanted to finish my thought and then I let them talk.'

> 'It was really difficult for me to communicate with the Slovak kids. I just did not seem to be able to get them to want to talk during our online lessons.'

One US-based PST found her two Slovak teammates 'very quiet' and was puzzled over whether they were 'just shy or did not really want to do the work'. A closer look at the two Slovak PSTs' reflection suggested that these non-native speaking PSTs felt insecure about their use of English. One of these teacher candidates described the laborious effort to prepare communicatively for the co-teaching aspect of the VE project:

> 'I had sent my parts of the lesson to my godmother who is an English teacher to check for mistakes and only after that I sent it to my group members. Before our lessons I was reading my parts several times just to make sure that I would not make some 'stupid' grammatical mistakes. I thought about possible questions of learners to make sure that I would respond in a grammatically correct way. I had prepared questions for learners beforehand, so I did not have to do it during the lesson to minimalize mistakes. But I have to say that our American colleagues were just amazing. They accepted our level of English and understood that we are not native speakers, so they were patient with us.'

The above PST's concern over grammatical accuracy as a high-stakes benchmark for effective communication and positioning of native speaking counterparts as superior project partners was echoed by several other Slovak PSTs, which stands in contrast to the fact that no US-based teachers ever mentioned the Slovak peers' grammatical competence in English. In fact, the mid-western PSTs appeared in awe regarding their peers' multilingualism, which stands in contrast to more deficiency-oriented views by PSTs in Cherrez and Gleason's (2022) study.

When communicating with Slovak learners of English, PSTs varied in the extent to which they encouraged learners to contribute responses, with some enthusiastically inviting oral responses and others resorting to accepting answers in the Zoom chat. Slovak students' relative reluctance to communicate during the online English lessons frustrated some PSTs, but others were able to adapt. As one PST commented, 'I could tell they wanted to participate, but I had to ask them personally'. A few Slovak PSTs translanguaged between English and Slovak as a way of supporting Slovak students' communication. Seeing the benefits of translanguaging as a communicative strategy was valuable for the PSTs from the US. One teacher candidate stated, 'I thought that was cool when they brung their language in the mix. I also learned how to say some of the words in Slovak'. Most PSTs were able to establish rapport with students through positively responding to or building upon students' answers, and through praise.

The fifth domain of global competencies involves *taking action* to address a globally relevant challenge and think about the impact of a possible intervention. PSTs took action by collaborating on different kinds of deliverables that benefited a community partner (e.g. ebooks about newcomers for use by English teachers, online lessons on well-being for secondary English learners in Slovakia). With each deliverable, they were guided to first engage in collective visioning, followed by collaborative development of materials, feedback and reflection on the impact of their work. In addition to the two main projects they produced, PSTs also engaged in rich communication as they worked on a final presentation of their project and a reflective 'Teacher-Citizen assignment' in which they shared how they addressed global competencies in their teaching and articulated a plan to take action in their own future classroom.

Research question 3: *How do TESOL teacher candidates enact pedagogy centered on global competencies in a VE project?*

The collaborative nature of the VE meant that PSTs were expected to plan, develop and deliver VE products in teams. Data from the recorded planning and teaching sessions indicate that most teams tended to 'divide and conquer' rather than collaborate collectively. Some PSTs said this was attributable to the 'time difference' between the two countries while others felt that doing so made task completion more efficient. For groups whose members took responsibility for parts of the project and did not spend time reviewing the whole project or rehearsing together ahead of the project delivery, this meant that at times, materials appeared to lack cohesiveness and/or appropriate transitions. The pedagogical materials and activities by teams that found ways to co-create or rehearse them in real time, tended to be more polished, clear and engaging.

In respect to addressing the specific domains of global competencies in their pedagogy, PSTs reported to have been best able to engage domains 2 (investigating the world) and 3 (recognizing perspectives) in their pedagogical materials and instruction. The Global Thinking Routine that PSTs engaged in themselves subsequently helped them frame their own lessons and materials – they often began with reflective questions that centered on their students' personal opinions and experiences, followed by discussions of the particular issue in their immediate and extended communities and finally broadening the issue to the global context. For example, when teaching an online lesson on physical well-being, PSTs guided their students to first share their own interpretation of what it means to be physically fit (personal dimension). Next, they thought about well-being in their community and imagined changes that would help improve local well-being. Finally, they examined school lunches from around the world and discussed which may be the most nutritious (global dimension). To cultivate global competencies and encourage communication, several teams also used globally oriented 'provocations'[2] such as short stimulating YouTube or movie segments, photographs and quotes.

The most common feedback related to global competencies that we found ourselves continually providing had to do with moving beyond surface-level conversational prompts. For example, the feedback on the PSTs' draft lesson on well-being included limiting yes-no questions that revolved around personal preferences (e.g. 'Do you like to do puzzles? Do you like to read?'). During a consultation, PSTs were guided to make the questions more open-ended and think beyond the personal sphere. The team's final breakout room discussion included revised questions that prompted more critical thinking around intellectual rights and equity (e.g. Do all kids and young people in Slovakia and around the world have access to literacy? Who is often excluded from being successful in reading and writing? In the United States, books can get banned because school administrators may find the language in the books to be inappropriate, or inclusive of LGBT issues, sexual content, etc. Should books be banned?)

Although the PSTs were open to our feedback and showed ability to improve drafts of materials and lessons in ways that made final products better aligned with goals around global competencies, they had a harder time responding to critical incidents in real time. For example, in analyzing available textbooks and instructional materials in Slovakia, PSTs struggled to notice the lack of diversity around race and social class. During the online lessons, PSTs failed to respond pedagogically to learner statements that reflected biases or stereotypes. For example, when a secondary learner said 'In Africa, not every single person has the internet', the PSTs leading the lesson acknowledged the statement without taking the opportunity to ask the student whether they thought that in developed countries all people had equal access to resources.

Our VE provided a model for how global competencies could be pedagogically enacted, but interestingly, no PST explicitly mentioned that they would employ VEs in their own teaching. Instead, they imagined enacting their future teaching as engaging students in thinking about the key issues through personal, local, global lenses. This quote from a PST from the US is representative of many:

> 'I feel very confident incorporating global topics, thinking routines, and activities into my future teaching. Because of the immense practice that I have done within this class, I believe that I can effectively implement my newfound knowledge into a real-world classroom with ease.'

Beyond the incorporation of the three-pronged global thinking routine, PSTs also saw themselves addressing global competencies in their future classrooms by:

> 'Watching a snippet of global news everyday.'

> 'Including specific facts, videos, texts for students to practice the individual parts of language learning and get to know the world around them, the people, what it offers and how it can be used and do something for others.'

> 'Including global topics and activities in my lessons to help my students develop these skills, talking about different cultures, learning about issues that affect the world, or doing activities that help us work together with people from different backgrounds.'

Discussion

Our VE study suggests that the program has successfully cultivated global competencies among the participating PSTs who showed ability to (1) engage global competencies as university students while learning about and discussing the selected topics, and developing projects in international teams, (2) enact global competencies pedagogically while producing instructional materials and co-teaching and (3) reflect on global competencies individually and collaboratively. Although the first four domains of global competencies were drawn upon much more frequently than the last one, follow-up VE projects can seek to center action. Indeed, fully engaging all domains in a singular, short-term VE program may not be realistic. Instead, a layered approach to global competencies may be more beneficial – an early TESOL course could introduce the global competencies with a VE that engages PSTs in the first two domains, a mid-program VE could center the next two domains and an end-of the program capstone or practicum project could help guide teacher candidates toward developing and implementing an action-oriented VE (the last domain). Throughout a TESOL program, a portfolio could capture PSTs' growth in respect to their thinking about and pedagogical enactment of global competencies.

In addition to the layering of global competencies as a way of systematically internationalizing TESOL curriculum with VEs, modeling of global competencies and unpacking criticality are the two areas that merit more intentionality during VE planning. Most of the globally oriented pedagogy we implemented as teacher educators, namely self-awareness activities, global routines, provocations and tools for collaboration (e.g. Jamboard), PSTs incorporated in their own online instruction of English learners. This points to the importance of modeling – PSTs benefit from experiencing as learners the kind of pedagogy we want them to use as teachers. In this view, TESOL teacher educators adopt the role of 'frontline mentors' (Hauerwas *et al.*, 2021: 185), helping PSTs navigate an interconnected world with the hope that one day, they will do the same for their own learners.

Despite their ability to apply the target content and strategies into their pedagogy, PSTs struggled to move beyond simplistic, surface-level discussion and evaluation of selected topics. This was especially evident in the early drafts of their materials and lessons which they improved following teacher educator feedback. Intensified modeling and explicitness around pedagogical criticality, rather than addressing the lack of it through feedback on drafts, is something we want to strive toward in our future VE programs. Deep engagement with educational decolonization efforts, critical thinking and critical literacy in TESOL courses that precede VEs would provide a valuable foundation upon which a VE could build. At minimum, supports such as Anderotti's (2012) HEADS UP tool can be adapted as a way of framing and scaffolding criticality in VE projects and activities. Comparative activities that engage PSTs in analyzing lessons and activities on the same topic, but with a varied degree of critical literacy and critical thinking could also catalyze more thoughtful pedagogical enactment of global competencies. Finally, TESOL teacher educators interested in designing VEs centered on global competencies can benefit from considering scholarship on timely critiques in this area (e.g. Engel *et al.*, 2019).

Although this chapter focused on the benefits of the VE on PSTs' global competencies, the teacher candidates in our VEs alluded to many other benefits they experienced throughout the programs. A large majority of PSTs credited the VE for increased confidence to plan and teach lessons. Several PSTs also appreciated the experiential nature of the program. Others commented positively on the service-component of the VE – they liked doing something as part of their coursework that benefitted an actual community of learners and teachers. The VE also offered incredibly rich opportunities for PSTs to cultivate their 'soft skills' – they were immersed in negotiating ideas, taking responsibility for tasks, working toward consensus, finding solutions to problems, adapting to challenges and practicing empathy, all while working in solidarity with peers from another country.

Future scholarship in this area could consider whether any global competencies that PSTs practice during a VE transfer to other TESOL coursework or the extent to which they may be correlated with the development of ethical and civic competencies. TESOL Teacher Education could also benefit from research on PSTs' understanding and application of criticality across curricular projects, but especially in internationalized VEs that seek to sensitize teachers to issues beyond content and language learning. Finally, future scholarship could explore the long-term impact of VE participation and examine the extent to which educators with pre-service VE experience incorporate global competencies in their own classrooms.

Conclusion

Online teacher preparation coursework has been on the rise over the past decade, with the COVID-19 pandemic accelerating this trend. Despite some of its benefits, the virtual format does not organically lend itself to what TESOL teacher educators consider effective teacher preparation practices such as internationalized curriculum, authentic application (i.e. teaching actual learners) or development of global competencies. A curricular innovation such as the VE can help address this gap by centering global competencies developed through active participation in collaborative, globally relevant and applicable pedagogical projects. Our research and experience suggest that VEs hold a great promise in improving the TESOL curriculum by making PSTs' experiences more authentic, practical and globally enriching.

Notes

(1) For examples, see https://sites.google.com/emich.edu/ipete/home.
(2) Provocations are visual tools designed to 'spark thinking and dialog around an issue of global significance' (Ramos *et al.*, 2021: 312). They 'engage learners at an emotional level, inviting them to think critically about how information is constructed and presented, and for providing opportunities to question messages embedded in images in the news. (2021: 321)'

References

Andreotti, V. (2012) 'Editor's preface: HEADS UP.' *Critical Literacy: Theories and Practices* 6 (1), 1–3.

Arndt, S., Madrid Akpovo, S., Tesar, M., Han, T., Huang, F. and Halladay, M. (2021) Collaborative online learning across borders (COLAB), Examining intercultural understandings of preservice teachers in a virtual cross-cultural university-based program. *Journal of Research in Childhood Education* 35 (2), 281–296. https://doi.org/10.1080/02568543.2021.1880994

Asia Society/OECD (2018) *Teaching for Global Competence in a Rapidly Changing World*. Retrieved from https://asiasociety.org/sites/default/files/inline-files/teaching-for-global-competence-in-a-rapidly-changing-world-edu.pdf

Association of American Colleges and Universities (2014) *Global learning VALUE rubric*. Retrieved from https://www.aacu.org/initiatives/value-initiative/value-rubrics/value-rubrics-global-learning

Boix Mansilla, V. and Jackson, A. (2011) *Educating for Global Competence: Preparing Our Youth to Engage the World*. Retrieved from https://asiasociety.org/files/book-globalcompetence.pdf

Boix Mansilla, V., Perkins, D., Ritchhart, R., Tishman, S. and Chua, F. (2017) *Global Thinking: An ID-Global Bundle to Foster Global Thinking Dispositions through Global Thinking Routines*. Project Zero, Harvard Graduate School of Education. Retrieved from http://www.pz.harvard.edu/resources/global-thinking

Burns, A. (2010) *Doing Action Research in English Language Teaching: A Guide for Practitioners*. Routledge.

Engel, L.C., Rutkowski, D. and Thompson, G. (2019) Toward an international measure of global competence? A critical look at the PISA 2018 framework. *Globalisation, Societies and Education* 17 (2), 117–131. doi: https://doi.org/10.1080/14767724.2019.1642183

Hauerwas, L.B., Kerkhoff, S.N. and Schneider, S.B. (2021) Glocality, reflexivity, interculturality, and worldmaking: A framework for critical global teaching. *Journal of Research in Childhood Education* 35 (2), 185–199. doi: https://doi.org/10.1080/02568543.2021.1900714

Jaramillo Cherrez, N. and Gleason, B. (2022) A virtual exchange experience: Preparing pre-service teachers for cultural diversity. *Journal of Digital Learning in Teacher Education* 38 (3), 126–138. doi: https://doi.org/10.1080/21532974.2022.2083732

Kang, J.H., Kim, S.Y., Jang, S. and Koh, A.R. (2018) Can college students' global competence be enhanced in the classroom? The impact of cross-and inter-cultural online projects. *Innovations in Education and Teaching International* 55 (6), 683–693. doi: https://doi-org.ezproxy.emich.edu/http://doi.org/10.1080/14703297.2017.1294987

Kopish, M. and Marques, W. (2020) Leveraging technology to promote global citizenship in teacher education in the United States and Brazil. *Research in Social Sciences and Technology* 5 (1), 45–69. doi: https://doi.org/10.46303/ressat.05.01.3

Lin, C. (2021) Leveraging virtual exchange for global learning in the classroom: TESOL Candidates' perspectives. *NYS Tesol Journal* 8 (1), 29–39.

Lenkaitis, C.A. and Loranc, B. (2021) The role of Intercultural Virtual Exchanges in global citizenship development. *Journal of International and Intercultural Communication* 15 (2), 222–234. doi: https://doi.org/10.1080/17513057.2021.1876241

O'Dowd, R. (2020) A transnational model of virtual exchange for global citizenship education. *Language Teaching* 53 (4), 477–490. doi: https://doi.org/10.1017/S0261444819000077

O'Dowd, R. (2022) *Internationalising Higher Education and the Role of Virtual Exchange*. Taylor and Francis.

Ramos, K., Wolf, E.J. and Hauber-Özer, M. (2021) Teaching for global competence: A responsibility of teacher educators. *Journal of Research in Childhood Education* 35 (2), 311–330. doi: https://doi.org/10.1080/02568543.2021.1880998

Rets, I., Coughlan, T., Stickler, U. and Astruc, L. (2020) Accessibility of open educational resources: How well are they suited for English learners? *Open Learning: The Journal of Open, Distance and e-Learning* 38 (1), 38–57. doi: https://doi.org/10.1080/02680513.2020.1769585

Syahrin, S., Akmal, N. and DePriest, J. (2023) Promoting intercultural competence in preservice teacher education through virtual exchange. *Studies in Media and Communication* 11 (1), 1–11.

9 Two Tales of Study Abroad: The Role of Class

Hyun-Sook Kang

This chapter explores how social class plays a role in Korean college students' ideology about English learning in relation to a short-term study-abroad program in the US. Class has garnered growing scholarly attention as a factor that shapes access to and the nature of a sojourning experience. This study examined how class, defined as global mobility and access to cultural and social capital, influenced the motivation for and beliefs about English learning, as illustrated in two participants, Larry and Fiona, who showed a contrast in international mobility. As part of a cohort of 10 teacher candidates from the same sending university, they participated in a four-week program that focused primarily on promoting students' English skills for classroom instruction purposes and cultivating their awareness of multiculturalism. Thematic analysis of student reflections and interviews during the program suggests disjunctures between the two participants in their prior international experience, their motivation for English learning, and their beliefs about an ideal English speaker they aspired to become. Implications for future research, study-abroad program development and the internationalization of Teaching English to Speakers of Other Languages (TESOL) programs are discussed.

Introduction

A growing body of literature has examined education abroad programs in relation to the internationalization of education (e.g. de Wit & Altbach, 2021; Streitwieser, 2014). Much attention has more recently been given to the intersection of educational justice and education abroad (see Kang & Shively, 2023). Included in this line of scholarly work is research that has addressed race/ethnicity (e.g. Goldoni, 2017), language status and values (e.g. Quan & Menard-Warwick, 2021; Sung 2022), socio-economic status (e.g. Hurst, 2019; Kang & Kurney, 2024; Kinginger, 2004), or their intersections in accessing and experiencing study abroad. To contribute to the growing body of scholarship on international education as a way to expand and enrich learning opportunities for all students, this chapter explores how social class plays a role in Korean college students' expectations and experiences in relation to a short-term study-abroad program hosted by a US university.

Adopting an interpretivist approach to the notion of social class (e.g. Sayer, 2018; Vandrick, 2014), this case study explores how class, defined as international mobility and access (or lack thereof) to different forms of capital – including economic, cultural and social (Block, 2012; Bourdieu, 1986, 1991) – shapes the expectations and experiences of students from the same sending institution in South Korea. While the students participated in a four-week summer program that focused primarily on promoting their English skills for classroom instruction purposes and cultivating awareness of multiculturalism, thematic analysis of their interviews and reflection entries (Braun & Clarke, 2006) demonstrates a disparity in learner beliefs, motivation and agency during study abroad. This case study focuses on two participants, Larry and Fiona (who showed a stark contrast in prior international mobility) and their experiences in relation to study abroad.

Short-Term Study Abroad in TESOL

In response to globalization, universities around the world are in a position to internationalize their curriculum and extracurricular offerings (de Wit & Altbach, 2021; Streitwieser, 2014). Among the internationalization efforts is the development and implementation of short-term study-abroad programs usually shorter than a typical academic term through which students visit a host institution for academic and cultural enrichment. Students enrolled in these short-term programs take credit-bearing courses for transfer to their degree programs at a home university, without matriculating to obtain academic degrees from the host university. Two salient themes that emerge in the recent literature on short-term international experiences are the impact of study abroad on (a) learners' language learning and (b) current and prospective teachers from non-English-speaking countries.

A longstanding line of research has examined the impact of study-abroad experiences on ESL/EFL learning and other related learner variables (e.g. Wang & Ren, 2022; Xu & Qiu, 2023). In a large-scale ($N = 465$) study on Chinese undergraduate students' listening strategy, Xu and Qiu (2023) uncovered that learners with study-abroad experience demonstrated a higher level of motivation for L2 listening, adopting more top-down strategies reflective of real-time communication, whereas those with no international experience adopted fewer top-down strategies and instead were more focused on test scores. In a cross-sectional study, Wang and Ren (2022) revealed significant effects of study-abroad experience on syntactic complexity and of L2 proficiency on appropriateness of learners' pragmatic performance, in addition to the interactions of study abroad and L2 proficiency on learners' use of refusal strategies.

Another line of scholarship in TESOL has documented the impact of study abroad in Anglophone countries on current and future teachers from regions where English is not widely used (e.g. Barkhuizen & Feryok, 2006; Chern *et al.*, 2022; Çiftçi & Karaman, 2018; Kang & Pacheco, 2020; Kang & Shin, 2024). Barkhuizen and Feryok (2006) reported on the personal and professional growth for a group of 15 pre-service teachers from Hong Kong in a six-week program hosted by a university in New Zealand. Written reflections elicited through a pre-program questionnaire, journal entries and a summative program evaluation were used to tap into participants' expectations and experiences, even including their complaints about the relative lack of interactions with local speakers. In addition to written reflections during study abroad, literature in this area has turned to participants' future-oriented preparation experiences before study abroad (e.g. Çiftçi & Karaman, 2019). Çiftçi and Karaman (2018) revealed that prospective teachers from Turkey who chose to participate in a four-week program in England exhibited their lived and imagined experiences during pre-departure activities, largely shaped by groundless optimism, intercultural competence or lack thereof and naïve ideas about an unknown international experience.

Social Class in Study Abroad

Socioeconomic status has typically been measured through parents' educational background, occupation type and annual income to account for the relationship between social structures and educational experiences, such as study abroad (e.g. Hurst, 2019). Distinct from socioeconomic status espoused by a positivist paradigm in education research, the notion of social class is often employed by scholars who take a critical or interpretive approach to the relationships of individuals, institutions (e.g. schools) and other social structures (e.g. Block, 2012; Sayer, 2018; Vandrick, 2014). This qualitative case study therefore adopts the term 'social class' as a construct that embodies the social status and practices afforded by a series of relationships and resources that individuals inherit or build (e.g. Block, 2012; Bourdieu, 1986), rather than just using clear-cut indexes of educational background, income level and vocation type.

Opportunities for global mobility and international education have long been associated with socioeconomically privileged students' pursuit of extra-curricular opportunities (see Gore, 2005; Hurst, 2019). Even if they obtain access to study abroad, students from economically disadvantaged backgrounds may not always feel included to benefit from the afforded opportunities (Ohito *et al.*, 2021). In South Korea, the sending country for this case study, native-like English skills developed through international travels and study abroad, especially for youth and their parents and guardians are often regarded as being indicative of middle-class family practices (see Kang, 2024; Kang & Pacheco, 2021; Park, 2009).

Conceptual Lens: Language Ideology

The current study is framed by the tenets of language ideologies, which are viewed as 'any sets of beliefs about language articulated by users as rationalization or justification of perceived language structure and use' (Silverstein, 1979: 193). As Piller (2015) has noted, language ideologies are not just beliefs and opinions formulated about language, but also are about speakers and their individual and group identities, including nationality, race and ethnicity. Language ideologies are associated with the notion of indexicality, which is viewed as 'the property of language that points to its context of usage' (Park & Wee, 2012: 38). The indexical meanings related to a particular language derive from the intersection of individuals' ideologies about a particular language and their attitude to a particular social group (Kang & Ahn, 2019; Pacheco *et al.*, 2019; Razfar & Rumenapp, 2012). Language ideologies in various contexts are multiple and sometimes conflicting. Pacheco *et al.* (2019), for instance, illustrate how US undergraduate students in their student-teaching placements viewed translanguaging practices as a scaffold to support multilingual student engagement in classroom activities, and at the same time, as a distraction from multilingual students' learning of the English language, the societal language.

The language ideologies manifested by an individual may change in relation to different communicative contexts, as well as over time. Language ideologies are also mediated through different modalities and forms of linguistic resources (e.g. written texts, oral conversation and gesture) sometimes in relation to power systems (Kroskrity, 2004). Language ideologies further shape or are shaped by practices, which, in turn, lead to opportunities for individuals to encode, negotiate and reify their beliefs and ideologies (Wortham, 2001). Discursive practice that encodes how individuals make sense of experiences provides a lens to understand their beliefs, as well as giving rise to evolving ideologies. Given the nature of language ideology mediated through various resources and practices, this study addresses the following question: How does class, viewed as global mobility and access to cultural and social capital, help shape learners' ideologies about English language learning in relation to study abroad?

Methods

This study adopted a case study approach, which is regarded as a research design suitable for an empirical investigation to unravel a contemporary phenomenon within its context (Duff, 2014; Yin, 2009). The current chapter reports on a comparative case study of two focal participants, named Larry and Fiona (pseudonyms). These two participants' cases were chosen for an in-depth analysis because they presented uniquely comparative and contrastive information, which could offer a contextualized understanding of a chosen phenomenon in this study, that is, learners' ideologies about English learning in relation to study abroad. Of further note is that a case study approach was utilized to achieve analytic generalization (Duff, 2014). The two focal participants as the selected cases could provide analytic or theoretical insights into the ways in which social class shapes learners' expectations, beliefs and practices associated with English learning during study abroad.

Setting and Participants

The study-abroad program was specifically developed for a group of 10 teacher candidates with two goals in mind: (a) to develop English skills for classroom instruction purposes and (b) to promote understanding of diversity in US schools and society. These programmatic goals were proposed by the sending university in consideration of South Korea's growing diversity in K-12 schools, in which the participants were trained to teach after graduation. To this end, the study-abroad program was composed of multiple visits to local schools and landmarks, as well as classes focused on classroom interaction purposes and different aspects of racial, cultural and linguistic diversity in the US. These activities constituted 20 hours per week for four weeks as agreed upon between the sending and host universities. Participants received three-credit hours toward their undergraduate degrees at the home institution.

Among the 10 undergraduate student participants, this comparative case study focused on two of them, Larry and Fiona (pseudonyms). At the time of data collection, Larry was a senior in physical education and Fiona was a freshman in chemistry education. Along with the other participants in the cohort, they were recruited by the sending university and selected from a large pool of applicants, based on grade point average (GPA) and individual interviews in English. The researcher developed and implemented the study-abroad program as a faculty member affiliated with the US host institution and as a Korean native who shares the first language and background upbringing with the participants.

Data Collection

While engaged in curricular and excursion activities, participants completed weekly written reflections on Band,[1] discussions in small groups of five during the program and individual interviews at the conclusion of the program, conducted by the researcher. Participants were invited to share their accounts and reflections with respect to different events and activities in line with the programmatic goals of L2 learning and awareness of diversity. The study drew on these sources of data from the two focal participants. The focal participants' Band reflection entries were in English, and their participation in the group and individual interviews were in Korean. The group and individual interviews were audio-recorded and transcribed verbatim.

Data Analysis

Thematic analysis was used to analyze the data to identify patterns across the dataset associated with Larry and Fiona (Braun & Clarke, 2006). The researcher read the interview transcripts and reflection postings multiple times, making notes of any significant aspects of the data and preliminary trends aligned with the research question. The interview transcripts were first coded with emergent semantic codes. The inductive coding process made it possible to identify relationships among the codes and divergences between the focal participants in global mobility resources and opportunities (or the lack thereof) that they were afforded. The coding process further uncovered a disparity between the two participants in their beliefs about English learning. Extracts from the reflection entries on Band and the interviews were then collated in relation to the theoretical framework of language ideology, which led to the development of themes. Analysis was conducted in a reflexive and reiterative way, based on the researcher's positionality as a program coordinator and former learner of L2 English originally from South Korea (Unluer, 2012).

Findings

This section describes three emergent themes around the focal participants' expectations and experiences in relation to short-term study abroad. In spite of the shared commonalities in EFL learning, let alone their participation in the study-abroad program hosted by a US university, the participants demonstrated disjunctures in their (a) prior international travel and expectations about study abroad, (b) ideology of English learning and (c) ideology of an ideal English speaker they aspired to become.

A globetrotter versus a first timer in international travel

The focal participants illustrated a contrast in the prior international travels. While they participated in the same program from the same sending university, Larry had multiple prior opportunities and resources to travel abroad even as a child in contrast to Fiona as a first timer in international travel. Larry revealed his background in international travel during an individual interview with the researcher at the conclusion of the program, as follows.

Researcher: Have you travelled abroad before?
Larry: I've been to more than 47 countries.
Researcher: When did you get to visit all those countries?
Larry: Before 20, I travelled with my Dad for his work-related trips. [Larry talks more about his Dad]
Researcher: Then, how many times have you visited the US?
Larry: More than five times.

Larry described having visited nearly 50 countries before he turned 20, which suggests the extensive resources and opportunities to travel abroad afforded by the economic, cultural and social capital of his family (Bourdieu, 1991). He further depicted his prior experience of studying abroad for a semester as space to get away from his daily routine, which led him to believe that the short-term study-abroad program in which he was participating would also be an opportunity for him to escape and relax in the US. Fiona, on the other hand, had not experienced opportunities to travel abroad before being chosen by her home university to participate in the program hosted by a US university.

Researcher: How did you like your stay here?
Fiona: I loved it as I had never been to such an open place as here before.
Researcher: What countries have you been to? Is it the first time to be in the US?
Fiona: I haven't been to any foreign country. I have not even been to Japan; I have never taken a flight.

During the interview, Fiona confessed that she had 'never taken a flight', let alone having been to any foreign country, even including Japan, which is distance-wise the closest foreign country for Koreans. She further remarked that she had the desire to travel abroad since her high school days, and that she was proactively seeking out opportunities like this study-abroad program. When she applied to the program as a freshman during her first semester in college (a new academic year starts in March in the Korean education system), she went on to describe her pre-departure expectations for the host culture.

> The US is a country we [Koreans] feel close to despite the physical distance as we always learn about the country at school. I heard many stories about it [the US], read books about it, and looked at pictures about it, which made me think of the US as a place of freedom and diversity. There is so many people in Korea, but everyone looks the same. Here in the US, however, everyone is different, and there is so much diversity. I realise my expectations [about the US as the host culture] were right.

Of note is that despite the lack of international experiences, Fiona was describing her longstanding interest in and exposure to the host culture through schooling in Korea. She appears to have formed her ideology of the US and Americans as an imagined community of diversity (Anderson, 1991; Kanno & Norton, 2003) even before her first visit. This study-abroad program provided her with an opportunity to verify her imagination about the US and its people and culture, which are physically distant but culturally close, in relation to her home country.

This section illustrated a difference between Larry and Fiona in their prior international travel and expectations about study abroad, which could be attributable to the disparity in resources and opportunities afforded by their family's economic, cultural and social capital (Bourdieu, 1991). Larry as a globetrotter appears to have perceived the US and study abroad as an escape from his routine in the home country, drawing on his prior international travel and study-abroad experiences. By contrast, Fiona had the imagination of the US and its people and culture as a community of freedom and diversity (Anderson, 1991; Kanno & Norton, 2003), and viewed study abroad as an opportunity to verify her imagination of the US and its people and culture.

English learning to study abroad versus to read textbooks in a college major

Beyond the disjuncture between the focal participants in their prior international travel and expectations about study abroad, Larry and Fiona also displayed a distinction in their ideology of English learning. Larry articulated his perception of English learning as an instrument for future international travel and study abroad. Fiona, however, indicated the usefulness of English proficiency as a means to deepen her knowledge in a college major of chemistry education. Larry delineated his motivation and strategies for English learning.

Researcher: How did you study English?
Larry: When I first went to Europe, I was selected (to study abroad) based on an interview. When I went to Canada, however, I had to take the TOEFL (Test of English as a Foreign Language). I enjoyed my semester in Europe, and it was too short. So I wanted to study abroad again, in Canada, which means I had to prepare the TOEFL. When preparing for the TOEFL, I became more interested in English and checked out things like Netflix.
Researcher: How did you study for the TOEFL? Did you attend a test prep school?
Larry: I studied alone for a short time. I spent four weeks of a winter break on the test prep, and scored higher than 80 points, which was a good score.
Researcher: How did you practice English while here?
Larry: I don't think I had much exposure to English during the program. Ten of us were together in the program, which was different from my previous study abroad and international travels where I had to use English to communicate with local people. I had few opportunities to be exposed to English during the program.

Even as a relatively motivated learner, Larry viewed English as a tool to achieve his next goals in traveling and studying abroad (Heller, 2010; Sung, 2022). With a singular goal of getting admitted to a study-abroad program hosted by a Canadian university, for instance, Larry put his time and effort into the task of improving his TOEFL score in a short time period, which he admitted motivated him to further seek out other sources for English learning. However, he pointed out that the study-abroad context where a cohort of 10 students from the same sending country had activities together was less optimal for English learning than the previous study-abroad opportunities in which he was alone in interacting with local speakers. In contrast, Fiona related her motivation for English learning to her college major.

Researcher: How did you like using English here?
Fiona: I have to read textbooks in English in my major program, so I always wanted to improve my reading skills. I feel I have more opportunities to practice speaking and listening comprehension than reading during study abroad.
Researcher: Did you make efforts to improve English reading while here?
Fiona: I looked up local Google news articles on the Internet. I also read a few children's books like Charlotte's Web and Charlie's Chocolate Factory.

Driven by the desire and need to read English-medium textbooks in her major, Fiona had placed greater emphasis on reading than other aspects of English. However, she further noted that study-abroad provided more opportunities for English speaking and listening comprehension than for English reading. To address this imbalance between reading and orality in opportunities available during study abroad, though, Fiona detailed her strategies, including seeking out additional reading materials, such as 'local Google news articles' and 'children's books'.

Both participants showed an ideology of English language as a commodity, which motivated them to improve English during study abroad (Heller, 2010; Sung, 2022). The participants exhibited a view of English as a tool essential for achieving future goals in college and the workplace, albeit of a different nature. While Larry put his time and effort into the task of improving his score on the TOEFL to pursue opportunities to study abroad, Fiona viewed English learning as an instrument to gain knowledge in the major program by reading original textbooks written in English. Despite the shared ideology of English learning as a tool, the manifestation of their respective language ideologies is therefore different between them.

'My own English accent' versus 'standard english' as an ideal English speaker

The schism between the focal participants was not merely limited to prior international experience, expectations for study abroad and ideology of English learning. Rather, they showed distinct visions when it came to the kind of English speaker they aspired to become. While Larry described his own English accent with which he was content, Fiona pointed to Standard English as the kind of English she strove to adopt. In a Week 2 reflection posting on Band in response to a prompt, 'What kind of English do you aspire to speak?'. Larry elaborated on how he chose his own accent as the kind of English he yearned for.

> My answer to the first question is that I want to speak 'my English'. Since I was young, I have been learning American English in Korea, so I became familiar with American accents and used them constantly. And then when I was in Ireland, I liked the Irish pronunciation that I followed. When I was in Canada, my roommate was an Indian. I have experienced an Indian accent more clearly than a Canadian accent. When I travelled to Quebec, I was amazed by the English of French tone. And when I travel to Belfast in [the] UK, I remember being frustrated because I couldn't hear any of the British accents that cut off and use the high tone. I thought the British accent was very cool. So it was a time when I practised English pronunciation in my own way. But the pronunciation that I thought was cool at the time was the pronunciation of British high society exposed in the media. In fact, everyone else in [the] UK had a variety of different accents.
>
> Now, I don't aspire to anything specific. I think I can say that it is the kind of English that I aspire that all of my previous experiences will become me and be able to speak my own English accent.

In his reflection posting on Band, Larry presented himself as a legitimate speaker of English (Bourdieu, 1991) while breaking away from the ideology of self-deprecation (Park, 2009) or the ideology of native-speakerism (Lippi-Green, 1997; Tavares, 2022). He acknowledged that he was taught the American variety of English in schools in Korea, and then listed the different accents of English he was exposed to when visiting different English-speaking countries. Larry further described his emotions when immersed in the different English varieties, such as 'cool' associated with the pronunciation of British high society, 'amazed' by the English variety used in Quebec and 'frustrated' when interacting with the English accent in Belfast (see Dewaele & Pavelescu, 2021). While alluding to the different values associated with different English accents, he shared his understanding of the elusiveness of one standard accent and his desire of constructing his own way of using authentic English as part of his identity that is emblematic of his international experiences. In contrast, Fiona revealed in her reflection posting on Band that she yearned to be a good English speaker, in hopes of making herself understood when interacting with different speakers.

> I think that the Standard English must make everyone who can speak English understand. So, I want to speak Standard English because I want

to be a good speaker. (Good speaker have the ability that makes good interaction.) English is a language. We have to interact [with] each other through language.

Displaying an instrumental view of English, Fiona exhibited the ideology of English as a lingua franca (Jenkins, 2007), identified as the common language used for speakers from different language backgrounds to communicate. Given its role and status as a global language for international communication, she put forth the so-called standard variety of English as the kind of English she aspired to adopt and embody (Lippi-Green, 1997). Distinct from Larry's beliefs about an ideal English speaker based on his direct experiences during international travel, Fiona illustrated her ideology of a good speaker being understood by other imagined English speakers (Anderson, 1991; Kanno & Norton, 2003).

Discussion

This comparative case study reports on two Korean college students from the same sending university who participated in the same study-abroad program hosted by a US university. In spite of the commonalities between the two participants, analysis of their interviews and reflection postings on Band showed divergences in prior international experience, expectations about study abroad and language ideology associated with English learning, as manifested in their motivation to learn English and goals as an English speaker (Kroskrity, 2004; Piller, 2015). Thanks to the resources and opportunities afforded by the economic, cultural and social capital of his family (Block, 2012; Sayer, 2018; Vandrick, 2014), Larry had extensive experience travelling abroad as a child and then studying abroad as a college student. Fiona, on the other hand, did not have opportunities to leave the home country until she was selected to participate in the short-term study-abroad program organized by the sending university. It was not attributed to a lack of her interest, but rather, she was not afforded an opportunity to travel abroad.

Despite the contrast in their backgrounds, both appeared to hold the ideology of English as a commodity for future international travels (Larry) and for deeper understanding of technical knowledge in a college major (Fiona) (Heller, 2010; Sung, 2023). However, the nature of their goals for English learning was rather different. Larry's articulated motivation to learn English was largely driven by his personal desire to pursue study abroad by scoring high enough on a standardized proficiency test of English to get admitted to an English-medium host university. Fiona, on the other hand, reported her desire to improve English, especially reading skills to be able to read textbooks in English for her college major. She further noted that study abroad presented opportunities to practice her speaking and listening comprehension in English, as she was seeking to interact with program staff members and local speakers. Fiona's beliefs about English learning afforded by study abroad could have enabled her chosen practice of seeking out and taking advantage of interaction opportunities with local speakers (Wortham, 2001).

In addition to the disjuncture in their ideologies of English learning, Larry and Fiona showed different perspectives on the kind of ideal English speaker they aspired to become. Drawing on his extensive experience of international travels, Larry conceived of an ideology of including himself as a legitimate speaker of English in the negotiation of his language identity (Bourdieu, 1991). This is inconsistent with the ideology of self-deprecation that is widely observed among Korean speakers of English (Kang, 2024; Park, 2009) or the ideology of native-speakerism (Lippi-Green, 1997; Tavares, 2022). Fiona's case, however, displayed the devaluation of non-native accents of English through the process of misrecognition (Bourdieu, 1991). Instead, she conveyed the reinforced ideology of an imagined native speaker recognized by other imagined speakers of English (Anderson, 1991; Kanno & Norton, 2003).

The current findings help expand our understanding of the role social class plays in shaping learners' international experience, expectations about study abroad and beliefs about English learning. Drawing on the view of class as a construct that encompasses the social status and practices afforded by resources that individuals obtain (Block, 2012; Sayer, 2018; Vandrick, 2014), this study illuminated how a difference in international experience was associated with divergent ideologies about English learning and an ideal English speaker. Considering that the two learners participated in the same study-abroad program from the same sending university, the disparity in language ideologies can be attributable to the schism in social class as manifested in the prior international experience or its lack thereof.

Conclusions

Findings from this case study suggest the significance of individual differences in developing and administering study-abroad programs. Despite the fact that both learners shared an EFL learning experience, situated in the same study-abroad context, Larry and Fiona exhibited distinct expectations and ideologies with respect to English and its speakers and culture, as well as English learning, which in turn shaped and were shaped by their orientation and attitudes toward study abroad. The use of a case study design made it possible to juxtapose and spotlight the personal backgrounds and language ideologies illustrated by the two learners. Insights gained from this case study help underscore the importance of paying attention to individual differences in program development on the part of a host institution. It is not uncommon for a host institution and program to categorize and lump together study-abroad participants in light of a sending country or institution when developing a program and its curriculum and activities. Findings from this case study help demonstrate the importance of curricular activities and excursions closely based on individual backgrounds, goals and identities.

Note

(1) https://band.us/en: An app familiar to Korean speakers

References

Anderson, B. (1991) *Imagined Communities: Reflections on the Origin and Spread of Nationalism*. Verso.

Barkhuizen, G. and Feryok, A. (2006) Pre-service teachers' perceptions of a short-term international experience programme. *Asia-Pacific Journal of Teacher Education* 34 (1), 115–134. https://doi.org/10.1080/13598660500479904

Block, D. (2012) Class and SLA: Making connections. *Language Teaching Research* 16 (?), 188–205. https://doi.org/10.1177/1362168811428418

Bourdieu, P. (1986) The forms of capital. In J. Richardson (ed.) *Handbook of Theory and Research for the Sociology of Education* (pp. 241–258). Greenwood Press.

Bourdieu, P. (1991) *Language and Symbolic Power*. Polity Press.

Braun, V. and Clarke, V. (2006) Using thematic analysis in psychology. *Qualitative Research in Psychology* 3 (2), 77–101. https://doi.org/10.1191/1478088706qp063oa

Chern, C., Lin, A.M.Y. and Lo, M.-L. (2022) Border-crossing and professional development of Taiwanese EFL teachers in a study-abroad program. In G. Barkhuizen (ed.) *Language Teachers Studying Abroad: Identities, Emotions and Disruptions* (pp. 111–122). Multilingual Matters.

Çiftçi, E. and Karaman, A. (2019) Short-term international experiences in language teacher education: A qualitative meta-synthesis. *Australian Journal of Teacher Education* 441 (1), 93–119. https://doi.org/10.14221/ajte.2018v44n1.6

de Wit, H. and Altbach, P. (2021) Internationalization in higher education: Global trends and recommendations for its future. *Policy Reviews in Higher Education* 5 (1), 28–46. https://doi.org/10.1080/23322969.2020.1820898

Dewaele, J.M. and Pavelescu, L.M. (2021) The relationship between incommensurable emotions and willingness to communicate in English as a foreign language: A multiple case study. *Innovation in Language Learning and Teaching* 15 (1), 66–80. https://doi.org/10.1080/17501229.2019.1675667

Duff, P.A. (2014) Case study research on language learning and use. *Annual Review of Applied Linguistics* 34, 233–255. https://doi.org/10.1017/S0267190514000051

Glass, C.R. and Gesing, P. (2022) Introduction - Study abroad and social mobility: Access and labor market inequality in a post-COVID-19 world. In C.R. Glass and P. Gesing (eds) *Critical Perspectives on Equity and Social Mobility in Study Abroad* (pp. 1–9). Routledge.

Goldoni, F. (2017) Race, ethnicity, class, and identity: Implications for study abroad. *Journal of Language, Identity and Education* 16 (5), 328–341. https://doi.org/10.1080/15348458.2017.1350922

Gore, J.E. (2005) *Dominant Beliefs and Alternative Voices: Discourse, Belief, and Gender in American Study Abroad*. Routledge.

Heller, M. (2010) The commodification of language. *Annual Review of Anthropology* 39 (1), 101–114. https://doi.org/10.1146/annurev.anthro.012809.104951

Hurst, A. (2019) Class and gender as predictors of study abroad participation among US liberal arts college students. *Studies in Higher Education* 44 (7), 1241–1255. https://doi.org/10.1080/03075079.2018.1428948

Jenkins, J. (2007) *English as a Lingua Franca: Attitude and Identity*. Oxford University Press.

Kanno, Y. and Norton, B. (2003) Imagined communities and educational possibilities: Introduction. *Journal of Language, Identity and Education* 2 (4), 241–249, https://doi.org/ 10.1207/S15327701JLIE0204_1

Kang, H.S. (2024) Learners' beliefs about English language learning: The case of Korean college students sojourning in the United States. *Study Abroad Research in Second Language Acquisition and International Education* 9 (1), 76–99. https://doi.org/10.1075/sar.22008.kan

Kang, H.S. and Ahn, S.Y. (2019) Broadening learners' perspectives on World Englishes: A classroom-based study. *Language Awareness* 28 (4), 268–290. https://doi.org/10.1080/09658416.2019.1673400

Kang, H.S. and Pacheco, M.B. (2020) Translingual competence and study abroad: Shifts in sojourners' approaches to second language learning. *Language and Education* 34 (5), 425–439. https://doi.org/10.1080/09500782.2020.1775246

Kang, H.S. and Pacheco, M.B. (2021) Short-term study abroad in TESOL: Current state and prospects. *TESOL Quarterly* 55 (3), 817–838. https://doi.org/10.1002/tesq.3014

Kang, H.S. and Shively, R.L. (2023) Researching language-focused study abroad through an equity lens: A research agenda. *Language Teaching*. https://doi.org/10.1017/S0261444823000149

Kang, H.S. and Kurney, L.T. (2024) Equity-focused education abroad in a community college: Practitioner perspective. *Community College Journal of Research and Practice*. https://doi.org/10.1080/10668926.2024.2330093

Kang, H.S. and Shin, D. (2024) Mobile-assisted language learning during short-term study abroad. *Frontiers: The Interdisciplinary Journal of Study Abroad* 36 (1), 288–313. https://doi.org/10.36366/frontiers.v36i1.787

Kinginger, C. (2004) Alice doesn't live here anymore: Foreign language learning and identity reconstruction. In A. Pavlenko and A. Blackledge (eds) *Negotiation of Identities in Multilingual Contexts* (pp. 219–242). Multilingual Matters.

Kroskrity, P. (2004) Language ideologies. In A. Duranti (ed.) *A Companion to Linguistic Anthropology* (pp. 496–517). Blackwell.

Lippi-Green, R. (1997) *English with an Accent: Language, Ideology, and Discrimination in the United States*. Routledge.

Ohito, E., Lyiscott, J., Green, K. and Wilcox, S. (2021) This moment is the curriculum: Equity, inclusion, and collectivist critical curriculum mapping for study abroad programs in the COVID-19 era. *Journal of Experiential Education* 44 (1), 10–30. https://doi.org/10.1177/105382592097965

Pacheco, M.B., Kang, H.S. and Hurd, E. (2019) Scaffolds, signs, and bridges: Language ideologies and translanguaging in student-teaching experiences. *Bilingual Research Journal* 42 (2), 194–213. https://doi.org/10.1080/15235882.2019.1596179

Park, J.S. (2009) *The Local Construction of a Global Language: Ideologies of English in South Korea*. Mouton de Gruyter.

Park, J.S. and Wee, L. (2012) *Markets of English: Linguistic Capital and Language Policy in a Globalizing World*. Routledge.

Piller, I. (2015) Language ideologies. In K. Tracy, C. Ilie and T. Sandel (eds) *The International Encyclopaedia of Language and Social Interaction* (pp. 917–927). Wiley-Blackwell.

Quan, T. and Menard-Warwick, J. (2021) Translingual and transcultural reflection in study abroad: The case of a Vietnamese-American student in Guatemala. *The Modern Language Journal* 105 (1), 355–370. https://doi.org/10.1111/modl.12701

Razfar, A. and Rumenapp, J. (2012) Language ideologies in English learner classrooms: Critical reflections and the role of explicit awareness. *Language Awareness* 21 (4), 347–368. https://doi.org/10.1080/09658416.2011.616591

Sayer, P. (2018) Does English really open doors? Social class and English teaching in public primary schools in Mexico. *System* 73, 58–70. https://doi.org/10.1016/j.system.2017.11.006

Silverstein, M. (1979) Language structure and linguistic ideology. In P. Clyne, W. Hanks and C. Hofbauer (eds) *The Elements: A Parasession on Linguistic Units and Levels* (pp. 193–248). Chicago Linguistic Society

Sung, C.C.M. (2022) Mainland Chinese students' multilingual experiences during cross-border studies in a Hong Kong university: From a language ideological perspective. *Journal of Multilingual and Multicultural Development* 43 (8), 715–730. https://doi.org/10.1080/01434632.2020.1767632

Streitwieser, B. (2014) *Internationalisation of Higher Education and Global Mobility*. Symposium Books.

Tavares, V. (2022) Neoliberalism, native-speakerism and the displacement of international students' languages and cultures. *Journal of Multilingual and Multicultural Development*. https://doi.org/10.1080/01434632.2022.2084547

Unluer, S. (2012) Being an insider researcher while conducting case study research. *Qualitative Report* 17 (29), 1–14. https://nsuworks.nova.edu/tqr/vol17/iss29/2

Vandrick, S. (2014) The role of social class in English language education. *Journal of Language, Identity and Education* 13 (2), 85–91. https://doi.org/10.1080/15348458.2014.901819

Wang, Y. and Ren, W. (2022) The effects of proficiency and study-abroad on Chinese EFL learners' refusals. *The Language Learning Journal* 50 (4), 521–536. https://doi.org/10.1080/09571736.2022.2088117

Wortham, S. (2001) Language ideology and educational research. *Linguistics and Education* 12 (3), 253–259. https://doi.org/10.1016/S0898-5898 (01)00055-9

Xu, J. and Qiu, X. (2023) Study abroad experiences count: Motivational profile of EFL listeners and its impact on top-down and bottom-up processing. *Applied Linguistics Review* 14 (1), 145–172. https://doi.org/10.1515/applirev-2020-0037

Yin, R. (2009) *Case Study Research, Design, and Method*. Sage.

10 Master's TESOL Returnees' Career Dilemmas in China: The Need to Prepare Teachers for Careers Beyond the United States

Jialing Wang

This chapter argues that ethnocentrism plagues Teaching English to Speakers of Other Languages (TESOL) programs in the US and impairs effective and adequate training for teaching English in international contexts. Concurrently, career outcomes of international TESOL graduates who leave the host country after graduation are opaque. This chapter critically explores the career paths of Master's TESOL holders who returned to China after completing their degree and examines the barriers to transfer western pedagogical practices to language classrooms in China. This study considers 11 semi-structured interviews with Chinese returnees who graduated from a TESOL master's program at a public US university between 2014–2021. Participants were employed in one of four types of educational institutions: private educational companies, public schools, international schools or higher education institutions. Regardless of their institution, they face challenges in applying the knowledge and skills gained from TESOL education in the US. Based on the findings, this chapter demonstrates how imperative it is for TESOL programs to better understand the contexts in which their graduates will teach, and provide professional development opportunities that prepare them for practical realities they may face teaching English outside the US.

Introduction

Master's programs in Teaching English to Speakers of Others Languages (MA TESOL) are rooted in the US context of influx of immigrants since the 1960s (Gray, 1997). After the Great Depression, the immigrant population in the US started to recover and increased from 528,431 in the 1930s to 3,321,0677 by the 1960s (US Department of Homeland Security, 2018). The Immigration and Nationality Act of 1965 marked the watershed moment that the US became more culturally, racially and linguistically diverse by abolishing the quota system based on national origin and ended preference for Western European immigrants (Vecchio, 2013). Under the influence of this policy, rising numbers of immigrants from Asia, Africa and South America arrived in the US and created an unprecedented demand for trained TESOL personnel. TESOL as a professional field developed during this era to support immigrants to improve English proficiency so as to fit in the country. With this context, TESOL programs have developed by targeting immigrants to the US who want to learn about the relationship between language and American society and politics.

However, with the increasing internationalization and the more salient status of English across the world, American higher education has also attracted many international students who hope to become English educators in their home country. There are concerns about whether MA TESOL programs in the US effectively and adequately train their students to teach English as a foreign language (EFL) by providing a wide range of courses that are marginally relevant to English teaching in foreign contexts (Govardhan *et al.*, 1999; Singh & Richards, 2006; Stapleton & Shao, 2018). Ingrained in American culture, academics and ideology, TESOL programs in the US need to make considerable modification in content and program structure to prepare international master's students to teach English in varied educational contexts. Universities also need to gear toward a more sophisticated global labor market to assist international students transition to work outside of the US.

The purpose of this chapter is therefore to explore the international MA TESOL returnees' early employment experience and examine the challenges faced by them in using the pedagogies acquired from the US-based TESOL programs in China. The main research question is: what are the barriers in teaching English faced by the international returnees in China?. This study investigated the external and internal challenges TESOL returnees experienced in the Chinese educational context. The findings have research and practical implications for international TESOL programs as well as higher education institutions.

Literature Review

TESOL education in US

English language teaching (ELT) dates back centuries before the establishment of TESOL as a formal professional community (Canagarajah, 2016). In the US, TESOL initiatives can trace their origins back over 300 years (Gray, 1997). Before it was recognized as a profession, English was taught for citizenship and religious purposes, under the notion that any English speaker could teach the language (Cowan, 1965).

A significant shift came in the 1960s when TESOL became a formal profession owing to international political and economic changes. The 1964 National Defense Education Act (NDEA) funded English language schools in 48 countries offering English courses to about 100,000 students each year, leading to a surge in demand for qualified English teachers (Croft, 1970; Russell, 1965). With post-colonialism influences aiming to enhance English supremacy (Rubdy, 2015; Tupas, 2015), the demand increased further, making English instruction pivotal for bringing national advantages in the economy, culture, diplomacy, research and technology (British Council, 2013).

The 1990s marked a key transition for TESOL, concomitant with the expansion of international higher education in the US. Driven by worldwide surging neoliberal ideology (Punteney, 2019), education shifted from public service to the driving force of the 'knowledge economy', represented by being listed under the service sector in the General Agreement on Trade in the Services (GATS) treaty of the World Trade Organization (WTO) in 1995 (Knight, 2008). Academic capitalism spurred universities to pursue market and marketlike activities, for instance, enrolling more international students as an additional revenue stream (Slaughter & Rhoades, 2004). In the US context, higher education has been more tactical in recruiting self-supporting full-fee paying international students. Consequently, TESOL programs continued to grow through strategically recruiting international students. As of 2020, there are approximately 450 TESOL programs in the United States and Canadian higher education institutions (TESOL, 2020). The history of TESOL in the US, against the backdrop of the power asymmetries in global economy and political dynamics, reveals a pronounced bias toward Anglo-centric perspective in teaching English (Phyak & De Costa, 2021).

Reflected in practice, whether the US TESOL programs produce effective teachers remains debated (Pakir, 1999; Singh & Richards, 2006; Stapleton & Shao, 2018). Rooted in its historical, economic and cultural context, US TESOL education has been criticized for its insular perception of ESL (Govardhan *et al.*, 1999; Raqib *et al.*, 2008), focusing predominantly on the social and cultural aspects of language learning within the American context while overlooking the global scope of English language education (Liu, 1998; Stapleton & Shao, 2018). For instance, studies in Bangladesh indicate that the contradictions between learner-centered curriculum and the tradition of centrality of the teacher in the classroom negatively affects the applicability of Western TESOL education in Bangladesh (Chowdhury, 2003; Chowdhury & Phan, 2008). These concerns are also echoed in Vietnamese (Nguyen, 2017). Similarly, China has deeply ingrained teaching conventions and philosophy in its own cultural history. Combined with the systemic reality of exam-driven and teacher-led large classes in a highly bureaucratic and hierarchical system, the applicability of US TESOL pedagogies in the Chinese context became questionable.

TESOL in China

Compared to the English-speaking countries, English education in China started relatively late. The commencement of China's Opening up and reform in 1979 witnessed the Chinese government recognizing the importance of English as a communicative tool. Consequently, they reinstated foreign language policies which were suspended during the cultural revolution. Landmarks such as joining the WTO in 2001 and hosting the Beijing Olympics in 2008 fueled English learning across the country (Lam, 2008). As mandated by the Ministry of Education, public schools introduce English no later than the third grade, continuing through nine-year compulsory education (Ministry of Education, 2001).

The emphasis on English in the Chinese educational framework is unprecedented as China was eager to connect to the world. It is a required subject in the national college entrance examination, holding equal importance to subjects like Chinese and Math. At the tertiary levels, every university student is expected to pass the national English proficiency exam College English Test (CET) Level 4 before they can graduate. The intensity of English education continues into postgraduate education and career opportunities (Pan, 2015). With more higher-paying jobs requiring certain levels of English proficiency, English has become a gatekeeper for education, job market prospects and professional advancement (Li, 2020). The emergence of the new middle class with broader global vision ignited a fever of English learning, and supplementary for-profit English education also experienced an upsurge during this era (Luo & Forbes, 2019).

However, there has been growing debate about the status and goal of English education in China and its threats to Chinese language and culture, particularly considering the current government's shift toward promoting 'telling Chinese stories' (Xinhua Press, 2013). Since 2013, amid the rising nationalism, the Chinese government frequently sent out signals of deemphasizing English. Education authorities in Beijing, Shanghai, Shandong and Jiangsu, the leading education municipalities and provinces, announced that they planned to shift the weight from English to Chinese or even remove English from the college entrance examination (Pan, 2015). Under current administration in China, formal English education has diminished emphasis, and most after-school English programs have been largely restricted (Mikesell, 2021). At the same time, the focus of English education has shifted toward promoting Chinese ideology and perspectives, amplifying Chinese voices and cultivating a positive image of China (Chang, 2021; Zhang, 2015). The divergent aims of English education in the US and China, each emphasizing exporting their perspectives while lacking receptivity to alternative viewpoints, represent fundamental conflicts within their educational frameworks.

Additionally, China's approach to English education has its own 'Chinese characteristics'. The primary goal of English learning remains for tests on paper (Zhang, 2022). A predominantly teacher-dominated, textbook-based and transmission-oriented pedagogy has restricted students' holistic language development. Additionally, regional disparities in China have led to a widening gap in the quality of English education provided to students.

Returning TESOL graduates

As international academic mobility rises since 2006, there has been an exponential increase in published research about international students. Most of the research delves into their language and cultural transition, mental well-being while studying abroad and migration to hosting countries (Jing *et al.*, 2020), scant attention has been paid to international students' postgraduate experience, especially those returning home after studying in the US.

A growing number of TESOL graduates are returning to China for employment, sparking increased interests on the impacts of study abroad experience on English language teachers. In general, teachers with study abroad experience have shown enhanced English proficiency, heightened intercultural competence, evolved pedagogy beliefs, increased awareness of their own identity and agency, and more open-mindness and inclusiveness (Hao *et al.*, 2016; Huang *et. al.*, 2023; Wang, 2014; Zhao & Mantero, 2018). Yet, little is known about whether these perceived improvements can translate to work opportunities and teaching effectiveness.

Moreover, current literature tends to examine changes in teachers' personal competence and beliefs in isolation (Suzuki, 2021). It overlooks how these changes, influenced by western contexts, play out in a different educational ecosystem. Teaching is a complex and dynamic process that involves many interactors: students, peer teachers, school administrators, parents and broader educational and sociocultural contexts. It is a situated contextual activity constrained by interconnected factors in the expansive educational system (Ilieva *et al.*, 2015). Hence, it is crucial to explore how the stakeholders influence and shape the teaching experience of returning TESOL professionals.

The TESOL education in the US and China differ fundamentally in historic, cultural and political origins, leading to contrasting educational contexts and objectives. However, the US-based TESOL programs often disregard the cultural contexts where many of their international TESOL graduates will teach. As a result, the ability to integrate the pedagogy in transnational context is sidelined in their graduate training. This study seeks to address this gap through a qualitative case study to explore the experience of international Master's (MA) TESOL returnees in China. Specifically, it aims to investigate how the knowledge, skill and educational beliefs acquired from the US-based TESOL program interact with the local educational realities, and how these interactions shape the early professional journeys of TESOL returnees in China.

Methods

This case study is conducted at a selective public university in the Northeastern US. From 2013–2021, 79 mainland Chinese international students graduated from the MA TESOL program at this university, representing 53% of the total graduates ($N = 148$). Eleven eligible graduates responded to a pre-screening survey, among which 10 were female, and one was male. The data for this study included 11 semi-structured postgraduate interviews conducted via Zoom. Each interview lasted approximately one to one and a half hours. The interviews were conducted in Chinese yet 'code-switching' between English and Chinese was allowed. The collected audio recordings were initially transcribed using an artificial intelligence (AI) supported software *Trint* and then manually edited to ensure accuracy. Key texts were manually translated to English after initial coding. Codes, preliminary analysis and reflective memos are documented in English. Back translation (Sperber, 2004) was used to ensure accuracy of the translation.

Data analysis proceeded with the data collection simultaneously and cyclically. During data analysis, categorical aggregation was used to find the common thematic patterns across the participants' experience, and direct interpretation was employed to draw meaning from the individual experience of a participant (Stake, 1995). Once patterns emerged from the analysis, I paid more attention to the same themes and took specific memos in the following interviews. Member checking (Maxwell, 2013) was exploited to enhance validity and reliability of the analysis.

Participants

All the 11 participants in this study graduated from an MA TESOL program at a selective public university in the Northeast US between 2014 and 2021. The MA TESOL program provides not only theoretical learning, but also offers opportunities to practice ESL teaching in an authentic environment under the supervision of faculty members. Following their graduation, they returned to China within three months. By the time of the interviews, the participants had been employed in China for a period spanning two months and seven years.

The majority of the participants are currently engaged in the language education sector in China. Their work experience spans across four main educational settings: private educational companies, universities (including both private and public universities in China, as well as global campuses of international universities in China), international K-12 schools, and public schools. Table 10.1 details the types of jobs each participant has held since graduation.

The initial jobs the participants secured were often constrained by the misalignment between their graduation time and the hiring cycle of teaching positions. Most formal educational institutions started recruitment process in the preceding fall semester, but the majority of international graduates only began their job applications after returning to China in the late summer. Two participants (PE and PL) were proactive and started job applications early in spring semester but soon realized *'it was already too late'*. As a result, most of them took on available positions but continued to search for opportunities that better aligned with their aspirations. Three participants switched jobs multiple times, and three more recent graduates (PB, PC and PG), although in their first jobs, are eager to explore other opportunities.

Three participants veered away from the language teaching profession. PA explored roles in language teaching and administration, before choosing to pursue a PhD in a different discipline in China. PI, following an unpleasant experience teaching English in a public university in China, chose to be a cartoonist. PJ quickly opted for a career in international business upon her return to China owing to personal considerations.

Table 10.1 Participants and job types

ID	Year of graduation	Private educational companies	Universities	International schools	Public schools	Others
PA	2015	X				X
PB	2021	X				
PC	2020	X				
PD	2017			X		
PE	2021		X			
PF	2014	X		X		X
PG	2021	X				
PI	2015	X	X			X
PJ	2017					X
PK	2020		X			
PL	2020				X	

Findings

Upon analyzing the interview transcripts, several themes emerged regarding the experience of the TESOL returnees in China. Regardless of the institutional types, subjects taught and student age groups, the returnees encountered challenges in implementing the pedagogy in their Chinese classrooms. They also grapple with the tensions with school administrators, students and parents, and peer teachers. The disparity between their educational beliefs and the prevailing educational contexts in China further induced moral distress, as they often had to compromise their teaching ideals to meet the requirements.

External tensions

In this study, external struggles arise from their working contexts in China. These challenges encompass factors such as students' English proficiency, motivation, learning approach, assessments methods, administrative structure within the institutions. These contextual disparities create tensions for the returnee teachers as they strive to effectively apply the theories, pedagogies and experience gained through their MA TESOL studies to their teaching role in China. The analysis reveals that the tensions stem from multiple stakeholders, including school administrators, colleagues, students and their parents.

Administration

One of the major external challenges originated from school administrators. All participants gained teaching experience in their MA TESOL program through a practicum course where they taught English to adult ESL learners in the US. However, when attempting to replicate a similar environment in China, the first hurdle they encounter is often the resistance from school administration. This challenge is pervasive across different educational institutions: public schools, universities and private educational companies.

Working in a private educational company, participant PB teaches an intensive program designed to prepare students for TOEFL, where students complete 30- or 45-day courses with the goal of improving TOEFL scores by 10–20 points. PB was particularly enthusiastic about teaching TOEFL speaking because she envisioned it as an immersive and interactive class where both students and the teacher will exclusively use English to communicate. She believes that language is learned through meaningful communication. However, in her school, teachers are directed to use Chinese as the language of instruction owing to perceived efficiency, as mandated by the administrators.

> In our EFL classes, they require us to use L1. I originally planned to give students more language exposure, like I speak English, and students

speak English too, but I found the teaching is very stereotypical. I argued with my supervisor, but it's useless...

All lesson plans need to be approved by the supervisor before implementation. PB's supervisor, a more experienced teacher, made significant revisions to her lesson plans, including the removal of all group discussions. The schools' instructional format is highly standardized. For instance, in a speaking class, the teacher 'explains the templates for a TOEFL speaking question type, provides a prompt for students to practice, corrects student's pronunciation and grammatical errors, and then repeats the process', as described by PB.

PI echoed PB's experience. Similarly, she was very enthusiastic in adopting a student-centered approach in her class when she taught college English in a public university in China. In her opinion, unlike high school students facing the cruel college entrance competition, college students should broaden their view about the language and its culture. She tailored her lesson plan by integrating external materials, rather than relying on the designated textbook. However, in the second semester, when the dean observed her class, it became a turning point in her career:

The main article in the textbook for that week was about (Stephen) Hawking, so I played a video clip from the Big Bang theory, and led students to analyze the use of phrases in the video. Since it's also related to the content, we had some class discussion around it. But the dean, I don't know why, I totally didn't anticipate it but he reacted so strongly and was extremely angry. He questioned me: why do you teach these irrelevant things? You don't teach what's in the textbook but adding these nonsense?... I had an argument with him in the lounge. I think the dean's view was too narrow... We held different philosophies but he wouldn't allow me to teach in my way.. Then I quit. This is the primary reason.

Although participants agree that English teachers with international background are generally welcomed in educational institutions (PB, PK), their expertise and perspectives on education and pedagogy tend to take a backseat to seniority within the school. Administrators in Chinese schools are constrained by their specific institutional goals, the criteria by which their education quality is evaluated and the vision of English education by the senior administration. When conflicts in pedagogies arise, the participants feel not prepared to negotiate the differences with higher ranked administrators, but instead express a sense of powerlessness.

Colleagues

While international returnees are generally more favored by private educational companies, participants who work in formal educational settings in this study frequently felt a sense of isolation, owing to lack of colleagues with similar overseas background. They found an international qualification is potentially disadvantaged in applying jobs in public schools and universities in China. PE and PL both highlight a preference for teachers trained from renowned Chinese normal universities when hiring:

> If you graduated from a top normal university, like Beijing Normal University in China, that would be better than international returnees. The teaching sector particularly prefers graduates of normal universities. (PE)

> Domestic graduates from normal universities in China already knew how to teach in Chinese schools. If they have good English pronunciation, they can easily stand out (PL).

On the other hand, TESOL returnees occasionally felt an unspoken tension from their domestically educated colleagues. With the test scores serving as the sole metric for evaluating student outcomes, the participants who adopt Western pedagogy may feel less confident in its effectiveness within the Chinese framework. PL recounted:

> I observed that my colleagues who were raised and educated in China are very accustomed to the test-oriented teaching…if I do not follow (their teaching mode), it may adversely affect my students' academic performance. And if my class doesn't perform well in exams, it absolutely will have impacts on my future professional advancements.

Although many participants initially envisioned the international TESOL qualifications as a significant leverage in the Chinese job market, the reality proved differently. Domestic credentials especially from top-tier institutions in China showed strong alignment with the needs and ethos of Chinese public school settings. Consequently, the under-represented TESOL returnees felt pressured to adapt their teaching style to align with the prevailing educational norms of the majority.

Students and/or parents

At the same time, participants encountered resistance from students about teaching practices deviating from traditional Chinese pedagogy. Participants found the methods effective for instructing immigrants or ESL speakers in the US differed considerably from those suitable for Chinese adolescent students. The MA TESOL program, which participants underwent, primarily focused on adult non-native speakers in English-speaking countries. These ESL students, influenced by their environment, tend to be more motivated to learn English and have ample opportunities to practice English in daily life. In contrast, Chinese students have limited exposure to authentic English and often lack intrinsic motivation to use the language. Additionally, they are affected by the intense educational environment that prioritizes rigorous English test preparation over interactive learning.

PC found her students in China are disinterested in communicating in English owing to their pressing needs to excel in the written exams, which shapes their language learning objectives. For many of her Chinese students, English is merely a subject that they need to achieve better grades. PC commented:

> I feel that only a very very small portion (of the knowledge I gained in the US) can be integrated into my classes because the classroom is totally different from the one that we did in practicum (in the US). The things we learned are suitable for teaching ESL speakers in the US, but it's different in China. Students need to take tests and score higher. I really try to implement what I learned but it's very limited.

Similarly, PB faced passive resistance from students who expected a more teacher-centered classroom. Accustomed to the setting where teachers serve as the source of knowledge, her students showed reluctance to engage. PB noted:

> The gap between ideal and reality is quite big… I feel it's hard to change the way to teach. In class discussion, for example, it's just impossible to get students to talk. Students always want the teacher to talk.

PL also experimented with interactive approaches in her high school English classes but students were reserved in participation. To ensure class efficiency, especially facing the pressure to prepare students for the college entrance exam, PL felt compelled to revert to more teacher-centered instructions. She explained:

> (my students) struggle with the interactive activities, and (activities) makes the class even less efficient, so you have to adjust your pedagogies, and use the more conventional approaches in China to teach.

It is further complicated with the large class size and the variance in students' English proficiency. PK highlighted that teaching advanced concepts to students with weak English foundations is inherently challenging and results in frustration for both teachers and students.

> The difficult part is some of my students' English level is very low. Some students only scored 20–30 points [out of 150 points] in the English exam for college entrance. For this group of students, you have to repeat the simplest things in class, but this makes it difficult for teaching college-level English, especially in a large class.

While parents normally do not interfere with specific class activities, they sometimes indirectly steer teachers toward exam-focus instruction. Most participants have not had an issue with the parents in terms of what and how they teach, but PC felt the weight of parents' expectations, especially while working in a private educational company. Paying a high tuition, parents are particularly keen on seeing quick improvements in their child's test performance. If students' grades are not improved significantly through an intensive program, the teacher may lose the students which could consequently impact their earnings. PC explained:

> Because the tuition is very expensive, parents wouldn't let you spend a lot of time teaching 'unimportant' things. They just want you to improve (the child's) scores so they can apply to a better school overseas. The parents can't talk to teachers directly here, but they will complain to the sales team, then the sales team will give me a little pressure, asking me to help the students achieve better scores.

The shared experiences illustrate the challenges TESOL returnees face when they attempt to introduce their US-based TESOL experience to the educational ecosystem in China. Despite the extensive learning and training in the US, participants experienced a reverse cultural shock in education upon returning to teach in their home country. The TESOL returnees' belief about English teaching has been significantly reconstructed by the US-centric, student-center and English-delivered TESOL paradigm. They viewed the US TESOL education as 'contemporary' contrasted the 'traditional' Chinese teaching, and developed a binary view of language teaching that is either progressive Western style, or conventional Chinese approach, while they struggle to find the middle ground. The TESOL programs, designed with typical Western ESL learners in mind, do not equip these international TESOL graduates for educational environments outside the US. When confronted with a different educational system, the returnees accentuated in the interviews that *'this is not what we learned in the US'*, suggesting that negotiating educational differences and teaching practices across cultures is a crucial aspect missing from international TESOL education.

Moral distress

The feeling of lack of control and lack of voice within their professional environment led to heightened moral distress for the participants. Teaching is fundamentally a moral activity (Thumvichit, 2023). Teachers face moral distress when they find themselves compromising or forgoing personal values amidst conflicting values (Glasberg *et al.*, 2016; Thumvichit, 2023). Studying in the US has profoundly transformed the participants' perspectives on language education. However, their evolving beliefs are so discordant with the entrenched educational practices and ideology in Chinese schools and the broader society, that several of them have shared their frustration about not being able to make positive and meaningful contributions to reforming Chinese education. Caught between the two disparate educational paradigms without adequate support from either, participants' sense of powerlessness intensifies their moral distress.

During the interviews, numerous participants underscored the critical role of fostering critical thinking through education. They call for English instruction that goes beyond test preparation, advocating communication and cultural exploration and developing world citizenship through language learning. Yet, the systemic constraints imposed on both the form and content of teaching stymied their efforts to find a mid-ground. Working in a public high school, PL articulated her internal battle:

> I think the biggest change for me is that I have seen a bigger world, experienced education outside China...they have more freedom, and emphasize more on learning motivation, so my teaching philosophy is more inclined to promote students' independent learning... I feel very frustrated to see my students' suffering and exhaustion (from rote learning), so, I am in a constant struggle.

While some participants try to find a balance between the western instructional techniques and the Chinese context in their job, some participants are seeking environments more in tune with their educational beliefs. PC, grappling with moral quandaries at a private education company, is actively exploring opportunities to work in an international school:

> I've been really down for months. I feel I've hit the valley of my life, because I really don't know, I don't know my job. I don't know how to teach... I'm not even familiar with TOEFL testing skills, and what we learned at graduate school was not about getting students to achieve higher scores...I think international schools should have a better environment, because they use American or British curricula, so I think they will prioritize a well-around development of their students. That environment probably is more suitable for me. I still expect that the knowledge I learned in the US can support students' personal growth somewhere, not only prepare them as a test-taking machine.

Through their narratives, the participants' emerging educational philosophy contributed to their sense of alienation from the Chinese educational context that they were once familiar with. The returnee teachers encounter moral dilemmas when balancing general practices and their personal beliefs in education. These conflicts encompass their empathy for students, compliance with school standards and navigating broader cultural expectations. The tension is exacerbated by uncertainties about career progression impacted by their students' test performance, and the challenge of balancing their professional integrity with the educational norms in China. Through their experience, there is a notable absence of preparation and support for international returnees to navigate and alleviate their moral distress in real-world teaching contexts outside the US.

Discussion and Implications

This qualitative case study represents an initial effort to explore the cross-cultural teaching experience of Master's TESOL holders who transitioned back to China to teach. The analysis of their early career experience provides a nuanced and comprehensive understanding of the barriers for them to translate West-based pedagogical practices to language classrooms in China. The findings suggested several implications for international TESOL programs.

First, the current TESOL curricula centering around US EFL classrooms lack adaptability in non-Western settings. There is a clear disconnect between West-based pedagogies and the actual teaching contexts in countries like China, characterized by distinct educational ecosystems, cultural contexts and learning objectives. The contextual differences underscore the necessity for global-minded TESOL programs that transcend an Anglo-centric perspective and embrace transnational teaching contexts.

Second, there is an evident lack of foresight in US TESOL programs about the practical challenges TESOL educators face when undertaking different teaching approaches in other countries. This oversight leads to a dearth of professional development opportunities tailored for practical realities outside the US. After the initial conflicts in teaching, the TESOL returnees often grapple with the resistance from different stakeholders and find themselves inadequately supported. These are partially attributed to the blindness of US TESOL programs, ignoring the contextual differences of international career pathways and administrative constructions outside the US. I argue here for the importance of being critically aware of international TESOL students' practical career trajectories and barriers, collaborating with global TESOL stakeholders to provide an alternative lens for examining effective English teaching, and integrate the lived experience of TESOL returnees to truly prepare students for diverse teaching landscapes.

Additionally, international returnees often find themselves unsupported after graduation. The lack of resources and validation leads to moral distress and jeopardizes their career advancement. A robust support system tailored to the needs of international TESOL alumni is imperative for their long-term success beyond graduation.

Conclusion

Despite repeated calls for internationalized curricula, ethnocentrism persistently plagues TESOL programs in the US and impairs effective and adequate training for teaching English in global contexts (Nguyen, 2017; Singh & Richards, 2006; Stapleton & Shao, 2018). Furthermore, there is very little evidence documenting the career experience of international TESOL graduates who leave the host country after graduation.

Drawing on the narratives of eleven international TESOL returnees' early career experience, this study contributes to filling the gap by documenting the international TESOL returnees' employment experience in China. In addition, this chapter contributes to TESOL research by calling for a comparative approach to look at TESOL curricula and research within the local teaching contexts. Language teaching is a complex system that we need to foreground it in a broader dynamic global context and prepare TESOL graduates to teach beyond the US.

In addition to its research implications, this chapter provides implications for stakeholders such as administrators and policymakers about the TESOL program design. This study underscores that negotiating educational differences and teaching practices across cultures is a necessary component of an international TESOL program. It illuminates the imperative for TESOL programs to better understand the contextual complexity in which their graduates will teach, and reconceptualize international TESOL and understand English teaching in different linguistic and cultural contexts.

In the end, as American universities are increasingly held accountable for students' employment outcomes, this study also calls for more outreach and career support to international graduates who leave the hosting country for employment. It is critical for American higher education to reflect on the quality of international education and how to better support international graduates to succeed in a global context. This study responds to the urgency for US TESOL programs to commit to more multicultural-minded curricula and robust infrastructure to support international students' postgraduate transition into the global workforce and their long-term success.

References

British Council (2013) The English effect. https://www.britishcouncil.org/research-insight/english-effect

Canagarajah, S. (2016) TESOL as a professional community: A half-century of pedagogy, research, and theory. *TESOL Quarterly* 50 (1), 7–41. https://doi.org/10.1002/tesq.275

Chang, H. (2021) Telling China's stories well in college English courses: Current situations, pathways, and methods. *Technology Enhanced Foreign Language Education* 5, 96–114.

Chinese Ministry of Education (2001) 教育部关于积极推进小学开设英语课程的指导意见 [Ministry of Education's Guideline for actively pushing English courses in elementary schools].

Chowdhury, R. (2003) International TESOL training and EFL contexts: The cultural disillusionment factor. *Australian Journal of Education* 47 (3), 283–302.

Chowdhury, R. and Phan, L.H. (2008) Reflecting on Western TESOL training and communicative language teaching: Bangladeshi teachers' voices. *Asia Pacific Journal of Education* 28 (3), 305–316. https://doi.org/10.1080/02188790802236006

Cowan, J.M. (1965) Opportunities for service in programs sponsored by nongovernment institutions. In *On Teaching English to Speakers of Other Languages. Series II* (pp. 9–13). Routledge.

Croft, K. (1970) *TESOL, 1967–1968: A Survey*. Washington, DC.

Govardhan, A.K., Nayar, B. and Sheorey, R. (1999) Do U.S. MATESOL programs prepare students to teach abroad? *TESOL Quarterly* 33 (1), 114. https://doi.org/10.2307/3588194

Gray, P.X. (1997) The formation and development of TESOL: A brief history. *International Education* 27 (1), 71.

Hao, J., Wen, W. and Welch, A. (2016) When sojourners return: Employment opportunities and challenges facing high-skilled Chinese returnees. *Asian and Pacific Migration Journal* 25 (1), 22–40. https://doi.org/10.1177/0117196815621806

Hsu, F. (2017) Resisting the coloniality of English: A research review of strategies. *CA TESOL Journal* 29 (1), 111–132.

Huang, Q., Cheung, A.C.K. and Xuan, Q. (2023) The impact of study abroad on preservice and in-service teachers' intercultural competence: A meta-analysis. *Teaching and Teacher Education* 127, 104091. https://doi.org/10.1016/j.tate.2023.104091

Ilieva, R., Li, A. and Li, W. (2015) Negotiating TESOL discourses and EFL teaching contexts in China: Identities and practices of international graduates of a TESOL program. *Comparative and International Education* 44 (2), 1–15. https://doi.org/10.5206/cie-eci.v44i2.9274

Jing, X., Ghosh, R., Sun, Z. and Liu, Q. (2020) Mapping global research related to international students: A scientometric review. *Higher Education,* 415–433. https://doi.org/10.1007/s10734-019-00489-y

Knight, J. (2008) *Higher Education in Turmoil: The Changing World of Internationalization.* Sense Publisher.

Lam, A.S.L. (2008) Language education policy in Greater China. *Encyclopedia of Language and Education* 1, 405–417. https://doi.org/10.1007/978-0-387-30424-3_30

Li, H. (2020) Changing status, entrenched inequality: How English language becomes a Chinese form of cultural capital. *Educational Philosophy and Theory* 52 (12), 1302–1313. https://doi.org/10.1080/00131857.2020.1738922

Liu, D. (1998) Ethnocentrism in TESOL: Teacher education and the neglected needs of international TESOL students. *ELT Journal* 52 (1), 3–10. https://doi.org/10.1093/elt/52.1.3

Luo, J. and Forbes, K. (2019) 'It's a plus rather than a must': Perspectives of mainstream teachers in China on the influence of advertised educational ethos in supplementary English education. *Compare* (1), 1–40. https://doi.org/10.1080/03057925.2019.1681937

Maxwell, J.A. (2013) *Qualitative Research Design: An interactive* approach (3rd edn). SAGE Publications.

Mikesell, D. (2021) The 'double reduction' crackdown and the future of private education in China. *The China Guys.* https://thechinaguys.com/china-double-reduction-policy-private-education-tutoring-crackdown/

Nguyen, M. (2017) *TESOL Teacher Education in a Globalised World: The Case of Vietnamese Teachers of English Author.* Griffith University, Queensland, Australia.

Pakir, A. (1999) Connecting with English in the context of internationalisation. *TESOL Quarterly* 33 (1), 103–114.

Pan, L. (2015) *English as a Global Language in China: Deconstructing the Ideological Discourses of English in Language Education.* Springer.

Phyak, P. and De Costa, P.I. (2021) Decolonial struggles in indigenous language education in neoliberal times: Identities, ideologies, and activism. *Journal of Language, Identity and Education* 20 (5), 291–295.

Punteney, K. (2019) *The International Education Handbook: Principles and Practices of the Field.* Association of International Educators.

R'boul, H. and Belhiah, H. (2023) Neo-nationalism and politicizing TESOL: Nationalist rhetoric and decolonial impulses in English teaching in Morocco. *TESOL Quarterly* 57 (3), 804–829. https://doi.org/10.1002/tesq.3230

Rubdy, R. (2015) Unequal Englishes, the native speaker, and decolonization in TESOL. In R. Tupas (ed.) *Unequal Englishes: The Politics of Englishes Today* (pp. 42–58). Macmillan.

Russell, T.W. (1965) Opportunities for service offered by government agencies. In *On Teaching English to Speakers of Other Languages. Series II.* Routledge.

Singh, G. and Richards, J.C. (2006) Teaching and learning in the language teacher education course room: A critical sociocultural perspective. *RELC Journal* 37 (2), 149–175. https://doi.org/10.1177/0033688206067426

Slaughter, S. and Rhoades, G. (eds) (2004) *Academic Capitalism and the New Economy*. The Johns Hopkins University Press.

Sperber, A.D. (2004) Translation and validation of study instruments for cross-cultural research. *Gastroenterology* 126 (1), 124–128. https://doi.org/10.1053/j.gastro.2003.10.016

Stake, R.E. (1995) *The Art of Case Study Research*. Sage.

Stapleton, P. and Shao, Q. (2018) A worldwide survey of MATESOL programs in 2014: Patterns and perspectives. *Language Teaching Research* 22 (1), 10–28. https://doi.org/10.1177/1362168816659681

Suzuki, A. (2021) Changing views of English through study abroad as teacher training. *ELT Journal* 75 (4), 397–406.

TESOL (2020) The TESOL directory of degree and certificate programs. https://www.tesol.org/enhance-your-career/career-development/beginning-your-career/finding-teacher-education-programs-in-tesol

Thumvichit, A. (2023) 'I'm aware of that, but…': Breaking the silence on moral distress among language teachers. *Language, Culture and Curriculum* 36 (3), 343–360.

Tupas, R. (2015) *Unequal Englishes: The Politics of Englishes Today*. Macmillan.

U.S. Department of Homeland Security. (2018) Persons Obtaining Lawful Permanent Resident Status: Fiscal Years 1820 to 2017. https://www.dhs.gov/immigration-statistics/yearbook/2017/table1

Vecchio, D.C. (2013) U.S. immigration laws and policies, 1870–1980. In E.R. Barkan (eds) *Immigrants in American History: Arrival, Adaptation and Integration* (pp. 1485–1502). ABC-CLIO.

Wang, D. (2014) Effects of study abroad on teachers' self-perceptions: A study of Chinese EFL teachers. *Journal of Language Teaching and Research* 5 (1), 70–79. https://doi.org/10.4304/jltr.5.1.70-79

Wang, S. (2022) The transnational in-between identity of Chinese student returnees from the UK: Mobility, variations and pathways. *British Educational Research Journal* 48 (3), 536–555.

Xinhua Press. (2013) National Conference on Propaganda and Ideological Work. https://www.gov.cn/ldhd/2013-08/20/content_2470599.htm

Zhang, C. (2015) How to tell China stories: On the translation of Chinese literature in a globalized world. *Foreign Language Learning Theory and Practice* 1 (4).

Zhang, Y. (2022) A review of the problems and the solutions in middle school oral English teaching in China. 2021 *International Conference on Education, Language and Art (ICELA 2021)*. Atlantis Press.

Zhao, Y. and Mantero, M. (2018) The influence of study-abroad experiences on Chinese college EFL teacher's identity. *Indonesian Journal of English Language Teaching and Applied Linguistics* 3 (1), 53–77.

11 Japanese Pre-Service English Teachers' Reflections on Study Abroad Experiences: Developing Intercultural Competence through ELF Awareness

Ayako Suzuki

Study abroad (SA) has become a recommended practice for English language teachers in many countries, including Japan, and has begun to be incorporated into university teacher training curricula. Although SA is widely perceived to enhance English language proficiency and intercultural competence, research has shown that without educational support to cultivate awareness of English as a lingua franca (ELF), SA participants may not be able to achieve these developments. This is because the lack of ELF awareness may challenge them in fully engaging in intercultural interactions, which are essentially multilingual and multicultural. The present study focuses on 10 Japanese pre-service English teachers who had the opportunity to develop ELF awareness before and after their long-term SA and explores their perceptions and evaluations of the significance of multilingual and multicultural experiences during SA through semi-structured reflective interviews conducted eight months after the completion of their SA. The findings revealed that those with developed ELF awareness were able to see their intercultural competence positively and locate their local ELT within the wider context of global English language use. Based on these findings, the study highlights the importance of integrating pre- and post-SA educational interventions to develop ELF awareness into teacher training curricula.

Introduction

Study abroad (SA) is increasingly seen as an attractive approach to cultivating competent English teachers in contemporary societies where English serves as an lingua franca (ELF) in various domains such as business, study and entertainment. SA in Anglophone countries is believed to provide immersive environments that enable teachers to practise the language with international peers and develop both solid knowledge of the language and intercultural competence to work with others. Research reports that SA positively contributes to participants' development in many areas including the target language proficiency, intercultural competence, teaching and management skills, cultural and political awareness, critical thinking and professional identity (Baecher, 2021; Barkhuizen, 2022; Morley *et al.*, 2019; Zhang & Wang, 2022). Consequently, many governments, particularly in East Asia where English has a limited role in the local society, see SA as an effective option for professional development and send their teachers overseas. For example, thousands of Chinese teachers have been sent to English-speaking countries, such as the USA, the UK and Canada, in recent decades (Wang *et al.*, 2019). Likewise, Taiwan (Chern *et al.*, 2022) and Hong Kong (Chan & Jackson, 2022) have organised SA programmes for both pre-service and in-service English teachers in Anglophone countries. Japan, the focus of this chapter, also values SA (Suzuki, 2021) and plans to send teachers overseas.

However, simply sending teachers to Anglophone settings does not ensure their development, as various factors, including the type of SA programme and participants' personalities, affect outcomes (Jackson, 2020). Another important factor to consider is teachers' awareness of the use of ELF in SA settings. Despite the widespread image of SA as a monolingual immersion experience, the reality of SA is often multilingual and multicultural (Diao & Trentman, 2021). Given the extensive role of English as an international lingua franca, Anglophone countries typically attract a diverse student population from around the world (OECD, 2022: 22). These students are often multilingual users, whose use of English may differ from that of native English speakers (NESs) in the host country. A lack of awareness of this reality can lead teachers to miss valuable opportunities for intercultural learning from and with their diverse peers (Baker & Fang, 2019; Boonsuk & Fang, 2021; Suzuki, 2021). It may also influence their interpretation of their international experience and its application in their future careers (Jackson & Oguro, 2018). Therefore, teachers' awareness of ELF can be a key to their professional development. However, it remains unclear whether this is actually the case. This chapter aims to explore how pre-service Japanese English teachers, who had the opportunity to develop their ELF awareness before and after SA, made sense of and evaluated the significance of their multilingual and multicultural experiences during SA, and how this awareness can enhance their teacher development.

Japanese English Teachers with SA Experience

To contextualise the present study, this section describes the situations surrounding SA among Japanese English teachers. At present, the number of Japanese English teachers with overseas experience is limited. A survey conducted by the Ministry of Education, Culture, Sports, Science and Technology (MEXT) in 2016[1] revealed that although more than 50% of the approximately 53,000 secondary school English teachers have undertaken SA, the majority have stayed for less than one month (Suzuki, 2021). Various factors contribute to this trend, including limited English proficiency, fear of living in a foreign country and financial constraints owing to the weak Japanese yen currency (Aspinall, 2013). Additionally, few degree programmes require language majors to spend a certain amount of time abroad to develop proficiency in the target L2 language. This limited exposure to international experience has led to the observation that Japanese English teachers often lack cultural knowledge and confidence in using English (Asaoka, 2019: 13).

Furthermore, it is widely argued that the country's teacher certification system discourages teacher candidates from pursuing long-term SA. The current system requires candidates to complete a minimum of 59 credits, including 27 credits of general education-related modules, 20 credits of subject-related modules, seven credits of pedagogical practice modules and four other credits, while completing a four-year bachelor's degree at an accredited university. Attending one class a week for 90–100 minutes over 14–15 weeks yields two credits, so it takes at least three semesters, or one and a half years, to fulfil all the mandatory modules. As a result, many universities advise their students that they may need more than four years to complete the bachelor's degree, obtain the certificate and participate in the long-term SA.

The Japanese government is well aware of this situation, which led to the issue of the new education plan in April 2023, entitled 'J-MIRAI: Japan-Mobility and Internationalisation: Re-engaging and Accelerating Initiative for future generations'.[2] The plan promises to increase the number of people participating in SA to 500,000 over the next decade, with a particular focus on English teachers. According to the proposal, sending both pre-service and in-service teachers overseas will enrich ELT and international understanding education in primary and secondary schools, and foster problem-solving skills in future students. This initiative is expected to reinforce the integration of SA into the four-year bachelor's degree curriculum. However, according to the author's research on the websites of accredited universities in Tokyo, as of September 2023, the integration remains limited, with only six out of 58 universities in Tokyo offering an embedded SA programme within their English teacher training courses. In this context, English teachers with SA experience are likely to be highly valued for their presumed advanced level of English proficiency and intercultural competence.

ELF Awareness for English Teachers

While teachers with SA experience are generally highly regarded, SA does not always guarantee their linguistic and intercultural advancement, as ELF awareness could potentially influence their SA outcomes. Sifakis (2019) outlines three key components of ELF awareness for teachers: awareness of language and language use, instructional practice and learning. The first component indicates teachers' knowledge of the differences between ELF and native English, along with the underlying reasons for these differences. The second is understanding of their own teaching practices, including their understanding of students' needs and the potential impact of local educational constraints on teaching practices and objectives. The last one concerns the awareness of how the use of ELF affects the learning process. At present, the ELF awareness among Japanese in-service and pre-service teachers may not be high owing to their training, which may subscribe to native-speakerism (Holliday, 2006). The national curriculum, or *the Course of Study* (MEXT 2017/18[3]), which is used as a guide for teaching by secondary school teachers, implicitly advocates a NES as the standard user, despite recognising that students' future use of English is more likely to be ELF (Naka, 2018; Suzuki, 2020).

However, signs of a shift away from this kind of ELT can be seen in the revised teacher training curriculum introduced in 2019: it now requires all teacher candidates 'to acquire a basic knowledge of the historical development of the English language in terms of speaking, writing, vocabulary and grammar, and to understand the reality of English as a global common language in the English-speaking world and throughout the world' (Tokyo Gakugei University, 2017: 114, author's translation). Although how much and what they learn is up to each university's decision, this change might have a positive impact on teachers.

Several studies suggest that SA itself may serve to increase teachers' ELF awareness. For example, Wang's (2014) study of 91 Chinese secondary EFL teachers revealed that SA in the UK led to increased confidence as competent users of English and greater acceptance of the linguistic and functional diversity of English, although the outcomes appeared to vary according to the length of SA. A longitudinal in-depth interview study by Mayumi and Hüttner (2020) of four in-service Japanese English teachers studying in the UK also highlighted that their multilingual and multicultural SA experiences challenged their beliefs about standard native English. They became more open and flexible and showed a preference for prioritising their students' communicative capability rather than achieving native-like proficiency in the classroom. For teachers in EFL contexts, SA can be an invaluable opportunity to reflect on and recast their conceptualisation of English as a teaching subject.

In contrast, the author's previous study of Japanese pre-service teachers showed more complicated outcomes (Suzuki, 2021): while the teachers displayed increased acceptance of diverse use of English through intensive interaction with international peers, they still perceived ELF communication as substandard. Suzuki suggested that it is desirable for teachers to acquire knowledge of multilingual English communication before undertaking SA. Moreover, other studies focusing on ELF and SA students from Asia (Baker & Fang, 2019; Baker *et al.*, 2022; Boonsuk & Fang, 2021; Ra *et al.*, 2022) also highlighted the importance of pre-departure preparation for ELF communication, although the participants were not necessarily English teachers. These studies found that SA participants often struggled to adequately assess their own English language skills owing to their idealised images of English speakers. Additionally, inadequate knowledge of different uses of English hindered their intercultural communication. Consequently, the studies emphasised the need to provide students with opportunities to develop awareness of English diversity before arrival to facilitate intercultural engagement.

The importance of pre-departure interventions has been discussed in many studies (for a comprehensive overview, see Goldstein, 2022; Jackson, 2020). Hanada's (2019) quantitative research on 303 Japanese SA students in North America examined the development of intercultural competence and found that participation in pre-departure preparation orientations exhibited the most significant association with the development compared to seven other variables, such as prior international experience, prior English proficiency, SA duration and type of stay. Pre-departure interventions may be crucial as they would facilitate students' adjustment to new environments, leading to more immersive experiences.

Although much less discussed, the value of post-sojourn interventions is recognised (Goldstein, 2022; Jackson, 2020). It is argued that educational support is needed to help sojourners articulate the knowledge they have gained from their time abroad (Thomas & Kerstetter, 2020). For example, as sojourners' understanding of intercultural experiences may remain superficial, it is important to encourage reflection to interpret how apparent cultural dissonance relates to implicit cultural values and norms. Zhang and Wang (2022) argued for the importance of a post-SA intervention in terms of the professional identity of Chinese English teachers. They insisted that even if international experience enhances their pedagogical knowledge and skills, positive changes will not occur naturally because teachers have to navigate various local teaching constraints in their home country. Therefore, embedding support mechanisms in their training curriculum appears to be essential.

In sum, it is crucial to provide opportunities for the development of ELF awareness and reflective practice before and after SA to foster interculturally sensitive teachers. Without this preparation, their experiences may simply be filed away as a lifelong memory (Jackson, 2020). With this in mind, the current study seeks to answer the following questions:

- How did pre-service Japanese English teachers, who had the opportunity to develop ELF awareness before and after SA, evaluate the significance of their multilingual and multicultural experiences during SA?
- In what ways did their ELF awareness contribute to their professional development?

The Present Study

The present study focused on exploring the perceptions of 10 Japanese pre-service English teachers (Table 11.1) who received support to develop their ELF awareness before and after their long-term SA. These teachers were undergraduate students at a university in Tokyo, which is one of the only six universities in the city that integrates long-term SA into its teacher training curriculum.

Pre-service teachers and long-term SA

The 10 teachers in the current study participated in the curriculum-integrated SA in the USA, the UK or Ireland from January to May/June 2022. The SA was organised with four main objectives: (1) to acquire language skills in English as a lingua franca, (2) to deepen understanding of the global reality and diversity of English, (3) to develop the ability to manage diverse values with a profound grasp of linguistic and cultural diversity and problem-solving skills and (4) to cultivate their identity as cosmopolitans. Teachers were also expected to learn about different ways of learning and teaching English to those at their home country and to apply the knowledge and skills they developed to their future profession.

Table 11.1 List of informants

No.	Informant (Pseudonyms)	Gender	Host university	Type of SA programme	Interview mode	
1.	Shizuka	F	USA A	Language + School Internship	face-to-face	(with Hikaru)
2.	Reiji	M				
3.	Izumi	F				
4.	Yoichi	M				
5.	Kohei	M	UK A	Language	Online	
6.	Taiki	M	Ireland A	Language + Special TEFL Module	face-to-face	(with Shizuka)
7.	Hikaru	M				
8.	Sayuri	F				
9.	Takemasa	M				
10.	Takashi	M	Ireland B	Language	Online	

The primary focus during the SA was English language learning, although some teachers also had the opportunity to take part in a school internship at local institutions or to learn in a specially designed sheltered TEFL module. About their SA, it should be noted that their sojourn was supposed to last nine months, starting in the summer of 2021, but was shortened by four months owing to the situation of the COVID-19 pandemic. During the four months of delay, they attended online courses offered by the host universities.

Ways of raising ELF awareness before and after SA

The opportunity for the pre-service teachers to raise their ELF awareness was also curriculum-integrated. Prior to SA, the teachers were introduced to the diversity of English and multilingualism in two main ways. One was their English language learning programme called 'ELF program', which is designed primarily for Japanese students who are expected to use English as a common lingua franca with a variety of English users from different backgrounds (see Suzuki, 2020, for details of the programme). All students in this university are required to earn a certain number of credits in the programme, which primarily focuses on developing intercultural communication skills, rather than attaining native-like proficiency. Because of this aim, the programme itself embraces diversity. As of April 2023, the programme had about 40 instructors with 14 different L1s, including Chinese, Finnish, Korean, Tagalog and Thai. Therefore, students are aware that their English instructors may not necessarily be NESs or Japanese. The pre-service teachers in the present research studied on the programme twice a week for three semesters during their first and second years and completed 12 credits before SA.

The other was a pre-departure pedagogical intervention conducted by the author just before their SA. This consisted of four lectures as a part of a one-semester-long introductory module on English linguistics. The lectures aimed to broaden the students' perspectives of English by presenting examples of linguistic diversity and key academic arguments about the global use of English, such as native-speakerism in ELT, World Englishes, English as a Lingua Franca and intercultural communication in English (see Suzuki, 2023, for details). Throughout the intervention, students were encouraged to consider, for example, why their English programme employs instructors from diverse linguistic backgrounds.

The post-SA opportunity was the second pedagogical intervention, an intensive English linguistics module offered within a month of the pre-service teachers' return to Japan. This module consisted of 15 lessons over five weeks and was delivered by three lecturers, including the author. Its main objective was to enable the students to interpret their experiences abroad through a theoretical lens. They were tasked with reading academic papers on various topics related to the global use of English, such as language variation and change, language attitudes, English medium instruction, ELF communication, language testing and translanguaging. In the final week, students gave a group presentation analysing their experiences through these theoretical perspectives.

Although these were the main ways in which the teachers were supposed to have developed their ELF awareness, they were not necessarily the only ones. For example, they took another pre-departure module focusing on the practical aspects of SA and honing self-management skills. Also, some of the pre-service teachers had experience living in a foreign country or travelling abroad with their families before their SA. Therefore, it is crucial to view their comments presented below as a synthesis of all their intercultural experiences.

Data Collection and Analysis

The 10 pre-service teachers were invited to participate in a semi-structured interview in February/March 2023, eight months after completing their SA. They were selected as informants based on their prior participation in two questionnaires about their perspectives on English and English education during the pre- and post-SA interventions, but these datasets are not discussed in this chapter owing to the scope of the paper. The purpose of the present research was explained in the interview invitation, and all informants agreed to take part and provided the author with consent forms. Their details, including gender, host university, type of SA programme attended and mode of interview, are listed in Table 11.1. Interviews were conducted either face-to-face or online, depending on their preference. Most interviews were conducted one-on-one, while Shizuka and Hikaru requested a joint interview. Each interview, typically lasting an hour, addressed core questions about the informants' interpretations of their SA experience, focusing on English language learning, intercultural communication and personal and professional development. The interviews were conducted in their L1, Japanese, and were recorded with their permission. The audio recordings were transcribed and analysed using thematic analysis (Braun & Clarke, 2022). First, the transcribed interviews were read several times to gain a general understanding of each informant's meaning-making of their SA experience. Then, between 10 and 13 specific themes were identified in each interview, and they were compared across all interviews and synthesised into six overarching themes. For example, three aspects (i.e. performative, linguistic and sociolinguistic) of the influence of pedagogical interventions in intercultural communication initially emerged, but these were intricately intertwined in the teachers' talks and difficult to separate neatly. They were therefore grouped together in order not to miss any of the complexity. This will be discussed in the section 'ELF awareness enhancing interactions' below.

Findings

This section discusses the findings that emerged from the interviews according to the two themes – SA for broadening horizons and ELF awareness enhancing interactions.

SA for broadening horizons

The interview data showed that all informants valued SA as an opportunity for personal and professional growth. As the SA they participated in was an integral part of the curriculum, that is compulsory for all students, the author asked them to recall why they wanted to do SA in the first place. Although the exact words they used to answer this question were different, their reasons were relatively homogenous, stating that they wanted to broaden their horizons by meeting various people, as English is used by many people in the world. For example, Reiji and Taiki explained that they wanted to go outside Japan, which seemed like a closed country to them, to expand their world because they were going to teach English in the future. For Shizuka and Sayuri who described themselves as 'stubborn', SA was seen as a good way to change their characters and broaden their perspectives, which they felt was necessary for teachers. This can be seen in Sayuri's comment below:

> When you study abroad, you'll have opportunities to interact with people from many different countries, so I wanted to broaden my horizons. I had a tendency to be a bit stubborn, which is difficult to describe, and when I think something was right, I tended to go straight for it. When becoming a teacher, I have to deal with a variety of students, and I wanted to change that a little more. I wanted to learn to be more flexible, and I wanted to broaden my perspective. (Sayuri)

In a similar vein, Yoichi and Izumi, for whom becoming a teacher was a long-cherished future goal, had *akogare*, or a sentiment to pursue one's own dream (Nonaka, 2018), for SA because they heard various stories from those who had experienced SA and thought that it would enable them to have different perspectives from other teachers. For Kohei, Hikaru, Takemasa and Takashi, who did not necessarily have explicit motives for participating in SA, English was the main reason: if you are going to become an English teacher, you should gain experience in actually using it by going abroad to become fluent in it. Kohei, Takemasa and Takashi added another reason, that it was 'cool' to be able to speak English. For example, Takemasa stated, 'I thought it was not too much to say that almost everyone in the world could speak English, so I thought it was cool to be able to talk to anyone in the world'.

Although there were some differences in the pre-service teachers' motivations for SA, the interview data indicated that SA was largely viewed positively in their context. English was regarded as a language for facilitating communication with others from different parts of the world, leading to an expansion of horizons, which was seen as an important disposition for teachers.

ELF awareness enhancing interactions

The linguistic, personal and professional benefits of SA are frequently discussed, albeit often idealized (Kubota, 2016), so the common motivations discussed above may not be unusual. How, then, did these pre-service teachers, who were expected to have developed ELF awareness, perceive the significance of their own SA experiences, which were inherently multilingual and multicultural?

The most striking finding was that all the teachers were generally positive about their intercultural competence. When asked about their self-evaluation of intercultural competence, six out of the 10 informants described themselves as open-minded. For example, Takashi said that he always tried to make efforts to understand others because he knew that intercultural communication was not easy and went on to say, 'I think it was significant that we went [abroad] with that kind of mindset. … I feel like that was one of the things we learnt before studying abroad'. Another example is Izumi, who portrayed herself as 'a type of person who accepts other people as they are' and continued talking about her use of multilingual and multimodal resources for communication as follows:

> I can talk to Chinese friends quite easily. Like, if I don't understand something, I can look it up, and there are things like this, or they show me a sentence in Chinese, and I then tell them I don't understand it. And they also can tell me when they don't understand me. (Izumi)

Later in the interview, Izumi added that she had 'no feeling of guilt' about using other resources besides English for her intercultural communication. She attributed this to her understanding, gained during the pre-departure period, that such communication practices which prioritised intelligibility were not uncommon (see Suzuki, forthcoming). Most informants seemed to have a relatively strong willingness to communicate in the L2 (MacIntyre *et al.*, 1998), probably stemming from their acceptance of various forms of English as a matter of course. They stated that when they had international classmates whose English was difficult to understand, they tried to pair up with them during class activities to improve their comprehension skills, although they admitted that they sometimes did 'let it pass' (Firth, 1996) when they did not understand.

Three informants, Taiki, Reiji and Kohei, showed a strong interest in learning about ELF at the time of the interviews, which was inspired by their participation in the ELF community of practice (Kalocsai, 2014). Taiki, for instance, spent a lot of time in a group that was 'incredibly multinational' because it included international friends from Africa, Asia, Europe and the Middle East. The time with them was comfortable for him because other languages than English were spoken, and they always encouraged him to speak in his own English. This experience taught him that it was acceptable for him to be himself at all times.

Reiji talked about a similar experience to Taiki's in an international student society where some members, including himself, were 'like, I'm here to learn English'. He characterised the communication within the society as 'a model of global communication' because they respected others and each other, explaining:

> For me, global communication is, well, let's say, the communication between people who have multicultural backgrounds and backgrounds, no matter what language they speak. ... I don't think it's possible to completely close the cultural gap between the two, of course, but I think we both understand that, like 'the person was probably very considerate and said these things to me'. If something offensive is said, I might say it, but the other person will probably understand, so I think that's the way global communication should be. (Reiji)

Kohei also recounted his involvement in a linguistically diverse group. He admitted that, during his pre-departure learning, he kept believing that NESs' English was the best and coolest. However, his perspective 'completely changed' after enjoying supporting his favourite football team with his international stadium mates during SA (see Suzuki, forthcoming). He attributed this change to his realisation that 'people over there [in the UK] don't expect me to speak English like native speakers' and that what he had learnt about ELF before SA was actually true.

These three informants told the author that their intercultural experiences were in line with the concepts they had learnt during the post-SA intervention, which covered language attitudes, ELF communication and translanguaging. Consequently, they were interested in furthering their understanding of ELF. Similarly, other informants, including Yoichi, Hikaru and Sayuri, said that the post-SA intervention helped them to conceptualise their interactions with international peers. For example, Sayuri noted that her understanding of her international friends' English was enhanced by the knowledge of language distance and variations. Yoichi described that 'my study abroad taught me that making mistakes is OK, and your lectures [in the post-SA intervention] were about not necessary to speak perfectly' and thus the lectures 'neatly summarised [my experiences]'.

Their positive accounts of intercultural communication seemed to have influenced some of the informants' ideas about ELT. For example, Taiki stated that Japanese ELT should prioritise how to cooperate with different others, rather than focusing on language. Reiji criticised the current ELT in Japan for lacking international elements and needing an ELF perspective. Kohei expressed a desire to teach that communication in English 'can be more flexible' as he felt that the current ELT forced students to prioritise native-like proficiency. Some others, however, still seemed to be striving for perfection. Shizuka and Hikaru mentioned the need to improve their grammatical knowledge before starting a teaching job, stating that English teachers 'cannot make mistakes'. Sayuri wanted to make her English 'perfect', although she admitted that she would never reach the level of NESs. Takemasa, who said that being able to speak English was 'cool', believed that as a teacher he needed to 'be like knowing everything' about English and still wanted to be like a NES. In contrast to Taiki, Reiji and Kohei, linguistic knowledge appeared to be one of the most important qualities for English teachers.

Discussion and Conclusion

The findings of the current study highlight the importance of fostering ELF awareness among pre-service teachers embarking on SA. While teachers' expectations for SA were comparable to those of SA participants with limited awareness, their self-awareness of intercultural competence appeared to be positive. Their proactive engagement with multilingual English speakers and their acceptance of linguistic diversity demonstrate the potential of an ELF-informed perspective to reframe one's values of English.

The role of ELF awareness in shaping these pre-service teachers' intercultural experiences was evident, and this can be explored in terms of analytical and experiential knowledge. The pre-departure learning of ELF equipped the teachers with a robust framework for interpreting their multilingual encounters (cf. Suzuki, 2021), which fostered an open-minded approach and a willingness to engage in ELF communication (see Fang et al., 2020, for the relationship between global perspective and a willingness to communicate). This attitude allowed them to embrace different communicative resources and to prioritise intelligibility over a monolingual approach to communication.

The favourable self-evaluation of intercultural competence further emphasises the influence of ELF awareness, fostering an appreciation of global communication. Particularly, the post-SA intervention, which supported conscious reflection, turned their experiential knowledge into reflective knowledge, which plays a role in facilitating the teachers to clearly articulate and make sense of their experiences and enabled them to envision their future teaching practices in a global context (see Hagar, 2018).

A clear implication of the current study is the vital role of comprehensive pre- and post-SA support procedures within the teacher training curriculum. An ideal approach of this support is to prioritise the development of intercultural competence and promote a nuanced understanding of linguistic and cultural diversity. It is important to note that some teachers in this study had continued to strive for a 'perfect' knowledge of the

English language, even though our knowledge of languages, even our own mother tongue, is always 'truncated' (Blommaert, 2010: 23). In the case of L2, the scope of knowledge can be more limited. Therefore, it is better to encourage the teachers to focus on utilising their limited linguistic resources effectively, rather than to acquire the full knowledge of the language. This can facilitate the active use of communication strategies, which is important for communicative success in multilingual environments (Cogo & House, 2018). By adopting such an adaptable view of English, SA as part of teacher training can nurture the intercultural competence of pre-service teachers, enabling them to successfully navigate the complexities of global communication.

While this study focused on a specific group of pre-service teachers in a particular teacher training context, it is essential to note that the findings may not be generalisable. Nevertheless, the author hopes that it can serve as part of a foundation for future research in the field of internationalisation of English teacher training. Further exploration of the long-term impacts of SA on pre-service teachers' professional development and intercultural competence would be beneficial in advancing our understanding of the transformative potential of ELF awareness within this field.

Acknowledgement

This research project is supported by JSPS KAKENHI Grant Number JP21K00659.

Notes

(1) The survey results are available in Japanese at https://www.mext.go.jp/a_menu/kokusai/gaikokugo/1384230.htm.
(2) An English version of the details of the plan is available at https://www.cas.go.jp/jp/seisaku/kyouikumirai/pdf/230427jmirai.pdf
(3) English versions are available at https://www.mext.go.jp/content/20220603-mxt_kyoiku02-000005242_003.pdf (junior high school) and https://www.mext.go.jp/content/20230328-mxt_kyoiku02_100014466_002.pdf (senior high school)

References

Asaoka, C. (2019) *Early Professional Development in EFL Teaching: Perspectives and Experiences from Japan*. Multilingual Matters. https://doi.org/10.21832/9781788923224

Aspinall, R. (2013) *International Education Policy in Japan in an Age of Globalisation and Risk*. Brill. https://doi.org/10.1163/9789004243729

Baecher, L. (2021) *Study Abroad for Pre- and In-service Teachers: Transformative Learning on a Global Scale*. Routledge. https://doi.org/10.4324/9781003004387

Baker, W. and Fang, F. (2019) *From English Language Learners to Intercultural Citizens: Chinese Student Sojourners' Development of Intercultural Citizenship in ELT and EMI Programmes*. British Council.

Baker, W., Boonsuk, Y., Ra, J.J., Sangiamchit, C. and Snodin, N. (2022) Thai study abroad students as intercultural citizens: Developing intercultural citizenship through English medium education and ELT. *Asia Pacific Journal of Education*, 1–16. https://doi.org/10.1080/02188791.2022.2096569

Barkhuizen, G. (ed.) (2022) *Language Teachers Studying Abroad: Identities, Emotions and Disruptions*. Multilingual Matters. https://doi.org/10.21832/9781788929950

Blommaert, J. (2010) *The Sociolinguistics of Globalization*. Cambridge University Press. https://doi.org/10.1017/CBO9780511845307

Boonsuk, Y. and Fang, F. (2021) Re-envisaging English medium instruction, intercultural citizenship development, and higher education in the context of studying abroad. *Language and Education* 37 (3), 271–287. https://doi.org/10.1080/09500782.2021.1996595

Braun, V. and Clarke, V. (2022) *Thematic Analysis: A Practical Guide*. SAGE.

Chan, S.Y.C. and Jackson, J. (2022) 'I thought it was really a no!': A narrativized account of an L2 sojourn with a homestay. In G. Barkhuizen (ed.) *Language Teachers Studying Abroad: Identities, Emotions and Disruptions* (pp. 120–131). Multilingual Matters. https://doi.org/10.21832/9781788929950-012

Chern, C., Lin, A.M.Y. and Lo, M.-L. (2022) Border-crossing and professional development of Taiwanese EFL teachers in a study-abroad program. In G. Barkhuizen (ed.) *Language Teachers Studying Abroad: Identities, Emotions and Disruptions* (pp. 111–122). Multilingual Matters. https://doi.org/10.21832/9781788929950-011

Cogo, A. and House, J. (2018) The pragmatics of ELF. In J. Jenkins, W. Baker and M. Dewey (eds) *The Routledge Handbook of English as a Lingua Franca* (pp. 210–223). Routledge. https://doi.org/10.4324/9781315717173-18

Diao, W. and Trentman, E. (2021) *Language Learning in Study Abroad: The Multilingual Turn*. Multilingual Matters. https://doi.org/10.21832/9781800411340

Fang, F., Chen, R. and Elyas, T. (2020) An investigation of the relationship between global perspective and willingness to communicate in English in a Chinese university context. *Journal of Language and Education* 6 (1), 39–54. https://doi.org/10.17323/jle.2020.10175

Firth, A. (1996) The discursive accomplishment of normality: On 'Lingua Franca' English and conversation analysis. *Journal of Pragmatics* 26 (2), 237–259. https://doi.org/10.1016/0378-2166 (96)00014-8

Goldstein, S.B. (2022) *Intercultural Learning through Study Abroad*. Cambridge University Press. https://doi.org/10.1017/9781009127011

Hagar, T.J. (2018) Role of reflective knowledge in the development of intercultural competence. *Journal of Intercultural Communication Research* 47 (2), 87–104. https://doi.org/10.1080/17475759.2018.1427615

Hanada, S. (2019) A quantitative assessment of Japanese students' intercultural competence developed through study abroad programs. *Journal of International Students* 9 (4), 1015–1037. https://doi.org/10.32674/jis.v9i4.391

Holliday, A. (2006) Native-speakerism. *ELT Journal* 60 (4), 385–387. https://doi.org/10.1093/elt/ccl030

Jackson, J. (2020) The language and intercultural dimension of education abroad. *The Routledge Handbook of Language and Intercultural Communication* (pp. 442–456). Routledge. https://doi.org/10.4324/9781003036210-34

Jackson, J. and Oguro, S. (eds) (2018) *Intercultural Interventions in Study Abroad*. Routledge. https://doi.org/10.4324/9781315276595

Kalocsai, K. (2014) *Communities of Practice and English as a Lingua Franca: A Study of Students in a Central European Context*. De Gruyter. https://doi.org/10.1515/9783110295511

Kubota, R. (2016) The social imaginary of study abroad: Complexities and contradictions. *The Language Learning Journal* 44 (3), 347–357. https://doi.org/10.1080/09571736.2016.1198098

MacIntyre, P.D., Clément, R., Dörnyei, Z. and Noels, K.A. (1998) Conceptualizing willingness to communicate in a L2: A situational model of L2 confidence and affiliation. *The Modern Language Journal* 82 (4), 545–562. https://doi.org/10.1111/j.1540-4781.1998.tb05543.x

Mayumi, K. and Hüttner, J. (2020) Changing beliefs on English: Study abroad for teacher development. *ELT Journal* 74 (3), 268–276. https://doi.org/10.1093/elt/ccaa020

Morley, A., Braun, A.M.B., Rohrer, L. and Lamb, D. (2019) Study abroad for preservice teachers: A critical literature review with considerations for research and practice. *Global Education Review* 6 (3), 4–29.

Naka, K. (2018) Professional development for pre-service English language teachers in the age of globalisation. In K. Hashimoto and V. Nguyen (eds) *Professional Development of English Language Teachers in Asia: Lessons from Japan and Vietnam* (pp. 76–91). Routledge. https://doi.org/10.4324/9781315413259-6

Nonaka, C. (2018) *Transcending Self and Other Through Akogare [Desire]: The English Language and the Internationalization of Higher Education in Japan*. Multilingual Matters.

OECD (2022) *Education at a Glance* 2022: *OECD Indicators*. OECD Publishing.

Ra, J.J., Boonsuk, Y. and Sangiamchit, C. (2022) Intercultural citizenship development: A case of Thai study abroad students in EMI programs. *Journal of English as a Lingua Franca* 11 (1), 89–104. https://doi.org/10.1515/jelf-2022-2071

Sifakis, N.C. (2019) ELF awareness in English language teaching: Principles and processes. *Applied Linguistics* 40 (2), 288–306. https://doi.org/10.1093/applin/amx034

Suzuki, A. (2020) ELF for global mindsets? Theory and practice of ELT in formal education in Japan. In M. Konakahara and K. Tsuchiya (eds) *English as a Lingua Franca in Japan: Towards Multilingual Practices* (pp. 71–89). Palgrave Macmillan. https://doi.org/10.1007/978-3-030-33288-4_4

Suzuki, A. (2021) Changing views of English through study abroad as teacher training. *ELT Journal* 75 (4), 397–406. https://doi.org/10.1093/elt/ccab038

Suzuki, A. (2023) Pre-service teachers' difficulty understanding English as a Lingua Franca for intercultural awareness development. In A. Sahlane and R. Pritchard (eds) *English as an International Education: Critical Intercultural Literacy Perspectives* (pp. 219–236). Springer. https://doi.org/10.1007/978-3-031-34702-3_12

Suzuki, A. (Forthcoming) The role of ELF-oriented ELT in preparation for study abroad. In T. Ishikawa, P. McBride and A. Suzuki (eds) *Developing English as a Lingua Franca Programmes for Language Teaching: Innovation, Resistance, and Applications*. De Gruyter.

Thomas, K.L. and Kerstetter, D. (2020) The awe in awesome in education abroad. *Frontiers: The Interdisciplinary Journal of Study Abroad* 32 (2), 94–119. https://doi.org/10.36366/frontiers.v32i2.469

Tokyo Gakugei University (2017, March) *Eigo kyoin no eigoryoku, shidoryoku kyouka no tame no chosa kenkyu* [Research on the development of English language teachers' proficiency and teaching competencies]. https://www2.u-gakugei.ac.jp/~estudy/28file/report28_all.pdf

Wang, D. (2014) Effects of study abroad on teachers' self-perceptions: A study of Chinese EFL teachers. *Journal of Language Teaching and Research* 5 (1), 70–79. https://doi.org/10.4304/jltr.5.1.70-79

Wang, F., Clarke, A. and Webb, A.S. (2019) Tailored for China: Did it work? Reflections on an intensive study abroad programme for Chinese student teachers. *Teachers and Teaching* 25 (7), 800–820. https://doi.org/10.1080/13540602.2019.1676224

Zhang, F. and Wang, J. (2022) Negotiating the impact of international experiences on professional identity development: A case study of Chinese college English teachers. *Frontiers in Psychology* 13, 1–10. https://doi.org/10.3389/fpsyg.2022.1007649

Part 4

Fostering Decolonization through Internationalization

12 Contesting Native Speakerism in Language Teacher Identity Construction: A Case Study of a Short-Term Study Abroad Program

Hyesun Cho

This chapter presents a qualitative case study of a short-term study abroad program co-founded and directed by the author at a Midwestern university in the United States. It examines language teacher identity construction from a critical perspective (Cho & Peter, 2017). Specifically, the study elucidates how native English-speaking (NES) student teachers negotiate their language teacher identity through critical reflections while teaching English as a foreign language (EFL) in Korean secondary classrooms during study abroad. It makes recommendations for teacher educators who aim to infuse a critical perspective into a short-term study abroad program by contesting the dominant language ideology perpetuated in the field of Teaching English to Speakers of Other Languages (TESOL), such as native speakerism.

Introduction

The internationalization of TESOL teacher education can take various forms, including study abroad initiatives as one means of internationalizing TESOL curricula. Notably, there has been a growing body of research exploring the impact of study abroad on professional development of TESOL educators (Cho & Peter, 2017; Kabilan, 2013; Palmer & Menard-Warwick, 2012; Trent, 2011). However, this body of literature has primarily focused on EFL pre-service teachers studying short-term in the countries like the United States, the United Kingdom and Australia, where English is the primary language of communication in everyday life (e.g. Çiftçi & Karaman, 2019; Kang & Shin, 2024).

The study presented in this chapter delineates the experiences of preservice teachers from the United States during a short-term faculty-led study abroad program. The six-week program takes place in one of the so-called 'Expanding Circle' countries (Kachru, 1985) – South Korea – in which English is not used outside the EFL classroom but carries significant value as social capital (Choi, 2021; Park, 2009). This chapter describes how a study abroad program focuses on challenging the hegemonic ideologies of English's global dominance while promoting the (re)negotiation of language teacher identity among participants (Cho & Peter, 2017). It contributes to the growing body of scholarship on the internationalization of TESOL curriculum in teacher education by highlighting the significance of critical reflections among native English-speaking (NES) teachers who taught EFL during a short-term study abroad program.

Conceptual Framework

Critical perspective on English language teaching and teachers

Since the inception of critically oriented paradigms on English language teaching (ELT) and the identities of ELT educators, scholars have scrutinized the global spread of English(es) and the roles of ELT educators in social, cultural and political contexts around the world (Selvi *et al.*, 2023). Not only have they recognized the varieties of English(es) used around the globe, but they have also challenged the discriminatory practice of hiring and working settings, based on 'nativeness' of ELT professionals. As a result, an increasing number of studies have examined the legitimacy of diverse ELT professionals considering racial, cultural, linguistic, religious, gender diversity (Selvi *et al.*, 2023). The binary distinction between NES and non-native English-speaking (NNES) may reify the deficit viewpoint about non-native speaker (NNS), assuming the limited linguistic competence of NNES based on distinct and oversimplified categories of NNS and NNES (Aneja, 2016). This essentialized dichotomy does not recognize the fluidity between privilege and marginalization in NES and NNES teachers (Rudolph, 2023).

Moreover, the hierarchical structure of ELT professionals solely rooted in the notion of 'nativeness' can have a detrimental impact on the (re)negotiation of teacher identity in that it may cause emotional struggles concerning the perceived illegitimacy of their professional identity (Song, 2016). As Dewaele *et al.* (2022) argue, it is unjust to determine one's linguistic and instructional competence solely based on the language they were born into, thereby categorizing individuals in deeply entrenched labels. Despite the critiques of the static, unidimensional, binary dichotomy between NES and NNES (e.g. Rudolph *et al.*, 2015), NES teachers continue to have a privileged status in instructional and institutional domains in ELT (Slavkov *et al.*, 2021). This observation has led to the emergence of terminology such as 'native speakerism', which will be explored further in the discussion below.

Native speakerism

Native-speakerism, a term coined by Holliday (2006, 2015), refers to a widespread ideology perpetuated in the ELT profession whereby those perceived as 'native speakers' of English are considered to be better language models and embody a superior western teaching methodology than those perceived as 'non-native speakers' in the periphery. According to Holliday (2006), native speakerism is based on the normalized values and practices about language and culture, primarily underpinned by the assumption that privilege and marginalization are categorically experienced across contexts. He argues that addressing native speakerism is essential in tackling the prejudices embedded in ELT practice as the binary and fixed categories of NES/NNES and the privilege of NES have been normalized in ELT practices, including NNES teachers (e.g. Whitehead & Ryu, 2023), administrators, parents and students, as well as the public in general. This essentialized and reified notion of language teacher identity has been one of the important precursors in the extension of language teacher identity research in TESOL and applied linguistics (Selvi *et al.*, 2023).

Language teacher identity

Language teacher identity (LTI) has recently garnered significant attention in the literature. In particular, scholars have theorized LTI from sociocultural and poststructuralist perspectives (Barkhuizen, 2016; Miller, 2009; Varghese *et al.*, 2005; also see the 2016 special issue of *TESOL Quarterly* on LTI). They frame LTI not only as the intricate interplay between teachers and students in a multifaceted and socially rooted process of identity (re)negotiation, but also an inherently power-infused engagement of teachers and students in a complex and embodied process of identity (re)negotiation. From a poststructuralist perspective, in particular, ELT is not merely a series of 'identity-neutral' instructional strategies or practices. Rather, being and becoming an ELT professional are fluid, dynamic, even contradictory processes of identity negotiation (Kanno & Stuart, 2011; Varghese *et al.*, 2005; Varghese *et al.*, 2016; Yazan, 2017). This perspective also problematizes the fixed categories by recognizing the fluid and embodied nature of identities intersected with various social markers including race, ethnicity, gender, nationality, religion and social class.

As Varghese *et al.* (2016) state, challenging the taken-for-granted assumptions about idealized versions as ELT professionals 'as white, middle class, heterosexual, inner circle speakers of English' (2016: 549) is important in the conceptualization of a critical perspective. Therefore, research pertaining to student teachers in international practicum contexts has focused on negotiating their teacher identity by contesting the assumptions and ideologies that are shaped by social, cultural, political and historical contexts (Kasun & Saavedra, 2016).

TESOL practicum abroad

Practicum plays an integral role in the professional development of prospective teachers in TESOL teacher education (Crookes, 2003). The burgeoning scholarship in TESOL underscores the importance of integrating practicum abroad as a pedagogical framework for teacher learning and professional development in TESOL teacher education (Baecher, 2020; Barkhuizen, 2022; Kabilan, 2013; Lindahl *et al.*, 2020; Pilonieta *et al.*, 2017). Numerous benefits of study/teaching abroad for prospective teachers have been reported in the literature, including developing intercultural competence (Bauler *et al.*, 2020), fostering empathy for their diverse students in the classroom, (Kasun & Saavedra, 2016) thereby undergoing transformative learning experience leading to personal and professional growth. These experiences can enrich the knowledge, skills and perspectives of teachers, making them become more aware of the complexities of teaching English in the global context.

While pointing to the limited number of international field experiences for pre-service teachers, Cruickshank and Westbrook (2013) discuss the benefits of practicum abroad including preparing prospective teachers for both global and local contexts. They contested the perception of international teaching practicum as mere 'cultural tourism' by demonstrating how the overseas practicum experience enabled pre-service teachers to develop a deeper understanding of new working cultures, particularly by placing them in minority situations.

Kasun and Saavedra (2016) argue that teacher educators must create spaces for teacher candidates to unpack their identities and their ways of knowing during TESOL practicum abroad. By analyzing coursework samples, student self-assessments, class discussions, focus group sessions and field notes, the researchers found that teacher candidates became socially aware, more empathetic toward language learners, and creators of safe classroom spaces. They illustrated how these predominantly white teacher candidates in Mexico exhibited positive learning in their LTI negotiations. However, as some studies have demonstrated (e.g. Palmer & Menard-Warwick, 2012), not all study abroad participants experience positive learning. For some, the experience may reinforce the deficit mindset that they already held toward minoritized student populations. This chapter describes a faculty-led study abroad program that encourages critical reflection among future ELT professionals while avoiding the risk of becoming a form of cultural tourism.

Program Context

A short-term study abroad program: *Teaching English in Korea*

Teaching English in Korea (TEIK) is a faculty-led study abroad program in which university students across multiple disciplines teach English in Korea over the course of six weeks in the summer (Cho & Peter, 2017; Cho & Hayes, 2024a; Cho & Hayes, 2024b). The participants from a large public research university in the US Midwest are selected to join the program based on a personal statement, letters of recommendation, scholarly records and interviews with program faculty. Participants attend a series of pre-departure orientations to learn basic Korean as well as to discuss professionalism in the Korean EFL context. The participants are enrolled in two courses, *TESOL Pedagogy* and *TESOL Practicum*, 3 credit hours each. While in Korea, participants observe classes taught by NES teachers and co-teach with a fellow participant in the Korean EFL high school classroom. Course meetings are held twice a week after dinner in a conference room at the dorm. During class meetings, participants engage in discussions centered around critical approaches to TESOL – approaches to contest the prevailing language ideology associated with native speakerism and the binary juxtapositions of NES and NNES.

The goals of the TEIK program are as follows (Cho & Peter, 2017):

- developing competency in intercultural communication and professional competencies associated with international TESOL standards;
- engaging in professional dialogue and critical reflection with cooperating teachers and university supervisors;
- comparing the American and Korean systems of education with respect to the role of English teaching and learning in Korean students' lives;
- investigating key TESOL issues in the international classroom;
- reflecting on a variety of linguistic and cultural experiences within the classroom and beyond; and
- experiencing being a foreign language learner in a foreign culture and thus developing empathy for such students in US schools.

Additionally, the course requirements for the TEIK program include the following:

- writing reflective and critical reviews of scholarly articles on TESOL theories, models and practices regarding English as a foreign language or an international language in Korea;
- completing two cross-cultural exercises to examine different perspectives in the global community, particularly related to ELT, where they

reflect on their own attitudes, beliefs and behaviors in contrast to those of their Korean hosts;
- designing and implementing culturally relevant instructional unit composed of a narrative and two lesson plans;
- taking weekly ethnographic field notes as teacher-researcher (e.g. critical incident reports and cross-cultural narratives);
- creating and presenting a web-based portfolio that encompasses the coursework during study abroad, along with their final reflection on the experiences in the program.

The portfolio development and presentation serve as a capstone experience for program participants to reflect on their learning and teaching during the program. Since reflection is an essential component of LTI negotiation, it is integral to study abroad programs (Stachowski & Sparks, 2007; Trilokekar & Kukar, 2011). The importance and the nature of reflection is explicitly outlined in the syllabus as follows:

> Reflection is an important part of teaching: reflecting on lesson plans, student engagement, your conduct as a teacher, etc. Therefore, every student teacher is required to keep a weekly teaching journal (five entries total). The content of the journal may include stories of student teaching: field notes of initial class observations and teacher shadowing, new knowledge and learning, success and failures, fears and stress, excitement/frustration; observations of teaching and learning, reflections on teaching behaviors; problems and solution, and last but not least, questions you have not been able to answer. Journal entries will be checked 3 times over the course of the practicum and will serve as artifacts in the portfolio.

Program site

The site for the TEIK is Jinsung Girls' High School (pseudonym), located in a satellite city outside Seoul in Korea. Jinsung has been selected as a site for TEIK owing to the author's professional connections, having previously worked as a secondary EFL teacher in Korean public schools as well as being an alum of a university renowned for its English language education (Cho & Peter, 2017). The private all-girls high school has a total number of approximately 1200 students and employs NES teachers to help students develop their conversational English skills. Under the onsite supervision of university faculty, the participants complete their student teaching in these conversational English classes taught by NES teachers. The school is dedicated to offering a high-quality education for students to become female leaders in a global context. As an endeavor to fulfill this mission, Jinsung has employed NES teachers since the 1980s, establishing itself as one of the pioneer secondary schools in Korea to have NES teachers on its staff.

Research Methods

Using a qualitative case study approach, the data were collected from students who participated in the program from 2015 to 2019. With the total number of 60 participants, all but three self-identified English as their first language. Many of the participants for each year's program were taking Korean language classes at the university (see Table 12.1 for language background). Most had little experience in a country outside the US and for some, it was the first time they had traveled outside their home state.

Data collection and data analysis

A range of course assignments, such as weekly reflections and web-based portfolios, were collected each year. All participants submitted the required course assignments each week and by the end of the program. The course assignments were compiled into a Word document for data analysis. To uphold confidentiality, identifiable indicators were removed from the assignments. Instead, participants were assigned numerical identifiers corresponding to their respective program years. In addition, the researcher, also serving as the program's co-founder and faculty director, took field notes during the program when she supervised the practicum in 2015, 2017 and 2019 on site. These firsthand observations and interactions provided insights into participants' experiences during the program.

Adopting both inductive and deductive data analysis approaches, the researcher identified salient themes pertinent to the issues of language teacher identity. For inductive data analysis, the researcher started with the raw data to look for themes while immersing herself in the data. By reading and re-reading the data line by line, the researcher developed several themes (e.g. *rapport with Korean students, respect for Korean culture, professionalism, Konglish*) that emerged from the data. For deductive data analysis, the researcher identified segments of data that correspond to several themes derived from critical perspectives of ELT (e.g. *native*

Table 12.1 Participants and language background

Year	Participants (N)	Language background
2015	9	7 Korean language learners
2016	14	12 Korean language learners; 1 multilingual with English, Hindi, Urdu and Punjabi
2017	14	11 Korean language learners; 1 Spanish/English bilingual; 1 Chinese as L1 speaker
2018	11	7 Korean language learners; Chinese as L1 speaker
2019	12	8 Korean language learners; 1 English/Urdu Bilingual

speakerism, roles of NES vs. NNES teachers; language ideology) and coded them accordingly. The following section presents the examination of language teacher identity through a critical lens, which entails challenging the prevailing norms inherent in ELT, such as native speakerism.

Findings

Consistent across assignments and course discussions, students reported that the study abroad influenced their perspectives of the status of English in the Korean context, NES and NNES teachers and their professional identity. Program participants experienced a range of shifts in their understanding of LTI throughout the duration of the study abroad program, as evidenced in the data collected over the years. While the findings demonstrate that student teachers initially subscribed to native speakerism, they started to challenge the dominant discourse in TESOL.

Challenging the dominant discourse in TESOL

As Lee and Jang (2023b) report, NES teachers in Korea, especially white teachers, tend to enjoy privileges that stem from their linguistic competence and cultural capital associated with western nationality and the NES status. During the first week while observing the Korean EFL classroom taught by an NES teacher, one student teacher wrote her opinions about the roles of NES and NNES teachers in her reflection journal:

> Would the Korean education system let the native English speakers do the communication and listening class and let the Korean teachers do the grammar and the reading classes? I feel like it would make a lot of sense doing it that way.

It appears that she subscribed to the binary oppositions of NES/NNES by endorsing the NES and NNES teacher dichotomy in terms of their divided teaching responsibilities for Korean EFL high school students. She commented that NES teachers would be at an advantage to teach listening and speaking while Korean teachers would be better to teach grammar and reading. This practice of splitting teaching roles is often used as a justification for favoring NES teachers over NNES counterparts, normalizing the marginalization of NNES teachers, rather than recognizing their expertise in language teaching. As Whitehead and Ryu (2023) found in their examination of the perceived pronunciations of Korean EFL teachers, even NNES teachers themselves in the Korean context may, to some extent, accept native speakerism, possibly stemming from a lack of confidence in their pronunciation. Similarly, one participant failed to acknowledge the pitfalls of native speakerism as well as the construct of standardized English:

> I know we have talked in-depth about native speakerism in the context of Korean EFL teaching, but I still struggle with it. I have a hard time wrapping my mind around why it is wrong. I don't want to say that other varieties of English, like Konglish, are wrong, but at the same time, I feel like it is important to be able to be understood when talking to other English speakers around the world. It feels to me like the best way to do that is to have a standardized English. Wouldn't you want the teachers at least of the upper levels to be native English speakers?

While making the assumptions that NES teachers are more proficient in teaching 'standardized English' at the advanced levels compared to Korean teachers, she overlooked the capabilities of NNES teachers, who might excel in teaching English as a lingua franca (ELF), considering that most ELF interactions occur among NNES users (Seidlhofer, 2005).

However, participants began to challenge this dominant ideology associated with essentialized/idealized (non)native speakerism through class discussion and interactions with Korean EFL students. By interrogating the hierarchical relationships between NES and NNES speakers and debunking the myth of native speakers as the ideal speaker and/or language teacher, program participants came to develop critical awareness of the power imbalance among English speakers and their teachers. One participant wrote:

> As we begin to consider English and the way it has spread all around the world, we see how it has crossed not just geographical boundaries but societal, political, cultural issues and more. Languages have a way of shaping our world and our understanding of this valuable tool within our communities is still one that needs a closer look. NES teachers must not assume the role of superiority simply because of their given understanding of the English language. This assumption can be detrimental to the education of the students as NES teachers could be unaware of essential steps to learning EFL. Therefore, in my position as a native English speaker intent on teaching English as a foreign language, self-reflection and an increased awareness of others' positions is not only valuable, but necessary.

By recognizing the fluidity of English in the global context, influenced not only by geographical boundaries but also by societal, political, cultural forces, she underscores the importance of languages as a means to facilitate deeper understanding and communication. She also argues that NES teachers 'must not assume the role of superiority' simply owing to their given understanding of the English language, calling for self-reflection and awareness of other teachers' perspectives and experiences. Another participant engaged in contemplating on LTI from a critical perspective, challenging NES teachers by questioning their 'charity and benevolence' as well as their 'tourist approach':

> I find the part of the quote that recognizes how many native English-speaking teachers took up identities of 'charity and benevolence'

interesting because at first evaluation such an identity seems great and altruistic. However, implied within this benevolence is a belief that American ways of life are superior and desirable when that is not always the case. I think the benevolence that teachers should have is one of interest in student development, and not in extending American standards. I found this quote important because it will help me recognize the tendency for Americans, Australians, etc. to regard the lesser-known parts of the world with a sense of hegemony and tourist-approach.

The data for this theme also suggest that the study abroad experience triggered reflective thinking and a heightened sensitivity to a pluralistic orientation to English. This led to question the monolithic views of English while embracing a range of English varieties, such as Konglish (Ahn, 2014):

> While reading the article about Konglish and Korean English and other similar formalities, I wondered how it could be technically wrong to speak it. It made me think how would it be considered wrong? If you can understand Konglish/Korean English and its components and that is what the majority of people speak, wouldn't it be easier to interact and communicate with them? Those were my thoughts as I read.

Through course readings about Konglish, this pre-service teacher began to question the dominance of American English in the global context, specifically in the Korean EFL context. Alternatively, he came to realize the legitimacy and significance of incorporating Konglish as a variety of English into the teaching context where he was working with Korean EFL learners.

Study abroad as a space for critical discussions on ELT

The findings indicate that participants found study abroad beneficial in engaging critical conversations with classmates and faculty while grappling with the global spread of English in sociopolitical contexts and the role of ELT professionals. Their appreciation of the study abroad experience was evidenced in the ways they wrote their final reflection on the program in their capstone portfolio. In her program reflection, one participant attributed her professional growth to the continuous critical discussions that took place both before and during the program as well as insights gained from the course readings:

> I believe one of the key benefits of this program is that we have discussions like this [hegemonic power of English inherent in the global and local context] not only in the classroom, but in the dorm, and even during excursions. I also remember we discussed this topic during the pre-departure orientations. We don't get to talk about it when we take classes at the university. Also, I think the readings about some critical issues around TESOL were informative and eye-opening.

The ongoing discussions, extending beyond the classroom, were readily evident throughout the program. Another participant acknowledged that the strong work ethics and motivation of Korean students to learn English with US student teachers had a profound impact on her construction of language teacher identity:

> During this practicum, I witnessed how hardworking Korean high school students were. They were so eager to learn and study hard all the time. I wanted to become a better teacher for them (and my future students in the US). At the same time, I learned so much from them! They motivated me to be a better teacher and advocate for those who may struggle with learning a new language.

Her interaction with Korean high school students prompted her to feel better equipped to teach both her Korean students and her future students in the United States. While many participants had studied Korean in college and a few were nearly fluent Korean speakers, there were some participants with no Korean language background. As with US pre-service teachers in Argentina who were not fluent in Spanish in Frieson et al.'s study (2022), the lack of language facility pushed participants to think about students in their future classrooms. One male pre-service teacher from the secondary English education program wrote:

> I did not learn any languages other than English growing up. I took some Spanish classes in high school but don't remember much. I have no Korean skills unlike some students who took Korean classes at [the university]. Now I have empathy for those who are entering the classroom with very little English in the US.

As with him, participants found themselves compelled to reflect on their experiences and perspective as future teachers, as they were in a minority position in a foreign country where they had no to little proficiency in the local language. This cultivation of reflective teaching has been identified as a gap in teacher education (Cruickshanka & Westbrook, 2013). By participating in study abroad programs, prospective teachers not only develop empathy for minoritized students in their teaching context, but also foster the development of reflective and critical teaching skills necessary for working with culturally and linguistically diverse learners in schools.

Discussion

This chapter, part of a larger qualitative case study on a short-term study abroad program, provides insights into how study abroad participants engage with the construction of language teacher identity through a critical lens. It contributes to the development and validation of a study abroad program for internationalizing TESOL curricula, fostering critical awareness of the realities of ELT. This study specifically focused on how study abroad experiences influence the professional identity negotiations of NES student teachers during their TESOL practicum in Korea. The reflections and class discussions during study abroad provided students with opportunities to cultivate a heightened awareness of the power dynamics perpetuated in TESOL. Taken together, the data revealed that their involvement in the TEIK program enriched their understanding of the roles played by English and teachers within the Korean context.

This study suggests that study abroad faculty encourage pre-service teachers to interrogate their own prejudices, privilege and assumptions they bring as NES teachers. This enables pre-service teachers to problematize conventional understandings of teaching English and reconceptualize the notion of LTI, which evolves with time, space and context (Lee & Jang, 2023a). In addition to reflective journals, study abroad participation warrants intentional opportunities for both individual and collective reflections before and during the program. For example, pre-departure preparation needs to include discussion on the relations of power, such as white privilege (Major & Santoro, 2016).

The findings also point to the need for carefully designed activities to facilitate critical dialogue among program participants. Instead of solely emphasizing the experience, incorporating reflection before, during and after critical dialogue is essential to the program (Bauler *et al.*, 2020). Furthermore, findings show that participants studying Korean tended to engage more frequently and comfortably with Korean high school students, finding enjoyment in practicing Korean while teaching English to them. This type of language exchange appeared to play an important role in negotiating their language teacher identity.

Nonetheless, this study does not argue that study abroad experiences will automatically lead to a heightened sense of critical awareness among participants. Examining identity shifts within the compressed timeframes of study abroad experiences presents theoretical and methodological challenges for TESOL teacher educators (Kang & Pacheco, 2021). Rather, it points to the significance of intentional criticality when designing and implementing a study abroad program in which participants go through sustained dialogue about the hegemonic power of English and TESOL educators between faculty and students and among students.

Also, it should be noted that study abroad programs in teacher education are mainly developed by individual faculty with personal passion for the work and building on their unique professional networks (Baecher, 2019; Parker *et al.*, 2022), such as the TEIK program discussed in this chapter. In particular, faculty-led study abroad programs are mostly developed by faculty who utilize personal connections and relationships to design and implement such programs. Therefore, study abroad programming for TESOL teachers may not arise from careful institutional planning in systematic and sustainable manners.

Additional challenges in the integration of study abroad experiences into teacher education stems from the lack of flexibility often inherent in teacher education programs that must align with the requirements for teaching licensure (Cruickshank & Westbrook, 2013). This inflexibility of teacher education curricula often leaves limited opportunities for most teacher candidates to engage in study abroad. Moreover, the uncertainties surrounding international travel, particularly in the wake of health crises like the COVID-19 pandemic have presented substantial impediments to the widespread adoption of such programs in teacher education.

Conclusion

Given the nature of the diverse student populations TESOL educators work with in the transnational context (Cho *et al.*, 2022), it is imperative that TESOL teacher educators internationalize the curricula to address the increasing diversity in the classroom and beyond. While many other internationalizing efforts might be fruitful, study abroad can have a positive impact on LTI negotiation by raising critical awareness of the power imbalance between NES and NNES as well as the varieties of World Englishes among prospective teachers.

Based on the findings of the multi-year case study, this chapter proposes recommendations for TESOL teacher educators to develop critical approaches to LTI negotiation during study abroad. Incorporating study abroad into TESOL teacher education as a critical and transformative pedagogy requires a high level of intentionality for teacher educators to continually (re)center the locus of learners and local contexts rather than privileging English as the priority for teaching. TESOL teacher educators should be purposeful about addressing the critical discussion about LTI, including the binary dichotomy between NES and NNES teachers and native speakerism. TESOL teacher educators should bring critical dimensions of LTI to the forefront of their pedagogical considerations during study abroad, moving away from the essentialist opposition via conceptualizations such as NES and NNES teachers (Rubin, 2020; Selvi *et al.*, 2023). With criticality and intentionality (Kasun & Saavedra, 2016), TESOL practicum abroad can become a critical space for disrupting the discriminatory discourses and practices in ELT.

This case study offers a heuristic for designing a program aimed at embedding the internalization of TESOL curricula. As Varghese *et al.* (2016) remind us, it is essential to explore how TESOL teacher educators can foster the fluid and agentive nature of LTI negotiations while actively attuned to the power dynamics that permeate the field of TESOL, particularly in study abroad contexts. It is of utmost significance to investigate how study abroad participants experience transformative learning not only during their time abroad but also in the period following their program participation. This extended examination can provide insights into the long-term impacts and sustainability of such internationalizing initiatives in TESOL teacher education.

References

Ahn, H. (2014) Teachers' attitudes towards Korean English in South Korea. *World Englishes* 33 (2), 195–222.

Ahn, S.J., Kim, M.J. and Lee, J.Y. (2020) Beyond the NS/NNS dichotomy: Exploring the potential of translanguaging in CPP practice by Korean EFL teachers. *Journal of Asia TEFL* 17 (2), 540–561.

Aneja, G.A. (2016) (Non) native speakered: Rethinking (non) nativeness and teacher identity in TESOL teacher education. *TESOL Quarterly* 50 (3), 572–596.

Baecher, L. (2019) Study abroad in teacher education. *Global Education Review* 6 (3), 1–3.

Baecher, L. (ed.) (2020) *Study Abroad for Pre-and In-service Teachers: Transformative Learning on a Global scale*. Routledge.

Barkhuizen, G. (ed.) (2016) *Reflections on Language Teacher Identity Research*. Routledge.

Barkhuizen, G. (ed.) (2022) *Language Teachers Studying Abroad: Identities, Emotions and Disruptions*. Multilingual Matters.

Bauler, C., Wang, X.L. and Thornburg, D. (2020) Developing global-mindedness in teacher education through virtual and international intercultural experiences. In L. Baecher (ed.) *Study Abroad for Pre-and In-service Teachers* (pp. 225–237). Routledge.

Çiftçi, E. and Karaman, A. (2019) Short-term international experiences in language teacher education: A qualitative meta-synthesis. *Australian Journal of Teacher Education* 441 (1), 93–119. https://doi.org/10.14221/ajte.2018v44n1.6

Cho, H. and Peter, L. (2017) Taking the TESOL practicum abroad: Opportunities for critical awareness and community-building among preservice teachers. In H. An (ed.) *Efficacy and Implementation of Study Abroad Programs for P-12 Teachers*. (pp. 149–171). IGI Global. https://doi.org/10.4018/978-1-5225-1057-4.ch009

Cho, H. and Hayes, J. (2024a) 'I hold the key to the cage, and nothing can keep me there without my permission': Exploring gender identity through identity journey mapping in a study abroad program. *Educational Forum* 88 (3), 309–323. https://doi.org/10.1080/00131725.2024.2339196

Cho, H. and Hayes, J. (2024b) Exploring the identities of Korean Americans through identity journey mapping in a study abroad program. *International Journal of Multicultural Education* 26 (1), 79–101.

Cho, H., Al-Samiri, R. and Gao, J. (2022) *Transnational Language Teachers in TESOL*. Routledge.

Choi, T.H. (2021) English fever: Educational policies in globalised Korea, 1981–2018. *History of Education*, 1–17.

Crookes, G. (2003) *A Practicum in TESOL: Professional Development Through Teaching Practice*. Cambridge University Press.

Cruickshank, K. and Westbrook, R. (2013) Local and global–conflicting perspectives? The place of overseas practicum in preservice teacher education. *Asia-Pacific Journal of Teacher Education* 41 (1), 55–68.

Dewaele, J.M., Bak, T. and Ortega, L. (2022) Why the mythical 'native speaker' has mud on its face. In N. Slavkov, S. Melo-Pfeifer and N. Kerschhofer-Puhalo (eds) *The Changing Face of the 'Native Speaker': Perspectives from Multilingualism and Globalization* (pp. 23–43). Walter de Gruyter GmbH & Co KG.

Frieson, B.L., Murray-Everett, N.C. and Parsons, M.J. (2022) Always outsiders, never insiders: A study abroad program for future teachers. *Teaching and Teacher Education* 112, 103632.

Holliday, A. (2006) Native-speakerism. *ELT Journal* 60 (4), 385–387.

Holliday, A. (2015) Native-speakerism: Taking the concept forward and achieving cultural belief. In A. Swan, P. Aboshiha and A. Holliday (eds) *(En)Countering Native-Speakerism: Global Perspectives* (pp. 11–25). Springer.

Kabilan, M.K. (2013) A phenomenological study of an international teaching practicum: Pre-service teachers' experiences of professional development. *Teaching and Teacher Education* 36, 198–209.

Kachru, B. (1985) Standards, codification and sociolinguistic realism: English language in the outer circle. In R. Quirk and H. Widowson (eds) *English in the World: Teaching and Learning the Language and Literatures* (p. 11–36). Cambridge University Press.

Kang, H.S. and Pacheco, M.B. (2021) Short-term study abroad in TESOL: Current state and prospects. *TESOL Quarterly* 55 (3), 817–838.

Kang, H.S. and Shin, D. (2024) Mobile-Assisted Language Learning during short-term study abroad. *Frontiers: The Interdisciplinary Journal of Study Abroad* 36 (1), 288–313. https://doi.org/10.36366/frontiers.v36i1.787

Kanno, Y. and Stuart, C. (2011) Learning to become a second language teacher: Identities-in-practice. *The Modern Language Journal* 95 (2), 236–252.

Kasun, G.S. and Saavedra, C.M. (2016) Disrupting ELL teacher candidates' identities: Indigenizing teacher education in one study abroad program. *TESOL Quarterly* 50 (3), 684–707.

Miller, J. (2009) Teacher identity. In A. Burns and J.C. Richards (eds) *The Cambridge Guide to Second Language Teacher Education* (pp. 172–181). Cambridge University Press.

Lee, H. and Jang, G. (2023a) Native English teachers' construction and negotiation of professional identities in the context of Korea: An analysis of multilayered nature of identities. *Teaching and Teacher Education* 122, 103981.

Lee, H. and Jang, G. (2023b) 'The darker your skin color is, the harder it is in Korea': Discursive construction of racial identity in teaching internationally. *TESOL Quarterly* 57 (1), 168–190.

Lindahl, K., Hansen-Thomas, H., Baecher, L. and Stewart, M.A. (2020) Study abroad for critical multilingual language awareness development in teacher candidates. *TESL-EJ* 23 (4), 1–13.

Major, J. and Santoro, N. (2016) Supervising an international teaching practicum: Building partnerships in postcolonial contexts. *Oxford Review of Education* 42 (4), 460–474.

Palmer, D.K. and Menard-Warwick, J. (2012) Short-term study abroad for Texas preservice teachers: On the road from empathy to critical awareness. *Multicultural Education* 19 (3), 17.

Park, J.K. (2009) 'English fever' in South Korea: Its history and symptoms. *English Today* 25 (1), 50–57.

Parker, M.A., Higgins, H., Jones, M., Chandler, C., Smith, K. and Stalls, J. (2022) Exploring the impact of a short-term study abroad experience: Learning in Ethiopia across the years. *Transformative Dialogues: Teaching and Learning Journal* 15 (1), 39–61.

Pilonieta, P., Medina, A. and Hathaway, J. (2017) The impact of a study abroad experience on preservice teachers' dispositions and plans for teaching English language learners. *The Teacher Educator* 52 (1), 22–38.

Rubin, J.C. (2020) Third spaces and tensions: Teacher experiences in an international professional development program. *Teaching and Teacher Education* 95, 103141.

Rudolph, N. (2023) Narratives and negotiations of identity in Japan and criticality in (English) language education:(Dis) connections and implications. *TESOL Quarterly* 57 (2), 375–401.

Rudolph, N., Selvi, A.F. and Yazan, B. (2015) Conceptualizing and confronting inequity: Approaches within and new directions for the 'NNEST movement'. *Critical Inquiry in Language Studies* 12 (1), 27–50.

Seidlhofer, B. (2005) English as a lingua franca. *ELT Journal* 59 (4), 339–341.

Selvi, A.F., Yazan, B. and Mahboob, A. (2023) Research on 'native' and 'non-native' English-speaking teachers: Past developments, current status, and future directions. *Language Teaching.* https://doi.org/10.1017/ S0261444823000137

Slavkov, N., Melo-Pfeifer, S. and Kerschhofer-Puhalo, N. (eds) (2021) *The Changing Face of the 'Native Speaker': Perspectives from Multilingualism and Globalization.* Walter de Gruyter GmbH and Co KG.

Song, J. (2016) Emotions and language teacher identity: Conflicts, vulnerability, and transformation. *TESOL Quarterly* 50 (3), 631–654.

Stachowski, L.L. and Sparks, T. (2007) Thirty years and 2,000 student teachers later: An overseas student teaching project that is popular, successful, and replicable. *Teacher Education Quarterly* 34 (1), 115–132.

Trent, J. (2011) Learning, teaching, and constructing identities: ESL pre-service teacher experiences during a short-term international experience programme. *Asia Pacific Journal of Education* 31 (2), 177–194.

Trilokekar, R.D. and Kukar, P. (2011) Disorienting experiences during study abroad: Reflections of pre-service teacher candidates. *Teaching and Teacher Education* 27 (7), 1141–1150.

Varghese, M., Morgan, B., Johnston, B. and Johnson, K. (2005) Theorizing language teacher identity: Three perspectives and beyond. *Journal of Language, Identity and Education* 4 (1), 21–44.

Varghese, M.M., Motha, S., Park, G., Reeves, J. and Trent, J. (2016) In this issue [of TESOL Quarterly, on language teacher identity]. *TESOL Quarterly* 50 (3), 545–571.

Whitehead, G.E. and Ryu, Y. (2023) 'I am not a native speaker…': Exploring the perceived pronunciation teaching difficulties faced by Korean public elementary school English teachers. *System* 115, 103056.

Yazan, B. (2017) 'It just made me look at language in a different way': ESOL teacher candidates' identity negotiation through teacher education coursework. *Linguistics and Education* 40, 38–49.

13 Toward Antiracist TESOL Teacher Education: Centering Transnational BIPOC Students and Communities

Eunjeong Lee and Chatwara Suwannamai Duran

This chapter discusses the praxis of cultivating antiracist Teaching English to Speakers of Other Languages (TESOL) teacher education. While laudable, internationalizing movement in TESOL programs has received criticisms for performing a 'lip service' to antiracism and social justice without challenging what and who counts as a legitimate language, speaker and teacher, keeping intact the working of colonial, monolingual ideology and nationalist frameworks (Charity Hudley & Flores, 2022; García *et al.*, 2021; Motha, 2020). What does pedagogical praxis to reorient to these efforts from racialized and language-minoritized communities-centered perspectives look like and entail? How can the efforts to internationalize TESOL teacher education simultaneously work against inequalities in English language teaching and learning? This chapter grapples with these questions, situating our discussion in a public-serving university in Houston – a city of the future with racioethnic, cultural and linguistic heterogeneity and transnational flows in the US South. We discuss our praxis to build antiracist TESOL teacher education and significance of a transnational, community-oriented perspective that centers our BIPOC, transnational and multilingual students' rich lived experiences and knowledge of different languages and literacies. We argue that beyond acknowledging onto-epistemological diversity, TESOL teacher education must center inequities and injustices entangled with variedly racialized communities to work toward antiracism and social justice.

Introduction

Scholars in TESOL teacher education and pedagogy have worked toward antiracist and decolonizing praxis for more just and equitable futures (Charity Hudley & Flores, 2022; Friedrich, 2023; García *et al.*, 2021; Kumaravadivelu, 2016; Lin & Motha, 2021; Motha, 2020). Still, the path toward such futures continues to encounter challenges. As of 2023, in our locale, Texas, where people of color are the majority of its population with Latinx communities now accounting for its largest (40.2%) makeup (US Census, 2022), the Texas Legislature passed SB17, which bans Diversity, Equity and Inclusion (DEI) offices and initiatives in state-funded, public higher education institutions. This law, along with attacks on Critical Race Theory, violence on migrants crossing the US–Mexico border, trans youth's right for gender-affirming care and women's reproductive right, to name a few, demonstrate the state's oppressive regime against those who are deemed as 'diverse', including our Black, Indigenous and other communities of color. Behind these bills lie colonial, white supremacist ideologies that hierarchize different communities and their belonging.

Residing and working in Houston, a home for more than 145 languages (Fairmont Homes, 2023), we, as TESOL teacher-scholars, acknowledge the inequitable realities we live in, and find it ever more significant to sustain, humanize, and honor our BIPOC multilingual communities' ways of being, knowing and doing language. What does the work of TESOL teacher educators to honor and sustain racialized and language-minoritized communities' ways of being, knowing and doing language look like and entail? What could our context of Houston inform TESOL teacher-scholars in their approach to internationalization of TESOL? This chapter grapples with these questions. As 'English language teaching and learning practices are completely meaningful when understood in the local contexts in which they occur' (Ramanathan, 2005: 120), we describe our praxis that attunes to our students, communities and their multilingual and transnational experiences in our locale.

We adopt transnational approaches, which normalize transnational flows and activities, including multilingual practice as a way of living. As two 'non-native' English-speaking, transnational, multilingual, immigrant-generation Asian woman scholars-educators – Eunjeong from South Korea and Chatwara from Thailand – our praxis is rooted in and emergent from our lived experiences of how our differences may be challenged, racialized and otherwise marginalized, in institutional and interpersonal spaces even more so in this era of oppressions (Flores & Rosa, 2023; Kubota & Lin, 2006). In all, our administrative and pedagogical practice aims to challenge the top-down, white, Eurocentric, monolingual norms and ideologies that dominate TESOL.

Houston: A Transnational City of 'Diversity'

Houston challenges the typical assumption of Texas and the homogenic US South. Being home to many business sectors, some of the largest oil companies and the largest medical center in the world, Houston witnesses an influx of professionals and workers from across the globe. Also one of the most racially and ethnically diverse cities in the US, Houston has approximately 29% of its population identifying themselves as foreign-born (1.7 million out of 7.2 million total residents), in comparison to 13.5% foreign-born residents in the whole nation (Greater Houston Partnership, 2023). The most common birthplaces outside the US include Mexico, India and El Salvador, to name a few, with varieties of Spanish, Vietnamese, Chinese, Arabic, French, Hindi, Urdu, Tagalog and other languages constantly spoken and heard.

With these data, Houston may easily seem like a *global* or an *internationalized* city at first glance. However, with a closer look, the city has a much more complex sociolinguistic makeup and history, with a multitude of transnational activities and flows of/across various ways of meaning making. For example, the University of Houston (UH), where we currently are working at, sits in the Third Ward – a historically Black neighborhood and also a site of Black communities' activism for racial justice. The neighboring Second Ward – also called El Segundo – was 'a hub of Mexican American social life' (McWhorter, 2010: 42) already in the 1910s, still largely populated by Mexican and other Latinx communities. Our Asian communities have grown from 1% to 26% in their population for the last 50 years, complexifying the city's racioethnic, linguistic and migratory history.

These growing transnational communities challenge whether or not the term 'internationalization' fits, and whose perspective it represents. For instance, Vietnamese communities in Houston, one of the largest in the US, keep their ties with their roots by traveling back and forth between the US and Vietnam, bringing their cuisine, expertise and faith into the Southeast region of Houston. They practice their bi/multilingual meaning-making while consuming Vietnamese cultural products, creating uniquely fusion dishes that represent multicultural Houston, and supporting their families financially both *here* and *there*. The same thing can be said to other cultural and racioethnic groups that maintain strong connections to their cultural heritage in their everyday practices.

In this sense, the complexity and dynamicity of Houston's sociolinguistic landscape and practices makes it imperative that we adopt transnational perspectives. The cultural abundance and the translocally complex, multi-faceted and dynamic forces make Houston a critical site with much potential to offer what transnational and anti-racist TESOL teacher education might look and work like. Transnational lenses allow us to investigate and weave threads of active and durable bonds between spaces more clearly, viewing people as important and interactive social agents (Glick Schiller *et al.*, 1995), unlike the top-down, unilateral, US-centered perspective as the notion of internationalization often conveys. In our transnational thinking, we also take up Wan *et al.*'s (2023) call to move away from the white-gazed notion of '(super)diversity' and ideological forces that erase the different racialized and language-minoritized communities' long presence and their language and literacy practices under the working of neoliberal ideologies (see also Flores & Aneja, 2017). In this way, our discussion also carefully considers how transnational perspectives further inform anti-racist praxis.

Antiracist TESOL Teacher Education in the Transnational World

The move to dismantle colonial ideologies and reimagine the field of TESOL with the anti-racist and decolonizing vision has been an ongoing struggle. As critical applied linguists have long problematized, TESOL and Applied Linguistics, as a field, are enmeshed with white supremacy and empire through their historical and ongoing participation in racio-ethnic stratification by way of (re)producing discourses of idealized language, speakers and teachers that are valued and contribute to the neoliberal global workforce (Flores & Rosa, 2015; García *et al.*, 2021; Kubota, 2020; Kumaravadivelu, 2016; Motha, 2020). As Motha (2020: 129) argues, we, teacher-scholars in TESOL and Applied Linguistics, need to be cognizant of how our work 'has functioned as an important and effective vehicle for white supremacy and relatedly empire'. And this commitment requires critical interrogation of how our work continues to adopt and extend race-neutral terms and frameworks as well as the logics and structure of settler colonialism (Flores & Rosa, 2023; Motha, 2020; Tuck & Yang, 2012).

Accordingly, anti-racist praxis in TESOL teacher education in the US has focused on disrupting the dominant language ideologies that undergird white supremacy and settler colonialism. To move beyond colonial, white-centered, monolingual-oriented frameworks, many have called for centering multilingual-oriented frameworks, such as translanguaging, plurilingualism and metrolingualism (Canagarajah, 2013; Pennycook & Otsuji, 2019). Often discussed as part of 'Trans/Plural' turn, these frameworks foreground multilingual meaning-making and identities on their own terms, emphasizing multilingual communication across borders – both visible and invisible – as a norm. In particular, as a theoretical orientation to language and pedagogical framework, translanguaging has received much attention in language teaching and teacher education, including TESOL teacher education (Flores & Aneja, 2017; Pontier & Tian, 2022; Seltzer, 2022; Seltzer & de los Ríos, 2018). In enacting translanguaging praxis, scholars have emphasized an epistemological shift toward 'translanguaging stance' (García *et al.*, 2017) or translingual dispositions (Lee & Cangarajah, 2019) in viewing emergent bi/multilingual students' language practices away from the monolingual, deficit perspective.

Yet, the epistemological shift must pay careful attention to the ontological difference. Critiquing the way translanguaging may obscure how differently racialized communities experience and practice language and 'raciolinguistic ideologies' (Flores & Rosa, 2015), Seltzer (2022) discusses how teacher educators can take up 'a critical translingual approach' (Seltzer & de los Ríos, 2018) – a translingual approach that also takes a raciolinguistic perspective in its conceptualization of language – to help teachers to understand how oppressive language ideologies operate on language-minoritized students. Emphasizing the role of teacher educators in culturally sustaining and revitalizing pedagogies (Alim & Paris, 2017), Domínguez (2017: 228) similarly argues that teacher educators must work toward '*affective* change, a shift in ontology, in how teachers see and value the diversity of experiences, ways of being, and realities that exist in the world'.

Shifting away from the dominating colonial and other harmful conceptualizations of language and relations takes constant and sustained reflexivity. Uncritical uptake with such frameworks can keep intact the systemic issues of racist, sexist and otherwise oppressive violence and the underlying dominant normativized ideologies, continue 'epistemological racism' (Kubota, 2020: 3) toward knowledges emergent from Global South (Pennycook & Makoni, 2019), or extend the settler colonial and neoliberal logics (Kubota, 2016; Motha, 2020; Tuck & Yang, 2012). As an important tool for reflection, learning and disrupting the working of dominant monoglossic and raciolinguistic ideologies, teacher educators in English education have discussed use of consciousness-raising activities such as autoethnography, written or multimodal storytelling of teachers' language learning or teaching experience, community-engaged inquiry, engaging with materials written by and from perspectives of BIPOC communities, semiotic or discourse analysis on examples of language use or metacommentary that demonstrates the working of dominant language ideologies (Baker-Bell, 2020; Caldas, 2019; Domínguez, 2017; Sánchez-Martín, 2021; Seltzer, 2022).

And such reflections and onto-epistemological shifts should extend to interrogation of the political nature of language teaching, and the role of pedagogy in disrupting the white-gazed, monolingual, English-only ideology. The onto-epistemological shift then necessitates in not just the way teachers understand language, speakers and their material and ideological conditions, and relations that constitute these conditions, but also how teachers themselves are implicated in the relations (Lee, 2021). As many Indigenous scholars and their allies have argued, we need to re-imagine the relations between teachers and students and their communities, away from the colonial pathologizing lens toward our communities (Patel, 2016;

Tuck, 2009). Cultivating 'answerable' (Patel, 2016) TESOL education through teacher education work demands teachers and teacher educators to recognize themselves in community with their students and communities, rather than gatekeepers of the boundaries and hierarchization of knowledge about legitimate language and language users between the institution and the community.

In our context of a historically Black city of Houston with linguistic and cultural richness of multilingual communities with varied migration histories and statuses, US police killing of Black and Brown bodies, anti-Asian racism resurgent during the COVID-19 and heightened visibility of white supremacy rhetoric and violence against refugees and migrants from the US–Mexico border make us all the more aware of our responsibility as TESOL teacher educators. We stand at a critical juncture where on the one hand, the demand for English continuously remains high and normalized, particularly with the increase of English as a medium of instruction globally; on the other, TESOL and its teacher education continues to be dominated by whiteness (Daniels & Varghese, 2019; Flores & Rosa, 2023; Motha, 2020; Sleeter, 2001). In this sense, TESOL practitioners have critical responsibilities to disrupt the normative discourses about English and colonial ideologies as well as cultivate new subject positions and relations that can work against the oppressive regimes against the global trend of a neoliberal take on internationalization of higher education (Lee, 2021).

Conscientious of the way coloniality functions as a transnational mechanism to categorize and hierarchize different bodies (Rosa & Flores, 2017), we work with an understanding that uptaking a transnational and anti-racist approach means recognizing both the complexity of multiple forces beyond one nation-state and language that shape our majority transnational, racialized and language-minoritized students, and working against colonial ideologies and the white gaze that racialize our students and communities (Alim & Paris, 2017; García *et al.*, 2021; Morrison, 1993; Wan *et al.*, 2023).

Praxis for Anti-racist TESOL Education and Teacher Preparation

As many scholars have emphasized, transnational language and literacy practices are entangled with many things, such as networks, ideologies and people and their identities (Duran, 2017; Sánchez-Martín, 2021). As transnational, racialized and gendered multilingual teacher-scholars ourselves, at the center of our praxis is our understanding of how our students' positionalities and language and literacy practices are part of the transnational networks and forces that variedly shape their everyday experiences, and their communities' historicities in Houston. Below, we discuss how we have worked toward anti-racist TESOL teacher education in our classroom and beyond.

Redefining 'teachers of English' based on local language ecologies and resources

The native speakerism paradigm forwards an ideal image of teachers of English as white monolingual 'native' English speakers. In this view, teachers also carry a mission to provide English education to speakers of other languages, as a speaker with authority and legitimacy over so-called standard English, often excused for the limited knowledge of other languages and cultures. As a result, teacher education often emphasizes how to prepare educators to understand and teach this particular construct of language to English language learners from various backgrounds. While many scholars have heavily critiqued the native speakerism, the myth is yet prevalent, even in a 'diverse' place like UH, if not Houston, continuously racializing our language-minoritized students and communities, who will potentially become future educators.

UH consists of an 'extremely diverse' student body, ranking No. 16 for 'Lots of Race/Class Interaction' (Princeton Review, 2023). With 80% of the student body institutionally categorized as racioethnic minority (University of Houston, 2022), the institution has been officially designated as a Hispanic-Serving Institution and an Asian American Native American Pacific Islander-Serving Institution (AANAPISI) by the US Department of Education. Diversity goes beyond race; UH serves many first-generation, veteran and the LGBTQIA+-identifying college students, with an increasing number of international students and growing exchange student programs.

Accordingly, we constantly hear multilingual practice, stories of learning, teaching and translating, as well as language loss, and other lived experiences of our students and their families, which involve locales other than the US. Yet, they do not always consider TESOL as a career path – the choice that is also often entangled with their own lived experience of linguistic racism and raciolinguistic ideologies (Flores & Rosa, 2015). For us, therefore, introducing TESOL as a career option for our students – particularly our racialized multilingual students – has been an ongoing advocacy act, not just for them but also for Houston, our public education and global ELT. In our effort to disrupt the traditional native speakerism in the TESOL profession, our privileged positionalities of being multilingual and transnational TESOL scholars has been important. Many minoritized and immigrant-generation students view us as someone with similar experiences of English learning, acculturation and/or migration trajectories, therefore seeing a possibility of becoming TESOL scholars regardless of country of origin and native language. For white monolingual 'native' English-speaking students, our positionalities as non-white, 'non-native' English speakers, yet qualified professionals and professors in TESOL, have broadened their views of an academic and professional domain.

Attuning to the various future educators in our classrooms and campus, we have worked to redefine TESOL teachers and what teachers of English must know and be able to do based on their rich lived experiences, transnational connections and understanding and hard-earned local knowledge, apart from the formal training. Moving toward antiracist TESOL teacher preparation, Chatwara and her colleagues designed a Teaching English as an Additional Language (TEAL) certificate program with a consideration of existing local conditions, including students' experiences and their desires in mind. That is, students from all backgrounds and majors, not limited to the English major, can enroll and complete this 15-credit program.

The required Practicum is also tailored to fit students' own research interests, needs and desire to collaborate with local communities, and career goals. For example, students who want to teach English abroad are supervised to assist international students in the intensive English program; students with Communication Disorder major work with bi/multilingual and/or disabled clients to complete the Practicum; students active in their communities can teach English for a non-profit organization to fulfill the Practicum. With this broader view of TESOL teachers and a contextualized practical curriculum in place, our pre-service teachers engage in and expand ecologies of language learning in their own way. The certificate program may be a small drive in the community to educate teachers of English from all backgrounds. But, such a localized and context-sensitive certificate program contributes to TESOL teacher education from the ground up and addresses the local needs, which differs from a generic certificate program that focuses on a mass production of TESOL educators.

Diversifying channels for English education and TESOL teacher preparation

Having one of the biggest numbers of immigrants and refugees in the US, Texas has seen increasing volunteering and internship opportunities to serve these newcomers (Pew Research Center, 2023). In Houston, universities and community colleges offer intensive English programs or ESL classes for academic and professional purposes. English tutors are in high demand for private tutoring sessions both for children and adults in affluent neighborhoods. Local libraries, churches, counties, government-funded sectors and non-profit organizations offer free English classes for adults. Amid abundant sites of education, TESOL teacher preparation should consider equitable access to these sites for communities, and go beyond a linear education program or a formal classroom as these spaces are often not accessible to many of our racialized and language-minoritized communities. A journey to become a teacher of English then should not be exclusively limited by a strictly designed experience of taking a series of mandatory content classes and a practicum, as often charted by the official teaching certificate program. While the TESOL certificate program is vital, we offer the following pathways that work to expand and sustain various sites and ways of language learning for communities while fostering relevant teaching experiences.

We encourage students to find teaching opportunities locally, beyond the formal classroom spaces. Chatwara recruited college students to teach English in Houston's communities, refugee and immigrant support groups, and non-profit organizations that provide English tutoring classes for K-12 and adult English learners in the underserved neighborhoods. With this community-centered approach, students recognize how English is used and learned among local learners for everyday living, jobs and academic purposes. They see the context-specific problems, understand how teaching English can be a practice for equity, and that sites of English education are not equally equipped and resourced. Understanding the local problems, some students created goal-oriented teaching projects such as Teaching ESL and mental health together for Black, Brown and Asian immigrant and refugee mothers, who are often new to the American healthcare and education systems. A group of students partnered with medical students and created an ESL class that included sex education for recently arrived refugee high school students. The community-based approach is grounded in antiracist pedagogy, raising pre-service teachers' consciousness to teach English for equity, centering real-world problems in classrooms and taking action that aligns with their beliefs. Producing teachers who see themselves as active community members then can support the underprivileged communities' access to English education.

Part of anti-racist educator work is to reveal the colonial and racist ideologies that uphold the structure and disrupt such structure. To this end, we have encouraged students to view their transnational experiences and disposition as valuable to teach abroad. UH has recently been one of the top Fulbright English Language Assistant producers. Chatwara has been a regular committee member, interviewing Fulbright English Teaching Assistant candidates for many years. Having witnessed successful Fulbright recipients coming from BIPOC immigrant-background communities and various fields of studies, beyond white middle-class families and English majors, Chatwara encourages students in her TESOL-related and Applied Linguistics courses to think of teaching English locally and abroad as a possibility. Chatwara invites Fulbright alumni/returnees to share their experience of teaching abroad in her classes. She offers students her support with job application processes and placement. By sending students from various cultural and linguistic backgrounds to teach abroad – especially BIPOC teachers, Chatwara challenges the white-dominant status quo of what teachers of English can be through her anti-racist advocacy work.

And even when our students' lived experience is filled with different ways of knowing and doing language, and translanguaging stance, as research has shown, it is not easy to 'translate' such disposition into practice (Flores & Aneja, 2017; García *et al.*, 2017; Pontier & Tian, 2022; Seltzer & de los Ríos, 2018). For this reason, in Eunjeong's class, students' projects focus on their praxis as community-engaged activist teachers. For instance, students have worked on a curriculum or a lesson plan that engages and sustains multilingual students' language practices through transnational, translingual and culturally sustaining pedagogical lenses (Alim & Paris, 2017; García *et al.*, 2017). They have also produced multimodal sociolinguistic activism work where they produce and share public-facing content to problematize linguistic violence and oppression that many of our communities have experienced and call for action.

Centralizing BIPOC students and communities' multilingual experiences in the classroom

Important in setting the tone for antiracist pedagogy is to start from acknowledging our sociolinguistic realities where our variedly rich multilingual students and communities experience and practice language and literacies. Many of our students already bring the critical sense of how this experience is connected to power, the discourse of which continues to discriminate and racialize their language in the racial capitalist society. Affirming their critical knowledge from lived experience in classrooms is crucial to extend the critical reflection and cultivate a space to translate the ideological understanding of language into practice, not just for racialized multilingual students but also students who view themselves as monolingual (Seltzer & de los Ríos, 2018).

To make visible different ways in which students experience and navigate inequitable multilingual realities, Eunjeong centers the discussion of bodily differences in experiencing linguistic realities. Regardless of what class Eunjeong teaches, the class begins with acknowledgement of how the key terms for the class, such as language, proficiency, correctness, norms, are never neutral. Throughout the semester, students read, watch and listen to materials that center BIPOC communities' multilingual experiences. They then further reflect on their own experience of language and how their experience is shaped by the dominant language ideologies that privilege a monolingual, homogenous group of people idealized as legitimate speakers – that is white, middle-class, able-bodied, cis-gendered people. While their experience with named languages varies, what often becomes common is how, despite their legal status, they and their communities all have experienced the deficit perspective on their language.

Part of taking an anti-racist approach to TESOL also means to understand and historicize our students' and their communities' varied lived experiences with multilingualism across different locales. As discussed above, TESOL Teacher Curricula and Certificate Program can be tailored to focus on local community-based practicum and sociocultural foundation for this endeavor. In the classroom, we used local news and historical events to connect students and pre-service teachers to their own surroundings and thinking about how and why racialization and ethnic conflicts locally occur. For instance, we turned to city maps of ethnically enclaved neighborhoods to discuss how the history of segregation has divided zones and neighborhoods, how migrations and refugee resettlements change the linguistic landscapes, and what these factors means for linguistic, cultural and educational resources in different parts of the city.

Another important dimension for us is to highlight and honor our racialized communities' language practice as part of the activism work in Houston. While they engage in transnational activities, understanding that their ancestors and community members have worked to fight for belonging affirms their sense of belonging as a transnational, racialized, multilingual. To situate language in our communities' ways of being and living, away from the neoliberal discourse of multilingualism (Kubota, 2016) or colonial discourse of language as 'a natural scientific object' (Heller & McElhinney, 2017: 117; see also Makoni & Pennycook, 2007), we have emphasized language and literacy practices as crucial activist work of shaping and transforming our sociolinguistic reality. Eunjeong's students have researched and examined activist history in the Third Ward, local Indigenous communities' (such as Karankawa and Akokisa) continual land stewardship and language documentation projects, Latinx communities' use of Spanish in their protest against immigration laws as well as in arts and music, LGBTQIA+ group activism, and community organizations' fight for language justice for Asian and im/migrant communities. Mindful of how their work is also often erased in language and literacy classrooms as critical language competence and literacies, Eunjeong's students have designed a short activity and longer units where their current and future students can learn about this history while learning English. They have also taken on activism work for language-minoritized communities by creating content and sharing it on their own social media.

To expand the conversation on our students' local multilingual experiences and knowledge as always connected to various historical and ongoing global forces, Eunjeong has had students conduct a sociolinguistic inquiry on each other, based on their shared interests and experiences. In Eunjeong's sociolinguistics class, students freely explore their past and current language experiences, focusing on memorable incidents, ideas, or thoughts in their reflection essays. They are then grouped together based on common themes, and read each other's essays to prepare for their language history interview. Together, students often explore various topics that are central in their own experience of language. Some of the past discussions included themes of changing relationships with and affective connections to their heritage language, the role of family language policies and dynamics in their language practice, bilingual schooling experience, migration histories and changing sense of home as tied to their language and racialized and gendered identities and their language practices.

Throughout their inquiry, along with discussions of the course material, our students developed understanding of complexity and richness of each other's transnational lived experience. By engaging in sociolinguistic inquiry on their classmates, the students not only had a chance to reflect on their own but extend such reflections beyond their own experience to understand varied historicities with different languages in Houston. But also importantly, they understand how the experiences of language, even in the same 'locale', are bound to differ based on their positionalities, their families' linguistic and cultural practices, socioeconomic conditions and racioethnic makeup of neighborhoods and educational institutions that they grew up in and attended, among others. This way, their inquiry is one that builds on and expands their own historicity as a transnational, multilingual language user and a community member, but also one that propels them to see their role as a future educator that crucially constitutes the sociolinguistic fabric of the city and has a responsibility to not participate in the inequitable sociolinguistic experiences that they and their peers have shared.

Conclusion

Despite the intention to respond to the inequities in the English language teaching and learning, internationalization of TESOL can reinforce white-gazed homogeneity of language and TESOL teacher education without taking up anti-racist and transnational approaches. Its efforts to 'diversify' and 'internationalize' its teaching force can keep intact the privilege of English that carries the colonial past and tradition. In this sense, disrupting the structure that is dominated by whiteness and white perceiving subjects inevitably requires a transnational thinking as its approach (Duran, 2017; Lee, 2021). Also importantly, developing TESOL teacher education based on the emerging translocal and transnational conditions also allows us to fight against this one-size-fit-all approach, expanding what language and literacy can mean and do for different people.

TESOL and language and literacy educators can either subvert or uphold the dominant language ideologies that continue to maintain the colonial structure within the global English language teaching. Therefore, English language teaching should not be presented just as a necessary capital important for neoliberal workforce but one that can reveal, disrupt and transform our sociolinguistic realities. Such advocacy efforts should also be cognizant of the multi-layered inequities and inequalities embedded in local communities' language historicities, experiences and practices. As we have shown, this work can occur on multiple levels such as mini-research and storytelling in the classroom, and administrative and institutional levels responsible for designing and implementing antiracist curricula that center real-world problems. Such work must also blur the boundaries of the institutional and community spaces, situating our communities' language in the actual struggles, livelihood and joy. With this drive, we hope our praxis can move toward decolonial, antiracist, and just possibilities (Charity Hudley & Flores, 2022; Meighan, 2022; Motha, 2020).

References

Alim, H.S. and Paris, D. (eds) (2017) What is culturally sustaining pedagogy and why does it matter? In D. Paris and H.S. Alim (eds) *Culturally sustaining pedagogies: Teaching and Learning for Justice in a Changing World* (pp. 1–21). Teachers College Press.

Baker-Bell, A. (2020) *Linguistic Justice, Black Language, Literacy, Identity and Pedagogy*. Routledge.

Caldas, B. (2019) To switch or not to switch: Bilingual preservice teachers and translanguaging in teaching and learning. *TESOL Journal* 10 (4). https://doi.org/10.1002/tesj.485

Canagarajah, A.S. (2013) *Translingual Practice: Global Englishes and Cosmopolitan Relations*. Routledge.

Charity Hudley, A. and Flores, N. (2022) Social justice in applied linguistics: Not a conclusion, but a way forward. *Annual Review of Applied Linguistics* 42, 144–154. https://doi.org/10.1017/S0267190522000083

Daniels, J.R. and Varghese, M. (2020) Troubling practice: Exploring the relationship between Whiteness and practice-based teacher education in considering a raciolinguicized teacher subjectivity. *Educational Researcher* 49 (1), 56–63. https://doi.org/10.3102/0013189X19879450

Domínguez, M. (2017) 'Se Hace Puentes al Andar': Decolonial teacher education as a needed bridge to culturally sustaining and revitalizing pedagogies. In D. Paris and H.S. Alim (eds) *Culturally Sustaining Pedagogies: Teaching and Learning for Justice in a Changing World* (pp. 225–246). Teachers College Press.

Duran, C.S. (2017) *Language and Literacy in Refugee Families*. Palgrave Macmillan.

Fairmont Homes (2023) At least 145 languages spoken in Houston Metro homes. https://fairmontcustomhomes.com/at-least-145-languages-spoken-in-hous ton-metro-homes/

Flores, N. and Rosa, J. (2015) Undoing appropriateness: Raciolinguistic ideologies and language diversity in education. *Harvard Educational Review* 85 (2), 149–171.

Flores, N. and Aneja, G. (2017) 'Why needs hiding?' Translingual (re)orientations in TESOL teacher education. *Research in the Teaching of English* 51 (4), 441–463.

Flores, N. and Rosa, J. (2023) Undoing competence: Coloniality, homogeneity, and the overrepresentation of Whiteness in applied linguistics. *Language Learning*. https://doi.org/10.1111/lang.12528

Friedrich, P. (2023) Anti-racist linguistics. In P. Friedrich (ed). *The Anti-Racism Linguist: A Book of Readings* (pp. 1–25). Multilingual Matters.

García, O., Ibarra Johnson, S. and Seltzer, K. (2017) *The Translanguaging Classroom: Leveraging Student Bilingualism for Learning*. Brookes Publishing.

García, O., Flores, N., Seltzer, K., Li, W., Otheguy, R. and Rosa, J. (2021) Rejecting abyssal thinking in the language and education of racialized bilinguals: A manifesto. *Critical Inquiry in Language Studies* 18 (3), 203–228. https://doi.org/10.1080/15427587.2021.1935957

Glick Schiller, N., Basch, L. and Szanton-Blanc, C. (1995) From migrants to transmigrant: Theorizing transnational migration. *Anthropological Quarterly* 68 (1), 48–63.

Greater Houston Partnership. (2023) Foreign-born population data. https://www.houston.org/

Heller, M. and McElhinney, B. (2017) *Language, Capitalism, Colonialism: Toward a Critical History.* University of Toronto Press.

Kubota, R. (2016) The multi/plural turn, postcolonial theory, and neoliberal multiculturalism: Complicities and implications for applied linguistics. *Applied Linguistics* 37, 474–494.

Kubota, R. (2020) Confronting epistemological racism, decolonizing scholarly knowledge: Race and gender in applied linguistics. *Applied Linguistics* 41 (5), 712–732.

Kubota, R. and Lin, A. (2006) Race and TESOL: Concepts, research, and future directions. *TESOL Quarterly* 40 (3), 471–493.

Kumaravadivelu, B. (2016) The decolonial option in English teaching: Can the subaltern act? *TESOL Quarterly* 50 (1), 66–85.

Lee, E. (2021) Transnationalism in TESOL teacher education and applied linguistics: Reflections and (re)imaginations. In A. Ahmed and O. Barnawi (eds) *Mobility of Knowledge, Practice and Pedagogy in TESOL Teacher Education* (pp. 13–37). Palgrave MacMillan.

Lee, E. and Canagarajah, A.S. (2019) Beyond native and nonnative: Translingual dispositions for more inclusive teacher identity in language and literacy education. *Journal of Language, Identity & Education* 18 (6), 352–363.

Lin, A.M. and Motha, S. (2021) 'Curses in TESOL': Postcolonial desires for colonial English. In R. Arber, R. Weinmann and J. Blackmore (eds) *Rethinking Languages Education: Directions, Challenges and Innovations* (pp. 15–35). Routledge.

Makoni, S. and Pennycook, A. (2007) (eds) *Disinventing and Reconstituting Languages.* Multilingual Matters.

McWhorter, T. (2010) From das zweiter to el segundo: A brief history of Houston's Second Ward. *Houston History* 8 (1), 38–42. https://houstonhistorymagazine.org/wp-content/uploads/2010/12/vol-8-no-1-Second-Ward.pdf

Meighan, P. (2022) Decolonizing English: A proposal for implementing alternative ways of knowing and being in education. *Diaspora, Indigenous, and Minority Education* 15 (2), 77–83. https://doi.org/10.1080/15595692.2020.1783228

Morrison, T. (1993) Interview with Charlie Rose. The Power of Questions: Charlie Rose. https://charlierose.com/videos/31212

Motha, S. (2020) Is an antiracist and decolonizing applied linguistics possible? *Annual Review of Applied Linguistics* 40, 128–133.

Patel, L. (2016) *Decolonizing Educational Research: From Ownership to Answerability.* Routledge.

Pennycook, A. and Makoni, S. (2019) *Innovations and Challenges in Applied Linguistics from the Global South.* Routledge. https://doi.org/10.4324/9780429489396

Pennycook, A. and Otsuji, E. (2019) Mundane metrolingualism. *International Journal of Multilingualism* 16 (2), 175–186. https://doi.org/10.1080/14790718.2019.1575836

Pew Research Center (2023) Just 10 states resettled more than half of recent refugees to U.S. https://www.pewresearch.org/short-reads/2016/12/06/just-10-states-resettled-more-than-half-of-recent-refugees-to-u-s/

Pontier, R.W. and Tian, Z. (eds) (2022) Paradigmatic tensions in translanguaging theory and practice in teacher education [Special Issue]. *Journal of Language, Identity and Education* 21 (3). https://www.tandfonline.com/toc/hlie20/21/3

Princeton Review (2023) University of Houston. https://www.princetonreview.com/college/university-houston-1023561

Ramanathan, V. (2005) Seepages, contact zones, and amalgam: Internationalizing TESOL. *TESOL Quarterly* 39 (1), 119–123.

Rosa, J. and Flores, N. (2017) Unsettling race and language: Toward a raciolinguistic perspective. *Language in society* 46 (5), 621–647.

Sánchez-Martín, C. (2021) Teachers' transnational identities as activity: Constructing mobility systems at the intersections of gender and language difference. *TESOL Quarterly* 56 (2), 552–581. https://doi.org/10.1002/tesq.3066

Seltzer, K. (2022) Enacting a critical translingual approach in teacher preparation: Disrupting oppressive language ideologies and fostering the personal, political, and pedagogical stances of preservice teachers of English. *TESOL Journal* 13 (2). https://doi.org/10.1002/tesj.649

Seltzer, K. and de los Ríos, C.V. (2018) Translating theory to practice: Exploring teachers' raciolinguistic literacies in secondary English classrooms. *English Education* 51 (1), 49–79. https://doi.org/10.58680/ee201829833

Sleeter, C. (2001) Preparing teachers for culturally diverse schools: Research and the overwhelming presence of whiteness. *Journal of Teacher Education* 52 (2), 94–106.

Tuck, E. (2009) Suspending damage: A letter to communities. *Harvard Educational Review* 79 (3), 409–427.

Tuck, E. and Yang, K.W. (2012) Decolonization is not a metaphor. *Decolonization: Indigeneity, Education and Society* 1 (1), 1–40.

University of Houston (2022) Facts at a glance. https://uh.edu/ir/reports/facts-at-a-glance/facts-at-a-glance.pdf

U.S. Census (2022) Quick Facts: Texas. https://www.census.gov/quickfacts/TX

Wan, A.J., Lee, E. and Alvarez, S.P. (2023) 'Queens is the Future': WPA horizons for transnational spaces. In C. Donahue and B. Horner (eds) *Teaching and Studying Transnational Composition* (pp. 305–322). Modern Language Association of America.

14 Future Preparers of TESOL Teachers: Construction of Decolonizing Community Space by Weaving International Identities

G. Sue Kasun, Saniha Kabani and J. Nozipho Moyo

The decolonizing community space was co-constructed by a transnationally oriented professor (e.g. Kasun & Mora-Pablo, 2022) and three doctoral students. Each student was from varying language, ethnic and geographic identities, united in their experiences of teaching in the United States' southeastern region (Urrieta & Noblit, 2018). Collaboratively, they purposefully developed a reading list which primarily focused on identity and its multi-faceted intersections with race, culture and raciolinguistics along with the positioning of identity in the international realm (Ladson-Billings, 1995; Muhammad, 2020). Through the student-led discussions, micro community cultural wealth developed (Yosso, 2005). During the learning process, the professor received a cancer diagnosis. As a result, the students were led to take ownership of their learning in dialog with their professor. Their community wealth (Yosso, 2005) extended beyond the learning environment in support of one of the community members: the professor. Authentic cariño was reflected as the students offered emotional support, coordinated a post-op recovery schedule, provided meals for the professor's family, care-taking and formed new relationships with extended members of the professor's community (Valenzuela, 1999). By upholding a decolonizing community space, the participants lived out the values of Ubuntu (Pennycook & Makoni, 2020) and ummah (His Highness Prince Karim Aga Khan, 2016). They modeled the ways in which internationalization extends far beyond learning environments. This critical auto-ethnographic reflective piece, framed through a weaving of the aforementioned global wisdoms of the importance of living in the collective, provides readers an opportunity to reframe roles of teacher/educator/caregiver in their international efforts toward creating spaces of learning.

Construction of Decolonizing Community Space by Weaving International Identities

As 'decolonial' professor and advisor, one wants to believe they are teaching decolonially. I, Sue, never expected a cancer diagnosis to serve as a catalyst in amplifying the decolonial teaching space, an event I turn to momentarily. Most of my doctoral students are future educators of TESOL teachers – TESOL educators in progress – and I embrace a decolonial approach to engaging them. They are all from rich cultural backgrounds as well, what serves as a source of inspiration for which I am grateful, thanks, in part, to our location in Atlanta, Georgia, US. When I teach my students, officially, this includes their own evaluations of themselves and/or my up-front explaining they will all receive an A – the highest score in the US education system – for their work to clear away the power differential created by the construct of a grading system. This approach to grading was a result from when co-author Nozi asked guest speaker Gustavo Esteva, during the Covid-19 pandemic and our synchronous, online course on decolonizing education, how he would decolonize education. He said he would stop making it compulsory and give everyone As. For doctoral students, this is something I decided I needed to take up, and for several years in my classes, I have achieved a sense of community and deeper learning as the students themselves take the power to decide what they learn. My reflection on and embracing of additional ideas beyond the white ways of knowing I grew up with is something I take on daily toward the goal of glimpsing into what Anzaldúa claims we can do as White women toward 'women of color consciousness' (Anzaldúa, 2002) while linking all my intersectional identities into a continued journey of growth, healing, and connection (Kasun, 2018).

Beyond the official moments of teaching, we meet regularly over zoom and more frequently in-person. Because in many ways I am 'elder' to the students, I am vulnerable with them without oversharing, creating a space where we can connect, but where I am available for counsel more than they are to me. We share meals together, usually at my house, even with my young children afoot. It is my politics to cook for my students and be hospitable (Esteva, 2018; Illich, 1973), a genuine effort to literally serve and with joy, while intentionally creating community. Throughout many years, my students have taken time to express gratitude for my care and concern for them as their advisor and as a person. To better illustrate, I provide a couple examples from each of the co-author writers of this chapter.

During one of my regular meetings with co-author Saniha in 2022, she expressed concerns about wishing she could study more math education instead of being locked into her originally slated track of a PhD program with a concentration in 'language and literacy education'. 'Oh, Saniha, we can totally address this!' I exclaimed. She was shocked to know she could change advisors, if necessary, as well as programs to one that aligned much better with her newer interest in hybridizing mathematics education and working with multilingual learners. She did not need to shift advisors, but offering the flexibility allowed her a new space of possibility, a hallmark of decolonial work and understanding.

Nozi (co-author) went to the expense of attending my second study-abroad course after finding the first two-week experience in 2022 to be both rich and decolonizing (Kasun *et al.*, 2024). There is absolutely no expectation on my part that students would, first, attend my study abroad (something not covered by regular tuition and fees) let alone come back a second time. 'Sue, there is so much to learn about Indigenizing language and education on your trip, I really want to go back,' she explained when she discussed her interest to return. Nozi was a source of comfort and wisdom during both trips, a student I could turn to for on-the-spot decision-making for the benefit of the group in moments where quick decisions had to be made.

Because I prioritize fostering authentic communication with my doctoral students, I realized three of them would benefit from a directed readings course where they collectively read and dialoged about identity, race, language and education from Global South and other adjacent perspectives. I am not seeking approbation by sharing this, but at my institution, there is no 'pay' for leading directed readings or other labor that does not constitute a formal course. So, any of this form of work is done strictly to do better mentoring, a role I take seriously when I consider myself a mentor to them in the field, as well. Initially, I helped facilitate their first discussions but saw they certainly did not need me there for fruitful discussion. And suddenly, at the end of September 2022, I realized my role would have to dramatically change.

'Nozi,' [one of my co-authors here] I began with the most senior of the three students. 'I don't know if I told you I had a rare form of cancer, sarcoma, in 2015. I do scans every year, and it's back – in my liver. I need a biopsy, but I'm pretty sure they'll have to cut out about 3 cm of my liver. I don't know how often I can join your reading group as I set up my life in advance of this,' I blurted, unsure of how it all sounded, worried about how she might take the news, and still in disbelief that this rare sarcoma had returned, knowing I was facing a serious and complicated surgical procedure for a growth that wanted to consume me. 'Sue, of course we are here for you. Let us know how we can help, and we can do the course ourselves just fine. We are enjoying it together already,' Nozi reassured me.

Two weeks later, one of my mentors, Shelley Wong (e.g. Lin *et al.*, 2004; Wong, 2022; Wong & Motha, 2007), also a lifelong decolonial TESOL teacher educator and Third World feminist activist of decades, offered me wise counsel. 'Sue, have your doctoral students help you. I have seen you work with them in the Critical Peace Education SIG [American Educational Studies Association], and they care about you. I'm sure they would love to help you'. I spent little energy wondering if this was true but rather trusting my gut, the resonance of her words with my heart, and the level of care I had established with the students. This trust of the gut and heart (Anzaldúa, 2002) – not to be mistaken for stridency – is a key facet of decolonial ways of knowing and being, and something much clearer than my mind reacted.

I asked the students to help build a calendar for people to stay over with me to take care of me and to bring food via text. They quickly responded, 'More than happy to help' and literally my care was in their hands. Their quick responses and earnest efforts to help reassured me that this life-and-death situation was something where these women, all with strong ties to the Global South, would be met with grace and authentic care (Valenzuela, 1999) through their efforts. Their learning, both formal and informal, and my learning as the one who had the role reversal of needing care, point toward the possibility of inverting formal institutional spaces and decolonizing learning into the field of TESOL teacher preparation.

Introduction

This chapter aims to connect into our own transnational and international backgrounds with a specific focus on decolonial perspectives which emanate from the Global South (e.g. Pennycook & Makoni, 2020) toward better internationalizing Teaching English to Speakers of Other Languages (TESOL) teacher education. To be clear, we aim not to cosmopolitanize this field but to harness the profound energy and wisdom from the Global South to help make an otherwise colonial tool and enterprise – English education (Lin & Motha, 2020; Von Esch *et al.*, 2020) – one that can be decolonial. Our goal is not to create a sliver of ultra-competitive and entitled humanity with 'flexible citizenship' (Ong, 2022) wherein they can lean into their English to be top-flight global consumers and businesspeople. Rather, we envision them using their English as a connector among many toward building a commons of relevance, of care, of community. English does not have to be taught in a way that provides entree into the Global North by forcing instruction related to media, consumerism, music and so on, but rather as a means for the language to be used for critical inquiry inward (e.g. Canagarajah, 2023; Kumaravadivelu, 2006) wherein they continue to value their heritage languages and cultures for the strengths granted from their native connections to heritage identities. Specifically, we explore through critical autoethnography the way we all designed the course as a collective, how we recalibrated and, most importantly, how this was achieved through the framing of Ubuntu and ummah – Global South framing concepts of ways of being that undergirded their reactions. We conclude with implications for the greater field with this one case as a signpost toward further decolonizing and internationalizing TESOL teacher preparation.

Background

Collaboratively, we purposefully had developed a reading list which primarily focused on identity and its multifaceted intersections with race, culture and raciolinguistics, along with the positioning of identity in the international realm (Ladson-Billings, 1995; Muhammad, 2020). Since Nozi and Saniha had different research foci, some of the readings also differed so that we could immerse ourselves in the literature that aligned with our area of interests. After engaging with the readings, we created an annotated bibliography as an ongoing reference for future research, teaching and our doctoral journey. We signed up to work with Sue individually, but she structured the course differently. She cultivated a decolonizing community space because each of us was from varying language, ethnic and geographic identities, united in our experiences of teaching in the United States' southeastern region (Urrieta & Noblit, 2018). Sue empowered us to critically discuss our reflections on our weekly readings, whether the readings were similar or different. She modeled the protocols for a healthy and productive discussion on the major takeaways of the readings in the first few weeks. Likewise, she encouraged us to constantly apply the readings to our own research interests to find the most benefit out of the course. We wrote a weekly reflection answering the following questions:

- How does this reading make me think about the field differently?
- How can I connect this piece to other readings in this course and other courses you've taken?
- Where do I still see gaps within the field?
- How can I put this reading in conversation with the other readings?

After a few weeks of modeling, Sue asked us to take turns facilitating the discussion to practice student-centered practices. Through these student-led discussions, micro community cultural wealth developed (Yosso, 2005). We shared our passion for internationalization with each other by also sharing a glimpse of our unique identities through these conversations. For instance, we discussed the origins of our own names and how those names embraced our linguistic and cultural identities.

During the learning process, as noted above, Sue received a cancer diagnosis; it was a recurrence of a rare form of cancer she had had in 2015 and would require a fairly serious surgery where she would stay in the hospital for three days. As a result, we were led to take ownership of our learning in dialog with our professor. Our community wealth (Yosso, 2005) extended beyond the learning environment in support of one of the community members: the professor. Authentic *cariño* was reflected as we offered emotional and post-surgery support, care-taking and formed new relationships with extended members of our professor's community (Valenzuela, 1999). By upholding a decolonizing community space, we lived out the values of Ubuntu (Pennycook & Makoni, 2020) and ummah (His Highness Prince Karim Aga Khan, 2016).

The opportunity to help our professor during her time of need was a demonstration of 'Ubuntu' which Pennycook and Makoni (2020: 108) define as 'I am what I am because of who we all are'. For me, Nozi, I grew up with Ubuntu and it was a normal and important part of our lives in my country of origin, Zimbabwe. We were educated on Ubuntu at a very young age. Ubuntu, whose origin is the Bantu people of Southern Africa, comprises body, air, spirit, heart and language (Pennycook & Makoni, 2020). Waghid (2020) further explains the elements of 'Ubuntu' by breaking them down to 'sharing, belonging, and participation'. Firstly, even though we are individuals we are compelled to share what we have because we recognize that we are not alone. Secondly, belonging creates the sense of interconnectedness. This sense of belonging was articulated by the late Bishop Desmond Tutu in a 'Newshour' interview where he stated 'I am human because you are human. My humanity is caught up in yours' (Uarez, 1999). Thirdly, participation encompasses being open and engaging in the community of which we are all a part (Waghid, 2020).

The late South African singer, Brenda Fassie, sang a song that was very popular in South Africa in the 1980s entitled, 'Umuntu Ngumuntu Ngabantu', (Fassie & Watson,1988) which means, 'We are one because we are there for each other'. This reiterates the action that we took as a group to look after our professor. We recognized that we are beyond being doctoral students and are one. Consequently, it is our human responsibility to assist each other and support each other. In 2012, in an interview with South African journalist Tom Modise, Nelson Mandela described 'Ubuntu' using the analogy of a traveler throughout the country whom at every village or town or city stops and doesn't have to ask for food and water but is nourished by the people. Ubuntu does not mean that people should not enrich themselves. It is the opposite in that individuals think of how to enable the community to grow and improve.

I, Saniha, drew from a concept I began to engage with at a very early age, a concept that continuously taught me the importance of unity in a diverse community. Within the Muslim world, 'diversity of identities is immense – greater than most people realize – differences based on language, on history, on nationhood, ethnicity and a variety of local affiliations' (His Highness Prince Karim Aga Khan, 2016). Even though diversity is an immense characteristic of the Muslim community, Muslims all over the world are bonded by their belief in the first pillar of Islam, the shahada (Mir, 2003). This fundamental principle 'is a verbal profession of God's unity and Muhammad's role as messenger' (2003: 7). The global Muslim community, also known as the ummah, unites as a collective group through the ethics of inclusiveness, sisterhood and brotherhood. The ummah represents the 'entirety of Muslim communities around the world' (His Highness Prince Karim Aga Khan, 2014) which aims to embody a peaceful, pluralistic community in which Muslims hope to coexist with one another so that 'diversity itself can be seen as a gift' (His Highness Prince Karim Aga Khan, 2016). The ethics of Islam provide Muslims with an avenue to create a 'meaningful global bond' (His Highness Prince Karim Aga Khan, 2016), in which Muslims care for each other by embodying empathy, compassion and kindness for one another. This framework elaborates on this idea of common humanity that unites people of various cultures, nationalities and identities. Similar to Ubuntu, ummah represents a framework that builds on the idea of the collective community coming together as one global community. While this concept of ummah is used among Muslims, I chose to extend this concept globally to everyone, regardless of their beliefs. Even though we each embodied different global wisdoms, we came together in this decolonizing community space to help each other through the challenging times that our professor faced with her cancer diagnosis. We carried out Ubuntu and ummah in these spaces so that we could support our professor in every step of the way as she dealt with her diagnosis. As a result, we modeled the ways in which internationalization extends far beyond learning environments.

Methods

This autoethnographic reflective piece, framed through a weaving of the aforementioned global wisdoms of the importance of living in the collective, provides readers an opportunity to reframe roles of teacher, educator and caregiver in their international efforts toward creating spaces of learning. Two doctoral students and one professor share their reflections on their journey of coexisting in a decolonizing space in which the students lived out the frameworks of Ubuntu and ummah. The authors use autoethnographic reflections as a 'methodology that turns the researcher's focus on themselves' (Esposito & Evans-Winters, 2021: 63) to engage in narrative and reflective writing that captures examples of Ubuntu and ummah in the decolonizing space that the professor and doctoral students cultivated throughout the semester.

For me, Kasun, I was compelled by the wisdom of one of my academic and life mentors, Dr Shelley Wong, mentioned previously. We spoke via phone about my diagnosis, and she explained that based on her observations of my mentoring of my doctoral students, I should ask for their support in organizing my care. Her words were highly resonant, and my intuition told me, 'Listen to her. Do just this'. Without thinking further, I reached out to the doctoral students and asked them to do just this. While there was a small amount of fear, there was comfort in knowing we had already grown together in our courses and shared spaces of convivencia, or meaningful shared lived experiences. I also felt a sense of confidence largely because they had lived among populations that still valued community and taking care of each other more deeply than we often do in the

Global North (at the risk of overly generalizing). Nozi and I had had many discussions, including academic ones, about Ubuntu, for instance, and I had witnessed Saniha's depths of generosity with other students and myself already. And like all of life, I also know I could not fully control any of the outcomes. I was interconnected with the students and realized they genuinely wanted to help in the ways they earnestly agreed to support me. At the same time, I knew they would complete the coursework with or without me, both out of their integrity and the sense of trust I had developed with them.

Nozi's perspective

Fall 2022 began like any other year. From the beginning, it was very busy with new classes and just general anticipation for the new year. I was quite excited because I was very fortunate to be involved as a GRA with the Fulbright program. There were 21 scholars from various countries who were in Atlanta for six weeks for professional development and to acquire new knowledge that they would utilize in their classrooms. I taught technology sessions on Friday mornings. This opportunity to participate in the program was attributed to Sue. She had been listening to me as I stated several times that I was interested in teaching preparation programs for my career path. I was very grateful to have an advisor who was very supportive and looking for opportunities for her advisees.

I remember vividly one Friday morning in September when I was to meet with Sue so we could exchange classroom keys. I noticed that she seemed somewhat distracted and not her normal self. She asked to talk to me in private. I assumed there was a problem with one of the Fulbright scholars or a class. She informed me at that moment that she had been diagnosed with cancer. The cancer which she had previously was back. I was shocked. I was not sure if anything I said would be adequate to relay my concern. However, I recognized at that moment that she would need my support. My concern went to her two young children. She then informed me that she would probably need surgery, but she was currently communicating with her specialist before anything was confirmed.

During our next Directed Reading class meeting we had a discussion with Sue regarding our way forward. Our priority was to support her and to use all the skills and knowledge which she had shared with us to ensure that the class continued. It was important that she attends her medical appointments and take care of not only herself but her children. We took control of our learning and continued with the schedule and the discussions.

Once Sue had her surgery date confirmed, in the spirit of Ubuntu we knew what we had to do. Knowing that we are one and we are because we are one. The interconnectedness made me not hesitate when a schedule was created to determine if we can prepare food for her or be available to assist her at home. I gladly volunteered to do both. It was so confirming to witness Ubuntu as Sue's friends and her students came together to support the member of our community who was in need. The students included not only present advisees but also those who had graduated. This was a true reflection of how the professor had impacted us all at some time during our journey. We all wanted her to recover and heal well without concern about the basics such as cooking.

Saniha's perspective

During the fall semester, I had the opportunity to interact with Dr Kasun more so than the other semesters. I served as her teaching assistant for an ESOL methods course she offered and had weekly touchpoints with her before the weekly class sessions. During the touchpoint, Dr Kasun mentored me to develop my own pedagogies regarding professorship. She continuously taught me how to plan instruction, guide student-centered activities, and challenge students to embrace criticality and joy while also serving as a compassionate and understanding instructor. I was able to learn through her own actions on how to create a positive classroom space in which students felt safe to share and challenge their learnings.

One day during our touchpoint, Dr Kasun seemed a bit stressed. I couldn't help but ask her, 'Is everything okay, Dr Kasun? Can I help you with anything?' She looked at me with a sense of comfort and shared that she just found out that she has been diagnosed with cancer. Being a single parent to her two beautiful children, she shared how the appearance of cancer immensely worried her since her own father passed away owing to cancer.

I could not believe that my advisor who has poured so much love into my development as an individual was diagnosed with cancer. I knew that the least I can do is offer support and assistance. I wanted to not only provide emotional support but also any kind of physical help since I knew she was alone. I went home and prayed immensely for her health. I knew that a person like her with such a pure heart will eventually be okay. I at least had faith.

During another touchpoint, she shared her surgery schedule, and I knew that she would need help with arranging care and food for a week as she recovers. I offered to create a schedule that outlined people signing up to stay with her overnight as well as people signing up to bring her food so that she could heal from the painful surgery. I asked Dr Kasun to share contacts of all those that were near and dear to her. I created a message thread and asked people to sign up if they were available to help her. Without a doubt, people signed up so quickly to help a community member, and her care schedule was complete even before her surgery. I also brought her several dishes that she could freeze in case she was ever in need of food. After her surgery, I continuously went to check on her, and I also tried to alleviate responsibilities of the university course by completing all the grading and guiding students in their final projects.

All of us wanted her to recover quickly and peacefully. Although we did not know each other before this situation, we united together in hopes of helping a member of our community, highlighting the concept of ummah.

Sue's perspective

While it was humbling to entrust care to these doctoral students, it was also a relief. I followed an intuition about their care (Anzaldúa, 2002) and the quality of the relationships we had established. The surgery was complex and required a 10 cm abdominal incision as well as the turning around of my liver to successfully extract a 3 cm tumor. This process was frightening, and the recovery required stores of energy I did not know I would need to engage. Having had a similar procedure with a first tumor in 2015, I was surprised at the level of fatigue I experienced this time for the following few months. I wonder how much was physical fatigue and how much was spiritual. As the mother of two school-age children, reckoning with an illness that will kill me if not managed inspires much grappling with mortality and meaning.

That said, I felt a sense of genuine care that helped me feel relief as I faced my physical and spiritual recovery. I also chose not to worry about if the students were learning what they needed from their readings and periodically asked the simple question if they felt they were learning. In the past, a stronger version of me would check in much more regularly and spend time with the students discussing the content and connections from the readings. On some level we can never know if their learning outcomes met their expectations before my September diagnosis; on another, we know they did things that were deeply meaningful. Their care taught them that the teacher in this case had to lean into being in the position of recipient, not the bearer of all the knowledge or wisdom. My body, in its recovery, looked weaker. I spent the first week on a couch near my kitchen from which my students and others brought me meals and helped me get to the bathroom. These are the most basic of needs and sharing them in all vulnerability also taught me to simply receive in that very moment. It is with gratitude I share that recognition – an intersection of the foundations of the global wisdoms undergirding the students' beliefs and what they shared, including with my extended community of caring others who also helped.

Our Key Learnings

Through the lens of Ubuntu and ummah, we were able to engage in a decolonizing space in which we brought our different identities and unique aspects of our culture within our group as assets. Even though we had quite varied backgrounds and identities, we came together as one collective community to leverage each other's diversities as a source of strength to overcome the adversities we all faced with our advisor's cancer diagnosis. As we engaged in readings that pertained to the role of language in shaping identity, we realized that identity is an essential aspect of our work. We are humans and come with our own positionalities, subjectivities and identities. Urrieta and Noblit (2018) discuss that identity is a self-constructed concept which is influenced by the individual as well as by sociocultural aspects that the individual engages in within society. As a result, people embody numerous identities, and these identities help create a work of belonging as people are categorized and positioned with others.

We can apply this to other aspects of internationalizing TESOL because even though students will bring in various identities that will intersect, it is our job to cultivate a classroom space that embodies the frameworks of Ubuntu and ummah. Considered through the lens of intersectionality, as educators we gain an understanding and analyze our student experiences and understand the complexities of these experiences (Collins & Bilge, 2016). Having the knowledge of the students' experiences and appreciating their backgrounds is important to us as TESOL educators and helps as we navigate our curriculum incorporating students' funds of knowledge. Ubuntu and ummah help us embrace this intersectionality as students and teachers bring their own identities in an environment where they are considered one because they are one.

Decolonization of education and this experience demonstrated how decolonization of the classroom can lead to an environment which is less traditional and allows more room for authentic student voices and experiences. Pennycook and Makoni (2020) address the need to not only restructure the curriculum but also incorporate multiple voices to prevent a monocultural approach, one of the key dangers of TESOL education and teacher preparation. In this situation, the professor helped decolonize the classroom by giving students power over their own learning. Therefore, the curriculum was not only reconstructed but pluralized student voices. With the decolonization of the curriculum, the students embraced the problem posing method (Freire, 1972). The profound problem was the professor's illness, and the students and professor came together to solve the problem. Ultimately, the experience allowed all involved to grow together; it also surely invited larger questions, perhaps life's most important questions related to mortality, care and connection. This experience as preparers of future TESOL educators was a reminder of the different methods in which student experiences can be enfolded into the curriculum and the community of learners.

Through this journey, we further disrupted the traditional power dynamics of formal education because we learned from each other. We became the custodians of our knowledge and the relationships we cultivated in this experience. Sue, the advisor and professor, became the recipient of care in which she had complete trust and faith in her doctoral students, Nozi and Saniha. We recognized the importance of being flexible so that we are prepared for unpredictable circumstances. We also realized the significance of leveraging those in our community spaces to help us move from one step to another. Since our professor respected her advisees through the relationships she had built with us, we were able to form a pluralistic community in which we valued each other's identities.

As TESOL educators, we need to be aware of the identities of our students and the various social, political and economic backgrounds that our students bring to our classroom. We need to be willing to learn from our students because they are the custodians of immense knowledge that can benefit everyone around them, including the educator. Similar to Sue, we need to have trust and faith in our students and allow them to bring their funds of knowledge (Gonzalez et al., 2005) into the classroom space to break the traditional cycles of power dynamics. Culturally relevant pedagogy cannot be truly implemented without the educator taking authentic time and space to get to know who our students really are, their identities, and their global wisdoms. Such pedagogy will surely involve questioning and breaking the norms of traditional approaches from the West of teacher-centered instruction that is unidirectional and full of knowledge centered in hegemony represented by the traditional transmission of English as *the* dominant language.

Implications for the Internationalization and Decolonization of TESOL Teacher Preparation

We have written this piece as an offering. We see how life-and-death matters can hook into the work of TESOL when we draw from the best of its potential, the drawing upon the cultural wealth of all its practitioners, the leaning into the global wisdom traditions which TESOL has settled into and has neither eradicated nor spoiled. In fact, TESOL is in a space where it can now recognize its folly as a colonizing project and instead reorient toward a global interconnectedness. We see that global interconnectedness in how Kasun leaned into these women and allowed their backgrounds to be part of the care-providing efforts they arranged. There was an authentic reciprocity in what she received after a more mentoring-oriented set of years spent with both co-authors. Indeed, she was largely the receiver of their care, from daal to beef stew to trusting that they were succeeding in organizing several people's efforts at care for her.

Kasun also relinquished a sense of control related to the outcomes of the students' formal learning objectives. Of course, as she continues to mentor, she is already activating her additional years of work in the field to help orient both co-authors. While she continues to feel a sense of responsibility to mentoring them, the quality of their relationship is now forever marked with the distinction of how they all worked together to care for her. This provides a more complex understanding of the mentees for Kasun, and certainly the reverse is also true. What we did was further humanize and enflesh (Hurtado, 2003) our understandings of each other. While we do not wish such adversity and illness on TESOL educators and their students, we recognize that the world over, people are facing remarkable challenges. Right now, TESOL educators are fleeing Sudan, for instance, as are those from Haiti. Other educators are answering to government mandates about how and when to prepare TESOL educators in ways that can preclude the full agency and professionalism of TESOL educators; we recognize there are urgencies which are enormous if not seemingly impossible. We invite TESOL educators to think of all the ways around and through these problems when challenges seem daunting, to say the least. What are the ways we can connect, including with our students, toward creating the decolonial space where language and love can flourish? We believe we have provided a humble and humbling example of that work in this chapter.

References

Anzaldúa, G.E. (2002) now let us shift… the path of conocimiento… inner work, public acts. In G.E. Anzaldúa and A. Keating (eds) *This Bridge we call Home: Radical Visions for Transformation* (pp. 540–578). Routledge.
Canagarajah, S. (2023) Decolonization as pedagogy: A praxis of 'becoming in ELT. *ELT Journal*, ccad017.
Collins, P.H. and Bilge, S. (2016) *Intersectionality*. Polity Press.
Esposito, J. and Evans-Winters, V. (2021) *Introduction to Intersectional Qualitative Research*. Sage.
Esteva, G. (2018) Struggling to live within the storm, with Ivan Illich. *The International Journal of Illich Studies* 6 (1), 189–214.
Fassie, B. and Watson, M. (1988) *Ubuntu Ngumuntu Ngabantu*. CCP Record Company.
Freire, P. (1972) *Pedagogy of the Oppressed*. (trans. Myra Bergman Ramos). Herder. [First published 1968.]
Gonzalez, N., Moll, L.C. and Amanti, C. (2005) *Funds of Knowledge: Theorizing Practices in Households, Communities, and Classrooms*. Routledge.
His Highness Prince Karim Aga Khan (2014) Address to both Houses of the Parliament of Canada in the House of Commons Chamber. https://the.ismaili/speeches/address-both-houses-parliament-canada-house-commons-chamber
His Highness Prince Karim Aga Khan (2016) Accepting the Adrienne Clarkson prize for global citizenship. https://the.ismaili/speeches/accepting-adrienne-clarkson-prize-global-citizenship
Hurtado, A. (2003) Theory in the flesh: Toward an endarkened epistemology. *International Journal of Qualitative Studies in Education* 16 (2), 215–225.
Illich, I. (1973) *Tools for Conviviality*. https://o500.org/books/ivan_illich_tools_for_conviviality.pdf
Kasun, G.S. (2018) Chicana feminism as a bridge: The struggle of a White woman seeking an alternative to the eclipsing embodiment of Whiteness. *Journal of Curriculum Theorizing* 32 (3), 115–133

Kasun, G.S. and Mora Pablo, I. (eds) (2022) *Applying Anzalduan Frameworks to Understand Transnational Youth Identities: Bridging Culture, Language, and Schooling at the US-Mexican Border*. Routledge.

Kasun, G.S., Marks, B. and Jefferies, J. (2024) *Decolonizing Study Abroad Through the Identities of Latinx Students: A Manifesto to Reclaim Identities and Heritage*. Taylor and Francis.

Kumaravadivelu, B. (2006) TESOL methods: Changing tracks, challenging trends. *TESOL Quarterly* 40 (1), 59–81.

Ladson-Billings, G. (1995) Toward a theory of culturally relevant pedagogy. *American Educational Research Journal* 32 (3), 465–491. https://doi.org/10.3102/00028312 032003465

Lin, A.M. and Motha, S. (2020) 'Curses in TESOL': Postcolonial desires for colonial English. In R. Arber, M. Weinmann and J. Blackmore (eds) *Rethinking Languages Education: Directions, Challenges and Innovations* (pp. 15–35). Routledge.

Lin, A., Grant, R., Kubota, R., Motha, S., Sachs, G.T., Vandrick, S. and Wong, S. (2004) Women faculty of color in TESOL: Theorizing our lived experiences. *Tesol Quarterly* 38 (3), 487–504.

Mir, A. (2003) *The American Encounter with Islam (Introducing Islam)*. Mason Crest.

Muhammad, G. (2020) *Cultivating Genius: An Equity Framework for Culturally and Historically Responsive Literacy*. Scholastic.

Ong, A. (2022) Citizenship: Flexible, fungible, fragile. *Citizenship Studies* 26 (4–5), 599–607.

Pennycook, A. and Makoni, S. (2020) *Innovations and Challenges in Applied Linguistics from the Global South*. Routledge.

Uarez, R. (1999) Newshour. Bishop Tutu's 1999 interview on NewsHour. South African History Online (sahistory.org.za).

Urrieta Jr., L. and Noblit, G.W. (eds) (2018) *Cultural Constructions of Identity: Meta-Ethnography and Theory*. Oxford University Press.

Valenzuela, A. (2005) Subtractive schooling, caring relations, and social capital in the schooling of U.S.-Mexican youth. In L. Weis and M. Fine (eds) *Beyond Silenced Voices: Class, Race, and Gender in United States Schools* (pp. 83–94). State University of New York Press.

Von Esch, K.S., Motha, S. and Kubota, R. (2020) Race and language teaching. *Language Teaching* 53 (4), 391–421.

Waghid, Y. (2020) Towards an Ubuntu philosophy of higher education in Africa. *Studies in Philosophy and Education* 39 (3), 299–308.

Wong, S. (2022) *Dialogic Approaches to TESOL: Where the Ginkgo Tree Grows*. Routledge.

Wong, S. and Motha, S. (2007) Multilingualism in post-9/11 US schools: Implications for engaging empire. *Peace and Change* 32 (1), 62–77.

Yosso, T.J. (2005) Whose culture has capital? A critical race theory discussion of community cultural wealth. *Race Ethnicity and Education* 8 (1), 69–91.

Index

accent 155
action research 107
adaptability 106
agency 96, 106, 207
American cultural knowledge 27
anti-racism 211
Asia 52
assessment 98
authentic English 170
awareness 90, 103, 178

British history 23

care 237
career 162
cariño 230
children's language learning 29
China 161
citizenship 133
class 146
classroom practices 113
colonialism 215
communication 203
communicative strategies 89
community 5, 234
community of practice 187
COVID-19 144
cross-cultural understanding 138
cross-cultural environments 103
cultural competence 39
cultural knowledge 180
curriculum 132, 186, 236
curriculum development 34
curriculum frameworks 43

decolonization 226
deficit 220
diplomacy 163
diversity 50, 74, 182, 188, 213
diversity of perspective 164

document analysis 22

efficiency 171
empathy 137
English as a lingua franca 42, 183
English as an international language 99
English for intercultural communication 121
Epistemology 1, 101, 215, 235
equity 212, 219
ethical citizenship 125
ethics 205, 232
excursion 150

feedback 143
flexible citizenship 229
frustration 155

gender 53, 141
gender socialization 119
Germany 63
global citizenship 85, 132, 135, 140, 164
global English 24
global English ideologies 48
global perspective 189
Global South 228
globalization 83
grammatical accuracy 139
growth 105

high school 200
higher education 64

identity 81, 97, 197, 206, 226
ideologies 222
ideologies of internationalization 69
immigrants 137
income level 148
institutional constraints 169
intercultural citizenship 116

intercultural citizenship awareness 123
intercultural knowledge 112, 115
intercultural tensions 121
international students 101
internationalization of the curriculum 33

Japan 51, 178
job applications 167

knowledge construction 3
Korea 199

language education 104
language ideologies 66, 149, 157, 162, 195, 214
Language ownership 1
language policy 70
language proficiency 39
liberal arts education 54
linguistics 184
listening comprehension 156
literacy 141, 221

methodological plurality 1
migration 217, 238
monolingualism 63, 73, 215
morality 86, 172
motivation 153, 187, 205
multiculturalism 147, 175
multilingualism 181, 220

narratives 173
native speaker 19, 49, 75, 195, 202
neoliberalism 18, 49, 58, 214
Norway 17

pedagogical competence 35
periphery 58
plurilingual speakers 51
policy making 57
practical experience 41
practicum 100, 198
pre-service teachers' professional development 190

privilege 202
professional community 59
professional development 39
professional identity 102, 179
proficiency tests 36

quality 38, 141, 196, 221

racial ideologies 30
reflection 87
refugees 120, 134
religion 231, 233
returning graduates 165

silence 56
Slovakia 136
social capital 152
standard varieties 20
STEM research 57
student teachers 66
study abroad 26, 146, 178, 195, 204
symbolic internationalization 54

teacher beliefs 65
teacher education 2, 118
teacher education curricula 82, 88
teacher identity 83
teacher ideologies 64
teaching methodologies 21, 37, 108, 168
textbooks 154
translanguaging 63, 71
translingualism 31, 84, 215
travelling 151

undergraduate course 117
university students 55

varieties of English 28
Vietnam 45
virtual exchange 3, 122, 131

Western culture 49
Westernized content 44
writing programs 124

www.ingramcontent.com/pod-product-compliance
Ingram Content Group UK Ltd.
Pitfield, Milton Keynes, MK11 3LW, UK
UKHW021826130225
455069UK00013B/105